Contemporary Performance Lighting

Performance+Design is a series of monographs and essay collections that explore understandings of performance design and scenography, examining the potential of the visual, spatial, material and environmental to shape performative encounters and to offer sites for imaginative exchange. This series focuses on design both for and as performance in a variety of contexts, including theatre, art installations, museum displays, mega-events, site-specific and community-based performance, street theatre, design of public space, festivals, protests and state-sanctioned spectacle.

Performance+Design takes as its starting point the growth of scenography and the expansion from theatre or stage design to a wider notion of scenography as a spatial practice. As such, it recognizes the recent accompanying interest from a number of converging scholarly disciplines (theatre, performance, art, architecture, design) and examines twenty-first-century practices of performance design in the context of debates about postdramatic theatre, aesthetic representation, visual and material culture, spectatorship, participation and co-authorship.

Series Editors

Stephen Di Benedetto, Joslin McKinney and Scott Palmer

Scenography Expanded: An Introduction to Contemporary Performance Design
Edited by Joslin McKinney and Scott Palmer
978-1-4742-4439-8

The Model as Performance: Staging Space in Theatre and Architecture
Thea Brejzek and Lawrence Wallen
978-1-350-09590-8

The History and Theory of Environmental Scenography: Second Edition
Arnold Aronson
978-1-4742-8396-0

Contemporary Scenography: Practices and Aesthetics in German Theatre, Arts and Design
Edited by Birgit Wiens
978-1-3500-6447-8

Sound Effect: The Theatre We Hear
Ross Brown
978-1-3500-4590-3

Immersion and Participation in Punchdrunk's Theatrical Worlds
Carina E. I. Westling
978-1-3501-0195-1

Consuming Scenography: The Shopping Mall as a Theatrical Experience
Nebojša Tabački
978-1-3501-1089-2

Digital Scenography: 30 Years of Experimentation and Innovation in Performance and Interactive Media
Neill O'Dwyer
978-1-3501-0731-1

Sites of Transformation: Applied and Socially Engaged Scenography in Rural Landscapes
Louise Ann Wilson
978-1-3501-9516-5

Contemporary Performance Lighting

Experience, Creativity and Meaning

**EDITED BY
KATHERINE GRAHAM, SCOTT PALMER AND KELLI ZEZULKA**

methuen | drama
LONDON • NEW YORK • OXFORD • NEW DELHI • SYDNEY

METHUEN DRAMA
Bloomsbury Publishing Plc
50 Bedford Square, London, WC1B 3DP, UK
1385 Broadway, New York, NY 10018, USA
29 Earlsfort Terrace, Dublin 2, Ireland

BLOOMSBURY, METHUEN DRAMA and the Methuen Drama logo are trademarks of
Bloomsbury Publishing Plc

First published in Great Britain 2023

Copyright © Katherine Graham, Scott Palmer, Kelli Zezulka and contributors, 2023

Katherine Graham, Scott Palmer and Kelli Zezulka have asserted their right under the
Copyright, Designs and Patents Act, 1988, to be identified as editors of this work.

For legal purposes the Acknowledgements on p. xv constitute an extension
of this copyright page.

Cover design by Burge Agency
Cover image: *All That Fall*, Pan Pan Theatre (© Ros Kavanagh)

All rights reserved. No part of this publication may be reproduced or transmitted
in any form or by any means, electronic or mechanical, including photocopying,
recording, or any information storage or retrieval system, without prior
permission in writing from the publishers.

Bloomsbury Publishing Plc does not have any control over, or responsibility for, any
third-party websites referred to or in this book. All internet addresses given in this
book were correct at the time of going to press. The author and publisher regret any
inconvenience caused if addresses have changed or sites have ceased to exist,
but can accept no responsibility for any such changes.

A catalogue record for this book is available from the British Library.

A catalog record for this book is available from the Library of Congress.

ISBN: HB: 978-1-3501-9515-8
PB: 978-1-3501-9516-5
ePDF: 978-1-3501-9518-9
eBook: 978-1-3501-9517-2

Series: Performance and Design

Typeset by Deanta Global Publishing Services, Chennai, India
Printed and bound in Great Britain

To find out more about our authors and books visit www.bloomsbury.com and
sign up for our newsletters.

Contents

List of illustrations vii
Notes on contributors x
Foreword xiii
Acknowledgements xv

Introduction: Thinking light *Katherine Graham, Scott Palmer and Kelli Zezulka* 1

SECTION 1 Experience 25

1   Theatrical atmospheres and the experience of light *Scott Palmer* 27

2   Felt dramaturgies of light *David Shearing* 46

3   Transforming visitor experience through light: Tivoli Gardens: A case study *Jesper Kongshaug* 64

4   Narratives, choreographies and felt experiences of light *Lucy Carter* 72

5   The unbearable brightness of beams: Light, darkness and obscure images *Yaron Shyldkrot* 82

SECTION 2 Creativity 101

6   Language, creativity and collaboration *Kelli Zezulka* 103

7   Northern Lights: Using natural light phenomena as stage lighting concept *Michael Breiner* 119

8 Light in contemporary Chinese opera *Psyche Chui* 130

9 RashDash: Fusing feminism and light *Katharine Williams* 145

10 Reflecting on light *Jennifer Tipton* 155

SECTION 3 Meaning 163

11 Aesthetics, materiality and meaning-making in scenographic light *Katherine Graham* 165

12 Storytelling with light *Paule Constable* 182

13 Tracing the light: A performance essay on space, light and the process of looking *Nick Hunt and Hansjörg Schmidt* 190

14 LX *ludens*: Mediations upon the play of light *Christopher Baugh* 200

References 219
Index 234

Illustrations

Figures

1 Interpretation of 'The Vision of Queen Katherine' from Charles Kean's *Henry VIII*. Princess's Theatre, London, 1855. *Illustrated London News*, 2 June 1855, p.532 31
2 *and it all comes down to this . . .* David Shearing, 2012. The space without participants 53
3 *Roskilde street lighting*. Data tracking footfall through brighter and darker areas. Lighting designer: Jesper Kongshaug 67
4 Tivoli Gardens. Guest data, tracking visitors to the Chinese area before and after lighting change. Lighting designer: Jesper Kongshaug 69
5 *Traces*. A participant's hand in the light, 2017. Lighting designers: Nick Hunt and Hansjörg Schmidt 192
6 *Traces*. Light viewed through the perspex viewfinder, 2017. Lighting designers: Nick Hunt and Hansjörg Schmidt 194
7 *Traces*. A dancer interacts with the light, 2017. Lighting designers: Nick Hunt and Hansjörg Schmidt 197
8 Camera obscura in Gemma Frisius's 1545 book *De Radio Astronomica et Geometrica* and an illustration of the principle of the camera obscura from James Ayscough, *A Short Account of the Eye and the Nature of Vision* (London 1755) 202
9 Georg Fuchs, *Twelfth Night*, Munich Artists' Theatre, 1908, *Dekorative Kunst*, XIV, 3 (December 1910), p.140 209
10 Computer visualization of Edward Gordon Craig's concept of moving screens (ca.1911) Cat Fergusson and Gavin Carver, University of Kent, 1999 210

Colour plates

1 *The Litten Trees*, St Just, Cornwall, 2021. Installation on the same tree at different times. Lighting designer: Joshua Pharo. (Joshua Pharo)

ILLUSTRATIONS

2   *The Litten Trees*, Alexander Palace Park, London, 2021. Lighting designer: Jackie Shemesh. (Hugo Glendinning)
3   *The Litten Trees*, Leek, Staffordshire, 2021. Lighting designer: Daniella Beattie. (Tim Vickerstaff)
4   *It Is Not the End of the World*. Superflex, 2019. (Scott Palmer)
5   *Ungdom* (*Youth*). Fix and Foxy, 2015. Lighting designer: Michael Breiner. (Per Morten Abrahamsen)
6   *Ungdom* (*Youth*). Fix and Foxy, 2015. Lighting designer: Michael Breiner. (Søren Knud)
7   *The Drowned Man – A Hollywood Fable*. Punchdrunk, 2013. Lighting designer: Mike Gunning. (Alex Palmer)
8   *and it all comes down to this* . . . David Shearing, 2012. Performance space without participants (David Shearing)
9   *and it all comes down to this* . . . David Shearing, 2012. Spatialized screens layout, with double-sided projection (David Shearing)
10 *and it all comes down to this* . . . David Shearing, 2012. Moments from the end sequence; paper birds with duo-tone light effect (David Shearing)
11 Tivoli Gardens, Copenhagen. 2015 visitor data tracking
12 Tivoli Gardens, Copenhagen. Visitors experiencing the twilight. Lighting designer: Jesper Kongshaug. (Jesper Konshaug)
13 The impact of light on the visitor experience of the Tivoli Gardens, Copenhagen. Lighting designer: Jesper Kongshaug. Clockwise from top left: 1. Daytime (Lasse Salling), 2. Nightime (Rasmus B. Hansen), 3. Chinese area with redesigned red lanterns (Lasse Salling), 4. Nimb Hotel decorated with historic coloured glass 'kuppels' (Jesper Kongshaug)
14 *Woolf Works*, Wayne McGregor. ©Royal Opera House, London, 2015. Lighting designer: Lucy Carter. (Photograph by Tristram Kenton)
15 *Woolf Works*, Wayne McGregor, Royal Opera House, London, 2015. Lighting designer: Lucy Carter. (Photograph by Tristram Kenton)
16 *Hidden 3* (Light Store) from *No Body*, Sadler's Wells, 2016. Lighting designer: Lucy Carter. (Richard Davies)
17 *F.LUX,* 2014. Lighting designer: Lucy Carter. (Richard Davies)
18 *J3RR1: Programmed Torture*. None Collective, 2018 (None Collective)
19 *Overcast*, Lighting designer: Yaron Shyldkrot, 2017. (Yaron Shyldkrot)
20 Creating the Northern Lights effect for *The Valkyrie*. WYSIWYG pre-visualization by lighting designer: Michael Breiner
21 *The Valkyrie*. The New Opera (TNO) Esbjerg, 2017. Northern lights as realized on stage. Lighting designer: Michael Breiner. (Marie í Dali)
22 *The Taming of the Shrew*, Hong Kong Academy for Performing Arts, 2014. Lighting designers: Psyche Chui and John A Williams. (Felix Chan)

23 *The Taming of the Shrew*, Hong Kong Academy for Performing Arts, 2014. Lighting designers: Psyche Chui and John A Williams. (Felix Chan)
24 *Two Man Show*, RashDash, 2016. Lighting designer: Katharine Williams. (The Other Richard)
25 *The Darkest Corners*, RashDash, 2017. Lighting designer: Katharine Williams. (The Other Richard)
26 *The Darkest Corners*, RashDash, 2017. Lighting designer: Katharine Williams. (The Other Richard)
27 *Necessary Weather*, 1994. (Restaged at Baryshnikov Arts Center, 2011) Lighting designer: Jennifer Tipton. (Photograph by Stephanie Berger)
28 *War Horse*, National Theatre, London, 2007. Lighting designer: Paule Constable. (Brinkhoff and Moegenburg)
29 *The Curious Incident of the Dog in the Night-Time*, National Theatre, London, 2013. Lighting designer: Paule Constable. (Brinkhoff and Moegenburg)
30 *Angels in America*. National Theatre, London, 2017. Lighting designer: Paule Constable. (Helen Maybanks, courtesy of ArenaPAL)
31 'The Trial of Queen Katharine, *Henry VIII*, Act II Scene 4 Covent Garden Theatre, 1831. (Painted in 1866 by Henry Andrews (1794–1868), courtesy of RSC Theatre Collection)
32 *We are Hull*. City Hall, Hull City of Culture, 5 January 2017. Installation by Zsolt Balogh. (David Graham/Alamy)

Contributors

Christopher Baugh is an emeritus professor of performance and technology at the University of Leeds, UK. He has worked extensively as a scenographer and has written widely on the history, theory and practices of scenography, including the monograph *Theatre, Performance and Technology: The Development and Transformation of Scenography* (2014).

Michael Breiner is a Danish lighting designer and educator. His work has mainly been focused on performance, contemporary dance and opera. Between 2017 and 2021, Michael was assistant professor and head of light design education at the Danish National School of Performing Arts. His research is focused on darkness and its relation to time and space. For more information, please visit www.michaelbreiner.com.

Lucy Carter is a light artist and multi-award-winning lighting designer. Her extensive work for theatre, ballet, dance, musical theatre and opera has led her to work with some of the top directors, choreographers and creative teams. She has also produced many solo light installations, light art works and devised lighting designs for fashion, pop and exhibitions. Her distinct abstract and vibrant style has led to an impressive international reputation.

Psyche Chui is a senior lecturer in theatre lighting design at the Hong Kong Academy for Performing Arts. She has worked as a professional lighting designer and theatre educator for over thirty-one years. As a lighting designer, Psyche has worked for every major professional theatre and dance company in Hong Kong and for many performing companies internationally.

Paule Constable is a multi-award-winning lighting designer working in drama and opera. She is also an associate director of the National Theatre and the Lyric Hammersmith, UK, as well as of Matthew Bourne's New Adventures. Her early career began working in music; she then spent time collaborating with Théâtre de Complicité, then with director Katie Mitchell. She has a highly collaborative working practice. Recent widely seen work includes *War Horse* – for which she won a Tony Award in 2011 – and *The Curious Incident of the Dog in the Night-Time* – for which she won the fourth of her five Olivier Awards in 2013.

Katherine Graham is a lecturer in the Department of Theatre, Film, Television and Interactive Media at the University of York, UK. Her research focuses on the agency of light in performance. She has also worked extensively as a lighting designer for theatre and dance and has published work about light in *Theatre and Performance Design Journal*, *Studies in Theatre and Performance* and *Contemporary Theatre Review*.

Nick Hunt is a digital research and innovation fellow at Rose Bruford College, UK. Nick began his career as a lighting technician and designer for theatre, dance and opera, before leading the lighting design degree at Rose Bruford College, where he later became head of the School of Design, Management and Technical Arts. His research interests include the performative nature of stage lighting, digital scenography and digital performance, the history of technical theatre and the roles and status of the various personnel involved in theatre-making and the relationship between scenography and photography.

Jesper Kongshaug is a radical and innovative international architectural and theatrical lighting designer who also teaches widely and is resident lighting director at Tivoli Gardens – an amusement park and pleasure garden established in 1843 and located in the centre of the city of Copenhagen. His lighting design for Hotel Pro Forma's *Operation:Orfeo* has been seen around the world since 1993. Examples of his large-scale work include the creation of a 14-kilometre installation, *Vinterlys* (*Winterlight*), for Copenhagen's European City of Culture (1996).

Peter Mumford trained as a stage designer at the Central School of Art in London, UK, studying under Ralph Koltai. Predominantly now known as a lighting designer, he works globally across drama, dance and opera, also as a set designer and occasional director. Recognition includes Olivier awards for Outstanding Achievement in Dance and also Best Lighting Design for *The Bacchae* at the National Theatre. He won Helpmann and Green Room awards for *King Kong* in Australia and a Knight of Illumination award for *Sucker Punch*. In 2019, Peter was nominated for Tony awards for *The Ferryman* and *King Kong*.

Scott Palmer is an associate professor in performance design and director of student education in the School of Performance and Cultural Industries at the University of Leeds, UK, where he teaches on the MA in Performance Design. His teaching and research focus on scenography, immersive theatrical environments and interactions between technologies and performance. His publications include *Light: Readings in Theatre Practice* (2013) that re-evaluates the historic role of theatre light and advocates new ways of thinking about lighting as a creative performance practice.

Hansjörg Schmidt is a lighting designer and educator. In his lighting practice, he regularly collaborates with performance makers and other practitioners on creating new landscapes and environments made of light. He runs the MA Light in Performance at Rose Bruford College in London and is actively engaged in exploring new ways to teach and learn about light in performance, particularly through cross-disciplinary working and knowledge exchange.

David Shearing is an artist and academic based in the UK. His research and practice explore the nature of audience engagement with design materials and spaces. He is a lecturer in experimental arts and performance at the Royal Central School of Speech and Drama. More details are available on his website, www.davidshearing.com.

Yaron Shyldkrot is a practitioner–researcher whose work explores the state of uncertainty in performance, the edges of sound and vision and the many possibilities in and of darkness. As a performance maker, he works as a director and dramaturg and co-founded Fye and Foul, a theatre company exploring unique sonic experiences, darkness and extremes.

Jennifer Tipton is an American lighting designer for theatre, dance and opera, and a leading figure in the field. She has designed lighting for numerous dance performances for such companies as the New York City Ballet, the American Ballet Theatre, Twyla Tharp Dance and the Paul Taylor Dance Company, among others. Her many awards include the Dorothy and Lillian Gish Prize in 2001 and the Jerome Robbins Prize in 2003. In 2008 she was made a United States Artist 'Gracie' Fellow and a MacArthur Fellow. She has taught lighting design at the Yale School of Drama since 1981.

Katharine Williams (they/them) is a lighting designer, writer and leader of projects. Extensive lighting design work in the UK and internationally includes a number of shows with RashDash and in venues ranging from London's Royal Opera House and Roundhouse to a lighthouse in Shetland, by way of Hong Kong, Mexico City and Stockton upon Tees. Katharine's projects are *Love Letters to the Home Office*, which used art, words and theatre to campaign against the UK's immigration policy; Crew for Calais, which mobilized people in creative industries to work with refugees; and People Powered, which lent support to the NHS and frontline services during the early part of the Covid-19 pandemic.

Kelli Zezulka is a lecturer in technical theatre (production and design) at University of Salford, UK. She has published in theatre and performance journals, as well as in applied linguistics. Her research interests include lighting design and scenography processes, theatre design pedagogy and creative collaboration. A practising lighting designer, she is also a non-executive director of the Association for Lighting Production and Design and editor of its bi-monthly magazine, *Focus*.

Foreword

Peter Mumford

This is a book about the use of light as a creative medium, just like oil paint or gouache is to the painter, or stone, plaster and steel are to the sculptor.

All art forms require a starting point of some kind. For the painter, it may be a clean white canvas, for the sculptor an empty space waiting to be filled, or for the filmmaker an unexposed reel of film. For the light artist, it is darkness, a space or a surface without light.

This is what I would refer to as the 'blank black canvas', and this is the starting point from which we create with light.

The first brush stroke might be a candle being lit, a cool shaft of light penetrating the darkness or a sudden massive lighting up of the space. Either way, the process of illumination begins, and with it the stimulation of perception, visual understanding and emotion.

It is, therefore, not for no reason that we darken our theatre before a performance commences. By doing so, we are taking away all previous visual references from the beholder and making it possible to start from scratch in terms of what is presented. Those images that are then confronted rely on using the imagination and the memory of how things look in order to propagate both recognition of references to 'reality' but also the introduction of entirely new ideas and concepts that may be more abstract or expressionist. It's a new and fresh look at life that, even when it appears to be naturalistic or realistic, is in fact working within its own world.

All theatre is realism in the sense that the theatrical act is a happening thing that creates its own reality and its own manipulated rules of perception. In this 'black canvas', light plays a central role through its ability to determine what one wants an audience to see, or to emphasize a particular aspect. This makes light a major controlling force and narrative contributor to performance.

Having this 'black canvas' also facilitates being able to rub out, as one might erase a drawing on paper. Remove all light, and one can begin again with an entirely fresh set of imagery. The big difference between this canvas and that of the painters is that one is dealing with a constantly changing canvas that can erase and recreate constantly, whereas the painter is, for the most part, creating a finite object. Even with film, a finished product is what is being created in the end, but theatre is more ephemeral, with light in a constant state of flux and subject to a wide variety of influences and conditioning, resulting in an ever-changeable chemistry.

Inevitably, inside this 'black canvas' is very often a highly complex structure of objects, shapes, surfaces and, of course, people. Thus, the act of introducing light to this darkened space is both an act of discovery, illustration and narrative as well as a creative contribution in its own right. Time of day, place, weather and psychological perception all become factors in the decision-making process of how to introduce and use light to create the right ambience to support and illuminate a theatre production. The important aspect to realize is, however, that one is also working and creating from memory too: memory of what a foggy street looks like, or light streaming through a window, light at the end of a day and so on. It's a referential process and is created within a new and fresh reality, re-formed out of darkness, so it's also crucial that what is created communicates images that the watcher can identify with, understand and be moved by.

This book explores, examines and explains the processes, functions and aesthetics of a wide variety of lighting practices and the work of artists who create using the medium of light. These essays are written by both practitioners and scholars, many of whom have not been published previously, drawing together a range of thoughts and creative philosophies and, in doing so, this volume defines a new art form.

Acknowledgements

We are grateful to the people who have contributed directly to this book, namely our contributors for their outstanding chapters, the photographers whose work illuminates the practice and the artists whose work is explored here.

We are also indebted to the many practitioners and thinkers who have indirectly contributed to the thinking and development of this volume. In particular, this has occurred via conference papers and discussions about light through international networks such as the scenography working groups of the International Federation for Theatre Research (IFTR) and the Theatre and Performance Research Association (TaPRA), as well as professional associations such as the Association for Lighting Production and Design (ALPD) and the OISTAT Lighting Design Working Group and Education and Research Commissions. In particular, we would like to acknowledge the contributors and attendees at the *Performing Light* events in Leeds in 2017 and at Scandlight in Malmö in June 2018 (organized by Ulf Nielsen and Anders Larsson), several of whom have contributed directly to this volume.

We are grateful for the support we have received from our institutions – the University of York, the University of Leeds and the University of Salford – and for the culture of scenography and light research at the School of Performance and Cultural Industries at the University of Leeds that has made this volume possible.

We would like to express our thanks to Mark Dudgeon, Ella Wilson and the team at Bloomsbury for supporting the volume. We would also like to thank the generous colleagues who read drafts of this work at various stages: Maria Kapsali, Jonathan Pitches, David Barnett and Joslin McKinney.

Our most profound thanks go to freelance lighting designers everywhere for continuing to find exciting ways of working with this most mysterious of materials.

Introduction
Thinking light

Katherine Graham, Scott Palmer and Kelli Zezulka

This is a book about light, about the work of lighting designers and about what light does in and for performance. To think about light in performance is also, inherently, to think about the experience of space and time, and the ways in which performances are assembled from their materials and for their audiences. Performance lighting, as explored here, is a phenomenon that expands beyond the boundaries within which it has previously been considered, connected to a wide range of practices from theatre and dance, to live and installation art and architectural and environmental encounters. Beyond – and through – thinking *about* light in performance, this book also sets out to think *with* light, exploring the ways in which the particularities of light – as a component of performance, a distinctively ephemeral material, and a mode of encounter – offer up new ways of understanding performance, art, materials and environments more deeply.

This volume collates, evaluates and develops current practice and research in performance lighting that encompasses the experiential, creative and meaning-making capacities of light. Recent years have seen an expanded cultural awareness of light as a material alongside recognition of the value of light and lighting practices in performance and associated literature. Where once publications about theatrical light focused largely on discussions of the craft and technical skill involved in mounting a lighting design for performance, there is now a growing critical understanding of the affective, dramaturgical and material contribution(s) of light to performance and the value of light as an area of research.[1] This expansion of research into the nature of light in performance is conversant with similar expansion in the wider area of scenography and performance design. In structuring this volume around the combined voices of academics, academic/practitioners and professional lighting designers, this project forms a provocation to institute scholarly framing for new conceptions of light in and beyond performance. In doing so, this book exemplifies an intertwining of theory and practice that evidences an ambition for light which we hope will have significance in and beyond the educational field to encompass professionals working with light and practitioners and thinkers across the cultural sector. The volume is arranged according to three critical analytical frameworks: experience, creativity and meaning. Each of these provides a mode of further understanding light, attendant to its material operation in creative contexts. Significantly, though each of these frameworks invites detailed possibilities for analysis, they are interconnected and the overlaps between them provide rich and fruitful insights about the nature and substance of light in performance. The approaches here demonstrate that light is significantly more complex as a material than has been acknowledged in previous writings in the field of performance and reveal ways in which light works as an aesthetic and dramaturgical meaning-making component of performance as well as an affective multisensory experience that can be harnessed in a rich variety of ways and creative contexts.

In this introductory essay, we scope the territory of the field, taking a contemporary snapshot of thinking in the area, providing a guide to the organization of the volume, and highlighting some of the key theoretical themes by drawing on specific examples. As such, this opening chapter aims to provide both a series of ideas through which to conceptualize the key concerns captured in our framing of ideas of light in, and beyond, contemporary performance and an introduction to the contributions that follow. In lighting terms, then, this introduction provides a 'general cover' and establishes the main areas of focus and key lighting, and the subsequent chapters can be seen as each providing 'specials', directing attention to specific ideas.[2]

Light and environment

Theatrical applications of light are increasingly evident beyond the stage and light is increasingly seen as a transformative material in environmental and cultural sectors, and as an integral aspect of the wider 'experience economy'.[3] Bille and Sørensen, for instance, discuss the ways in which light can manifest social relationships, noting that 'the materiality of light has the ability to alter human experiences of space, and to define sensations of intimacy and exclusion' (2007, p.174). In the fields of cultural geography and architecture, analyses of the cultural and social significance of light and dark include the work of Schivelbusch (1988) and Edensor (2017); studies on light in the built environment (Isenstadt et al., 2015); and writing on environmental light and psychology (Laganier and van der Pol, 2011; Aardse and Alben, 2016; and Kries and Kugler, 2013).

Drawing on traditions of spectacular firework displays and *son et lumière* events, there is a growing popularity of public cultural events that are centred around light. Bringing communities together, light festivals and displays have enabled greater attentiveness to the social power of light, as well as its aesthetic form. Lyon's famous annual *Fête des lumières* evolved from the community practice of placing candles in domestic windows into an annual festival and permanent interventions that transform the city. Lyon's status as a 'city of light'[4] has inspired similar light festivals in many cities including Amsterdam, Berlin, Durham and Helsinki. Moreover, many cities use light to transform the experience of the urban environment year-round, such as in *A Symphony of Lights*, a daily light show in Hong Kong's Victoria Harbour.

An interesting example of theatrical light operating beyond the theatre, and in public and social settings, can be seen in Fuel Theatre's *The Litten Trees* (see Plates 1, 2 and 3). In March 2021, eight British lighting designers were commissioned to light up a tree that had been local to them during the coronavirus pandemic while theatres had been closed. While this was a national project, it operated at a fundamentally local level; the installations were not widely advertised, for fear of social gathering, but were instead intended to be encountered in local communities, happened upon by chance, as an interruption, or a kind of 'gift', to lift the spirit (Fuel, 2021, n.p.). For the designers involved, the scale of this work, lighting solitary trees or clusters, is likely to have been much smaller than the kinds of complexities demanded in their previous work for live performance, without the full team of collaborators and the many moving parts involved in a stage production. Yet, the gesture of this project, these eight invitations to encounter an element of a local landscape in a new or unexpected way, illustrates the three key areas that we focus on in this volume: experience, creativity and meaning. *The Litten Trees*, both literally and metaphorically, provided light in darkness and aimed to generate feelings of community and shared experience amid the isolation of the pandemic, 'artfully navigating complex social rules to deliver something unique, creative, beautiful and surprising to people all across the country' (Daw, 2021, p.11). This was not only achieved in the physical encounter with light but also in the digital experience, multiplying the modes through which audiences were invited to both experience and contemplate the work and its metaphorical resonances. *The Litten Trees* presented the work of lighting designers as offers to experience, creating conditions in which the familiar might be seen anew. In doing so, these installations used light to sculpt the appearances of the trees in a way that moved beyond the visual image, allowing for a more complex experience of encounter. Fittingly, for that most ephemeral of performance materials, the installations remained in situ for only a short period of time, emphasizing light as a distinctly temporal art form.

Operating at a relatively small scale, this contemporary light work exemplifies the ways in which this volume thinks with and about light. The three themes under which this volume is organized – experience, creativity and meaning – are each reflected in this example, which also, crucially, acknowledges the fundamental ways in which these areas are interconnected and interwoven. In creating an experience beyond the everyday, light in *The Litten Trees* offered a physical transformation of the locale and a remote, digital mode of engagement. As a distributed creative project, involving a number of different lighting designers, *The Litten Trees* highlighted both the active power of light and the creativity of the people who make it. In terms of meaning, the installations also offered a metaphorical exploration of light in the dark, an invitation for the audience to rethink their world in the time of the pandemic and find new relationships in/to their habitual environments. These solo pieces positioned light as an active agent, a performer and also offered a sense of the power of light as an individual, as well as a collaborative, art form. Significantly, the project also recognized the important creative labour of lighting designers, especially in the context of the artistic and financial constraints as a result of closed theatres and a global pandemic.

The (dramaturgical) power of light

Practitioners often attest to the power of light in ways that speak to its experiential or dramaturgical capacities. Canadian theatre-maker Robert Lepage, for instance, states that theatre and opera are fundamentally a 'celebration of light' and that 'the idea of theatre is first of all to bring people in a dark room and do [sic] the festival of light' (quoted in Delgado and Heritage, 1996, p.157). American director and designer Robert Wilson, whose work is often lauded for its use of light (Abulafia, 2016, pp.126–37; Crisafulli, 2013, pp.166–74; Di Benedetto, 2010, pp.35–62), has frequently emphasized the dramatic power of light, describing it as 'the most important actor on the stage' (quoted in Holmberg, 1996, p.128). The use of the word 'actor' in Wilson's statement is significant because it implies that light is an active force in performance, one that may dynamically and creatively contribute to the dramaturgical progression of the performance in question. There remains a great deal to be said, however, about the kind of 'actor' that light may be, and about precisely how it contributes to performance. As the German theatre director Dieter Dorn articulates, part of the potency of designed light lies in the ways in which it is marked as distinct:

> in everyday contexts, light serves to make existing things visible. On stage, however, it creates a new reality. 'Created' light helps us to thrust forward into spaces that establish and nurture their own reality, helps us to thrust forward into dimensions that are different from the ones we experience every day. (1999, p.10)

Dorn's comparison points to the ontological particularity of light in performance. His evocative description of light working to thrust us forward into new realities certainly attests to the power of light, but it is perhaps his description of stage light as 'created' that most succinctly accounts for the artistic role of light in performance. In general, light in performance is light that has been specifically introduced for that performance. Light that has been produced (or manipulated) artificially can be retracted as easily as it can be applied, and it can shift from one moment to the next in a way that is markedly different from our implicit understandings of the cycle of light and dark. This in part explains the power and particularity of theatrical light and why any performance staged in an interior space has to account for its agency.

While this distinction is important in thinking about the creative properties of light in performance, conceptual and aesthetic experiences of light in other contexts also profoundly impact our understanding of light as a material in and of performance. Technology allows us to create artificial brightness, prolonging the hours of visibility in our homes, offices and social spaces. Arnold Aronson argues that a consequence of this is that darkness has been banished from modern Western cities, meaning that the social and cultural context of theatrical lighting has utterly changed since the time of Adolphe Appia's still influential writings about passive and living light (Aronson, 2005, p.33). Neither is this a new phenomenon: a century ago Edward Gordon Craig observed: 'It is quite unnecessary, all this glare in theatres, because there is a glare in the streets at night and a glare in our houses too. And, leaving these, we have to be met by a greater glare or we grow depressed' (1925, p.144). Edensor notes that the re-emergence of urban darkness, in part due to economic limitations, might be 'conceived as an enriching and a re-enchantment of the temporal and spatial experience of the city at night' (2015b, p.436). Edensor's essential argument here is that, in public spaces, light and dark do not present a clear oppositional binary and that the experience of each is infused with strong cultural and social practices. As Edensor affirms, both light and dark offer myriad possibilities for affective experience. The use of light that permeates social and cultural life can transform rhythms of light and dark, suspending darkness or extending the light, allowing extremes of light and dark to coexist, and enfolding experiences of light and dark. In performance, darkness can appear and reappear multiple times, at irregular intervals, and the quality of light can shift in almost infinite ways. The uncanny interplay of light and dark marks the reality of the stage as fundamentally different from our own. This is what Dorn means by spaces that 'establish and nurture their own reality' (quoted earlier), and the instability of changeable light in an artificially managed space is at least part of the active role of light in performance. The artificiality and createdness of performance light mark it as both an aesthetic and an artistic phenomenon that works on its audiences in significant ways. This book presents these capacities of light as significant meaning-making interlocutors in performance, operating on multiple dramaturgical and affective levels.

The distinct dramaturgical power of light has been long recognized by designers, directors and playwrights. In the late nineteenth century, Adolphe Appia created lighting scores for Wagner's operas and Ibsen's plays that were highly influential in advocating for a radical new potential of light as both an essential and an integral element of performance. In the twentieth century, directors such as Max Reinhardt seized on light as a key expressive material in their productions, while Eugene O'Neill's *Long Day's Journey into Night*, for instance, is an example of a play that is framed through a dramaturgy of light where, through the structure of the play, light telescopes towards darkness, both literally and metaphorically. Richard Palmer notes the importance of script analysis in lighting design, advocating for the ability of light to create a kind of dramaturgical score, 'which shows how changes in the lighting over time will interact with scene shifts and actor movement to establish tempo and mood and to enhance the themes of the production' (1985, p.152). As we explore through this volume, light works in complex, multiple and overlapping ways, operating as both a component of performance and a material condition of performance, shaping how a work might be understood as well as how it might be experienced or felt.

Light fulfils a strange role in the theatre. As soon as light appears on stage it takes on multiple, symbolic meanings. It becomes, as the Austrian playwright Peter Handke observes, 'brightness that pretends to be another brightness [. . .] light that pretends to be another light' (Handke, 2002, p.30). Traditionally light's main role in the realistic theatre of illusion was to replicate the conditions of the natural world – most frequently pretending to be sunlight or the light reflected from the moon or recreating artificial light for interior spaces by 'cheating' onstage visible light sources with hidden stage lighting that is pretending to be 'another brightness'. Elsewhere, reflecting on the dramaturgical potential of light in dance and theatre, Jean Rosenthal writes that light 'provides important shortcuts to comprehension' and that in drama the 'most important role of lighting is to expose the nature of the struggle, to set the atmosphere for its development, and to underscore its resolution' (1972, p.60). In this way, Moran argues that the lighting designer plays a key dramaturgical role as the 'guardian of the story' (2017, p.110), shaping the way in which an audience sees a performance. For Moran, and in much writing about light in performance, this is an explicitly visual operation, acknowledging the power of light to direct attention and to signal meaning. This is a kind of dramaturgy of recognition that aligns with semiotic analyses of light – such as Abulafia's *The Art of Light on Stage* – that advocate for the power of light as a readable language of the theatre and one with significant responsibility for the way in which an entire performance is understood.

However, to focus solely on representational or semiotic capacities of light would be to reduce the meaning-making qualities of light to its pictorial qualities. Light might represent or reproduce certain settings, seasons or times, but it is never simply an image that transmits information. As lighting designer Lucy Carter notes, audiences attending to an unfolding performance are 'looking for more than just the story', and are receptive also to psychological suggestion, wider references, and the sensation of seeing and feeling 'things shifting so fast and telling more than one story' (quoted in Moran, 2017, p.115). Such questions of phenomenological experience are especially pertinent to light because of its distinct (im)materiality and its imbrication with perception and experience, and because of the particular ways in which light reveals making sense of performance to be a richly complex and embodied process. Gernot Böhme persuasively argues that the phenomenology of light troubles the notion that we cannot see light in itself, noting that to attend phenomenologically to light is to attend to colour, space and specific qualities of light, as a substance that can be encountered, through 'glowing, brilliance, flickering, shadow, and much more' (2014, p.64). Contributions in this volume take this argument forward, explicitly positioning the phenomenology of light as a distinctly bodily experience, comprising spatial, kinaesthetic and felt affects. We contend that light is especially interesting as a vital phenomenon of performance, a substance that emerges at the confluence of affective, sensual and symbolic apprehension, and one that is inextricably enmeshed with all other materials of performance.

Light in research and practice

Lighting designers have long been the custodians of the aesthetics and status of light in performance. This has rendered lighting something of an oral tradition, propelled by practical and technical experimentation that has been handed down from one generation of designers to the next. Innovations in the use of light in performance have been documented since Renaissance Italy, when 'architect/designers' explained their practical and aesthetic solutions for lighting the stage (Bergman, 1977; Palmer, 2013). Examples from the last century or so include Loïe Fuller's live performance experimentation with light, fabric and the body from the 1890s; Josef Svoboda's spatial experiments with light and projection to create 'psycho-plastic space' from the 1960s (Burian, 1971, p.126), and Wilson's considerations of light as an actor (see Holmberg, 1996, p.128). More recently, in universities, there have also been experimentations focused on the creative possibilities of light and projection, which have then been translated from the academy to the international stage. Palmer and Popat's research with projection designers KMA, for example (Popat and Palmer, 2007 and 2008) began with light-focused investigations in a black box studio and later evolved into material for public performance (e.g. DV8 Physical Theatre's *To Be Straight With You*, 2008–9).[5] This collaboration reflects a shift in the field, which has begun to initiate an exchange of insights between lighting designers and researchers. Also significant here is the synthesis between teaching and practice, with a number of important practitioners developing their work and thinking about light through regular teaching, including Kathy Perkins and Fereshteh Rostampour (United States), Kimmo Karjunen (Finland), Flaviana Sampaio (Brazil), and Nick Moran (United Kingdom). The reciprocal relationship between the academy and professional lighting design has a long tradition that is also reflected throughout this volume. Nick Hunt and Hansjörg Schmidt's chapter exemplifies a laboratory approach, with light emerging from practice into research, Jennifer Tipton's chapter acknowledges the rich connections between her teaching and creative practices, and Psyche Chui's creative work in pedagogical settings enables intercultural experimentation with new forms. It is also significant to note how many of the academic contributors to this volume, in addition to the editors, are also practising lighting designers. This book exemplifies these new connections, building, in particular, from fora where research and practice have been shared – namely, the Performing Light Symposium at the University of Leeds in January 2017, and Scandlight[6] in Malmö in June 2018.[7] These meetings have instigated new conversations about the role and nature of light in performance, beginning to push the boundaries of knowledge and experimentation in the field that this book expands and develops.

The prevalence of technical and instructional textbooks on theatrical light speaks to the complexity and skill involved in the craft of lighting design. Many of the books that for a long time dominated the field of stage lighting publication (e.g. Bentham, 1968; Pilbrow, 1970) focus almost exclusively on the technical and practical decisions required in realizing light on stage as well as the ways in which designers might best use the technology that facilitates that work. While these texts serve to show that the skills of lighting designers have been understood – at least in some corners of the field – for some time, a historical over-emphasis on the technical process of the mechanics of the discipline has left less space for consideration of the affective, aesthetic and creative role of light in performance. It is only in recent years that performance light has begun to receive more sustained scholarly interest. The recent expansion of study in this field, which this volume celebrates and extends, has brought new attention, new questions and new insights about the nature and value of performance light. Salient discoveries from this contemporary flourishing of light research include the profound ways in which the evolution of lighting practice has impacted on, and co-evolved with, wider theatrical developments and dramaturgy (Baugh, 2005; Palmer, 2013; Gröndahl, 2014); the depth of work and thinking that lighting professionals engage in (Hunt and Melrose, 2005; Moran, 2017; Zezulka, 2019); the complexities of images created with light, and the ways in which these might be read or understood in the context of performance (Crisafulli, 2013; Abulafia, 2016); and the imbrication of experiential and meaning-making processes in the phenomenological encounter with light (Aragay and Escoda, 2012; Zerdy and Schweitzer, 2016; Graham, 2018). Productively, each of these insights raises further questions and extends the understanding of light itself, inviting new ways of analysing performance and related creative practices.

The language used in existing lighting literature reveals the evolution of attitudes towards lighting design, designers and their practice.[8] The fact that many of these books prioritize procedure over creative process is indicative of the difficulty that many practitioners have in articulating both their process and the impact that light can make to a production, dramaturgically as well as affectively.

In many of these sources, it is evident that lighting has traditionally been relegated to a 'support' function, making the lighting designer's role merely facilitative. Even if this is not quite so explicitly stated, the structures and systems within which a lighting designer is expected to work necessarily dictate light's relegation in the majority of Western approaches to theatrical practice. In *A Syllabus of Stage Lighting,* McCandless writes, 'Once the artistic approach has been decided upon, then the practical problem of designing the visual effects [. . .] can proceed' (1941, p.4). Though he does later concede that lighting design is a form of 'artistic expression', he repeatedly maintains that the main purpose of lighting is 'to convince an audience without its being aware of it as lighting, per se' (McCandless, 1941, p.78). Interestingly, a former student and life-long friend of McCandless, the pioneering lighting designer Jean Rosenthal referred to McCandless as 'the granddaddy of us all' because of his work in establishing a method for organizing lighting ideas. At the same time, however, she notes that, though he was 'simply enamoured of light', McCandless 'could not communicate about it', nor did he know 'how to apply it dramatically' (Rosenthal, 1972, p.16). An outlier in the field of lighting textbooks, Richard Palmer's *The Lighting Art* (1985 and 1994) gives thorough consideration to the aesthetics of stage lighting, rooted in an understanding of the play text and the ways in which light might contribute to the dramatic experience.

The oft-repeated maxim that lighting is at its best when unnoticed is, thankfully, part of a (slowly) dying attitude towards light. Theatre critic Lyn Gardner notes that lighting 'no longer seems an afterthought, but is integral to the whole look and feel of the production' (2009, n.p.) and can become 'its own character in the unfolding drama' (Gardner, 2009, n.p.). Journalist and writer Mark Fisher notes that descriptions of light in popular criticism as 'atmospheric' or 'evocative' are essentially meaningless without a fuller contextualization about the nature of the atmosphere in question, or the emotions or associations evoked (2015, p.179). Another critic, Matt Trueman, has also commented on the dramaturgical significance of light, noting that light animates and punctuates performance, while at the same time observing that lighting design is 'all too easy to overlook' and also 'bloody hard to write about' (2016, n.p.). However, not all critics are comfortable discussing light: it was only after serving as a judge for the Knight of Illumination (KOI) awards in 2018 that 'Britain's longest serving theatre critic', Michael Billington, 'realised that lighting can fulfil different functions in different art-forms' and appreciated 'the sheer diversity of possibilities within theatrical lighting' (2018, n.p.). This revelation exposes a historical bias in UK theatre towards the literary and a negation of how all of the elements of theatre coalesce to make meaning in performance. For Billington, direct engagement with professional lighting designers (following a lighting masterclass for critics instigated by the Association of Lighting Designers[9]) and the focused seeing that being a KOI judge required of him enabled him to see performance with a new sensibility, even after fifty years of nightly theatre visits. Though this sensibility may have felt new to Billington following this experience, light will still have been a material condition of the theatre that he had engaged with to that point but had almost entirely ignored in making sense of these performances for readers of his newspaper columns. As lighting designer and contributor to this volume, Jennifer Tipton puts it: '99.9 percent of an audience is not aware of the lighting, but 100 percent is affected by it' (quoted in Robertson, 1984, n.p.). Moran notes the 'intimidating' (2017, p.22) nature of specialist technical knowledge that is seen to be needed to understand what light is doing in performance. This preoccupation with the technical in a way that prioritizes its perceived impenetrability over light's dramaturgical and affective potential does a disservice to both the profession and the material.

Beyond the immediate field of light there has been a deep and exciting expansion of ways of thinking about scenography 'as a mode of encounter and exchange founded on spatial and material relations between bodies, objects and environments' (McKinney and Palmer, 2017, p.2). This critical expansion has been referred to as a recent 'scenographic turn' in academic thinking that is highlighted in the editors' introduction to the first issue of the *Theatre and Performance Design* journal – a publication that itself provides:

> an assertion that scenography, as a way of reading performance that takes account of the interrelationship of all its constituent elements, is formally instated as a significant contributor to the production of knowledge, not only in performance studies but across a range of closely related fields. (Collins and Aronson, 2015, p.1)

The chapters in this volume contribute to this perceived 'turn' by expanding current conversations around the role and value of light in performance (Baugh, 2013; Crisafulli, 2013; Palmer, 2013; Abulafia, 2016; Zerdy and Schweitzer, 2016; Moran, 2017; Graham, 2018; Zezulka, 2019). This brings light into wider conversations across the disciplines of theatre and performance studies in which scenography is no longer dismissed as craft-focused, stage decoration (e.g. Parker and Smith, 1963; Reid, 1996) but has become recognized in its own right as a vital, central aspect of understanding and making performance. This recognition has coincided with a growing awareness of and interest in aspects of performance studies that have placed greater emphasis on the non-written elements of theatre and on the phenomenological, the kinaesthetic and associated areas such as audience reception.

In performance, light 'is interwoven with space, time, material and affect' and is 'the material that binds together all other scenographic elements' (Zezulka, 2019, p.16). This makes it an extremely potent force that is both creative (Palmer, 2013) and scenographic (Graham, 2016). As cultural anthropologist Tim Ingold reminds us, even 'though we do not see light, we do see in light' (2005, p.97), drawing attention not only to the necessity for light on stage for basic illumination but also to how light affects and is affected by other production elements, as well as its potential power to affect audience perception, to direct attention and to become a discrete dramaturgical force in its own right. Yet, even in publications that focus primarily on scenography (e.g. Howard, 2002; Lotker and Gough, 2013) surprisingly little attention has been paid to the role of light as a fundamental scenographic material that conditions an audience's reception of performance. Light is barely mentioned in Howard's seminal *What is Scenography?* (2002), and while the 2013 special edition of *Performance Research*, 'On Scenography', purports to address the 'many faces' of scenography (Lotker and Gough, 2013, p.3) and advocates a 'spatial dramaturgy' (Lotker and Gough, 2013, pp.4–5), there is not a single contribution in the volume that addresses light in the theatre. More recent research (e.g. McKinney and Palmer, 2017; Hann, 2019; and, since

2015, *Theatre and Performance Design*) has productively extended critical conversations about scenographic practice and addressed key aspects of scenographic relationality, affectivity and materiality that are directly relevant to considerations of light. There remains a need for further consideration of light in the kind of depth that our contributors are able to do in this volume because light conditions the experience of all other elements in performance and has not yet been fully explored in these terms.

Contemporary performance lighting

This volume seeks to extend the depth of the field by taking light seriously, as a substance of the theatre, as an integral practice of performance-making, and as a distinct and meaningful mode of encounter. While each of the following chapters represents a unique perspective on the practice of light, the collection builds on much recent scholarship in performance studies by following an approach grounded in phenomenological and material analysis. The materiality of light is difficult to qualify and often eludes direct description. Edensor (2015a) maintains that light 'transcends the cognitive and moves into the nonrepresentational, the realm of the affective and sensual' (p.139), highlighting the visceral and often inexpressible impact of light in performance. Light is, paradoxically, an immaterial material; its materiality is obtained by proxy, by coming into contact with an object in space. Light's materiality is inherently bound to the spatial and temporal conditions in which it is employed.

These tensions and paradoxes mean that light is not only a component of scenography, which might be productively thought of in relation to the relationality, affectivity, materiality (McKinney and Palmer, 2017) and temporality (Nibbelink, 2019) of performance materials that have been revealed by the 'scenographic turn' (Collins and Aronson, 2015), but also a distinct phenomenon that serves to enrich understandings of the nature of affectivity and ephemerality in performance. What is at stake in this volume, then, is not only a greater expansion of the ways in which light operates as a significant and consequential element of and for performance, but also an examination of what the analysis of light might offer to performance studies widely. In the sections that follow, we attend to this provocation through three overlapping concepts that frame deeper engagement with light: experience, creativity and meaning. In this volume, experience refers to both bodily encounters with light and the ways in which experiences are inflected and shaped by light as a material. The second core principle we examine here relates to creativity: the agency of lighting designers and the active dramaturgical contributions that underpin lighting designers' creative practice. The final critical framing we put forward in this volume is meaning, by which we mean the ways in which light shapes and generates meaning-making processes in performance. We are proposing these three core principles as distinct yet overlapping lenses for the analysis of light in performance, and these allow for an expanded understanding that is attendant to the affective, dramaturgical and material potential of light as a medium for and of performance. Individually, these areas – reflected in the sections into which this book is organized – provide a means of thinking through the operation of light in performance, and in combination, they provide a framework for the holistic study of light as a creative material in performance.

Pan Pan Theatre's touring production of Samuel Beckett's *All That Fall* (2011–18), an image of which graces our cover, is an example of the ways in which this framework might operate. Written as a radio play, *All That Fall* presents a score of light in a context where previously none was defined, creating 'an intermedial reimagining, highlighting a tension between light and darkness' (Johnson and Heron, 2020, p.48). Interestingly, this same production is used by Alston and Welton (2017) as an example that draws on the power of darkness in performance, and by Yaron Shyldkrot in this volume in relation to the 'hazy vision' (p.88) afforded by the intermingling of crafted brightness and darkness. Alston and Welton characterize the darkness in this piece as 'thick and pervasive', noting that the intermittent glowing of the light provides an 'affective counterpoint' to the darkness, resulting in a sensual entanglement of 'enigma and foreboding' (2017, pp.2–3). That this production is equally pertinent to a study of darkness as it is to one of light demonstrates that the phenomena of light and dark in performance are interdependent and indivisible.

All That Fall places its audience within a shared environment, described by the artists as a 'theatrically tuned listening chamber'; the performance creates a sense that the whole space is somehow responding to the sounds of the voices from the text. This production collapses the audience and performance space together; the audience sits on rocking chairs scattered throughout the space while the theatrical materials of light and sound permeate the room and (human) actors are present only sonically. Within this environment, light enfolds the audience completely; it skims across the carpet under our feet, light bulbs hang and glimmer above our heads and a solid wall of light in front of us commands attention. The darkness, when it comes, feels equally encompassing.

Experience

Fundamental to this volume is a focus on the experience of light, comprising phenomenological accounts of light in performance as well as analyses of the affective impact of light in a range of performance contexts. This focus serves to advance conceptions of light beyond the procedural or semiotic accounts that have dominated the field heretofore. This centrality of experience significantly advances understanding of light as a material of performance, and through this core theme contributors consider the ways in which light influences the experience of performers and audience members alike.

Returning to the example of Pan Pan's *All That Fall* through the lens of experience, it is worth noting that this production creates a realm in which light becomes a significant material in the encounter, but one that relates to the content more obliquely than might be the case in other theatrical examples. The multiple overlapping scores of light, sound, space and voice emerge as a kind of synaesthetic experience, in which light and dark seem to extend as bodily presences in the space. Within this encounter, the light occasions a continuum of sensual experience, from the inviting glow of a barely shining bulb to the wall of lanterns – visible on our cover image – blazing directly into the audience's eyes at key moments in the performance, to the seemingly tactile presence of the encroaching darkness. Thinking through the experience of this production, and more specifically, the ways in which light is experienced in this performance reveals a complex sensory dramaturgy, in which this 'tuned' space for active listening becomes a site of synaesthetic engagement where the whole body of the spectator is invited to participate. The shifts in light, and the patterns and shapes of light that emerge throughout the work, clearly mark the substance of light as a kind of creative actor in the piece; light is a force that interacts with all other performance elements and that shapes the vignettes in the story visually, rhythmically and kinaesthetically.

The shifting flow of light in *All That Fall* produces a bodily engagement with light, layered over the content of the text. The bodily engagement extends from the visual experience of watching the configurations of light change, to the physical sensation of moving from light to dark and to light again. The brightness of the light ranges from a soft glow to an uncomfortable glare, and this forms part of a distinctly bodily reaction to the work. The sensation of light here incorporates an awareness of the lanterns, and the means by which light is produced, but remains principally an environmental encounter that multiplies rather than clarifies the textual interpretation. This multiplicity in the process of encounter in *All That Fall* is central to this volume's foregrounding of bodily experience as a key mode of light analysis more widely.

Artist Olafur Eliasson has embraced the theatrical potential of light to work directly on the body in many of his works. In *The Weather Project* (London 2003), for example, visitors to Tate Modern stepped into the vast space of the Turbine Hall to face a dazzling sun. The theatrical illusion of the sun was created by a semicircle of mono-frequency lamps reflected in a mirrored ceiling. The narrow wavelengths of light restricted the audience's sense of colour and the quality of light was enhanced by fog which was introduced to the air and appeared to make the light tangible. This installation, in which the technical components deliberately revealed themselves in close-up, created a playful theatrical atmosphere through light, which directly affected how audiences behaved in the space. Bodies rested, sat down on the bare concrete floor, and enjoyed the experience of being bathed in the unusual yellow light. At one level the light created a nostalgic space of contemplation but other participants felt that the light gave them permission to relax in a public space. Some lay down looking at their reflection and played games, making connections with other strangers in the mirrored ceiling, and in groups worked together to create patterns or used their bodies to spell out rude words. The particular quality of light, made more tangible through the haze and the mirrored ceiling, worked to create a social space of play in which everyday behaviour might be altered. The experience of light therefore both foregrounded our own bodily relationship to the sun and the fundamental role that weather plays in shaping our society and every aspect of our lives.

All That Fall and *The Weather Project* reveal complexities in the analysis of light, demonstrating how vital experience is in the analysis of light. This is an area that is only beginning to be understood. These two examples (and many more in this volume) illustrate the significance of the experiential encounter and the ways in which light is felt by audiences. This volume argues for the consideration of the experience of light as a vital part of an analytical framework for performance light. In this way, attending to the spatial relationships between spectators and light sources, observed relationships between performers and light, between light and materials all form key considerations in a performance analysis that is alert to the possibilities of material performance.

The experience of light, and darkness, is attended to in this volume in a number of exciting ways. Scott Palmer's chapter explores how multiple qualities of light and dark may shape the audience's experience of performance, drawing on a range of examples including installation and 'immersive' relational performances. Similarly, David Shearing and Yaron Shyldkrot both explore bodily immersion in light, examining the kinaesthetic operation of light and the framing of perception and new perspectives that light may afford. Shearing reflects on qualities of light in his own performance-making practice, and Shyldkrot interrogates notions of visual obfuscation in his own and others' performance work. Lucy Carter's chapter draws on her experience in contemporary dance to posit a framework for lighting design that connects to experiential and choreographic scores of performance. Moving further beyond the theatre, Jesper Kongshaug's chapter examines the impact of light in public spaces – including his detailed design work in Copenhagen's Tivoli Gardens. Kongshaug's theatrical understanding of the potential of light to affect experience is supported by significant empirical evidence to demonstrate how this has directly influenced public behaviour.

Creativity

In establishing light as a component of performance, both the creative, performative capacities of light, as well as the creative practices of lighting designers, need to be explored. This section of the book advocates for the role of the lighting designer as integral to collaborative performance practices while also providing scholarly analyses of work and working practices in the field.

Creative and dramaturgical agency may occasionally be attributed to light as a scenographic element, but authorial agency is rarely granted to lighting designers themselves. This is partially due to the fact that, as Hann argues, 'set designers have historically cemented their status as lead designers through the holistic qualities of scenography' (2019, p.49). Often, light is described in a way that is separate from the authorial agency and creative contribution of the lighting designer. This can be seen in some theatre criticism, in which a particular property or quality of light, or light's effect on a production, might be described in varying levels of detail, but the lighting designer (that is, the person responsible for creating that effect/affect) is not mentioned. For instance, in a recent review of *The Animal Kingdom* at London's Hampstead Theatre, theatre critic Claire Armitstead writes about 'the fizz of the electric lighting' (2022, n.p.), without naming lighting designer Holly Ellis.[10] Sometimes, the lighting is described as a thing that belongs to and is somehow separate from the lighting designer, rather than something they have actively created. In Susannah Clapp's review of *The Sun, the Moon, and the Stars* (Theatre Royal Stratford East, London, June 2021), she describes how the central character is 'trapped in Peter McKintosh's fine box design – hard-edged, made golden and finally starry by Oliver Fenwick's lighting' (2021, n.p.). While it is the light that initiates this transformation of the space, the designer's contribution is minimized in this construction. Where light – and therefore the lighting designer – is afforded a much more active and dramaturgical role, its potential is brought to the fore. The shift towards a view of light as a material 'thing', what Graham, borrowing from Harman (2011), articulates as an 'object oriented ontology' (2018a, p.123) of light, can be seen throughout this volume, while this section focuses explicitly on the creative practice of lighting artists.

As Peter Mumford advocates elsewhere, 'contemporary dance has led the way in the development of lighting as a visual language' (quoted in Palmer, 2013, p.250). Dance practices have proved a fertile ground for the development of the creative potential of performance lighting, as evidenced in Loïe Fuller's experiments in the late nineteenth century and reflected in this volume in chapters by Jennifer Tipton, Lucy Carter and Katharine Williams.[11] One key reason why dance has led the way has been the recognition that light is central to the performance experience and consequently a significant and integral part of devising processes and rehearsals. A recent volume by Finnish lighting designers, practitioners and artists (Humalisto, Karjunen, et al., 2019) has also advocated the benefits to creative processes when lighting designers are integral to collaborative processes of performance-making and the critical importance of playful experimentation and creative 'flow' (after Csikszentmihalyi (1990)) that emerges as a result.

There are long-standing structural hierarchies in theatre practice that lighting practitioners must work within and against. Pilbrow, for instance, often advocates for the role of light to go beyond a merely functional role, though there are some passages in his influential book, *Stage Lighting Design: The Art, the Craft, the Life,* that demonstrate some still-prevailing attitudes towards light. For instance, he maintains that 'lighting supports the storytelling process' (Pilbrow, 2010, p.9) but also that it is 'clearly no part of [the lighting designer's] job to do anything but enhance the appearance of the set and costumes' (Pilbrow, 2010, p.36). This deference to the director and what is sometimes, reductively, referred to as their 'vision' is an attitude that lingers from the early days of lighting design as a profession. Moran (2007, p.78; 2018, p.84) advises that 'when the lighting designer and the director significantly disagree, the lighting designer has only two real choices – do what the director asks or quit'. While he acknowledges that persuasion may be possible, this attitude only serves to perpetuate these existing hierarchies. Interestingly, Moran follows this, in both editions of *Performance Lighting Design* (2007 and 2018), with the provocation that 'there is no reason other than tradition why the designers cannot lead the interpretation of the text onto the stage' (p.78 and p.84, respectively). Moran describes designers who would undertake this role as 'a vanguard for a new practice that will refresh live performance for a much more visually orientated generation' (2007, p.78; 2018, p.84). The fact that this is posited as a 'new practice' in both editions of this book, eleven years apart, speaks volumes about the industry's entrenched hierarchies and resistance to change. It is worth noting, however, that while this deference to the figure of the director still features prominently in many design textbooks, a more collaborative approach is clearly advocated for in a number of texts on directing. Anne Bogart, for instance, tells the story of an occasion where, following a design meeting: 'To my horror, the designers and the crew built exactly what I described' (2014, p.49). Through this anecdote, Bogart is implicitly allowing space for a much more lateral power structure that recognizes 'designers require the freedom to experiment and search' (Bogart, 2014, p.84). This volume advocates for greater attentiveness to the potency of design that will allow for a more nuanced approach to collaboration in theatre-making and therefore co-creation in relation to light.

Thinking about the creative role of light in *All That Fall* also extends to the work of the artists who created it. In this, it is perhaps especially important to note that this production, like the company itself, was driven by the artistic partnership of company founders and co-artistic directors Aedín Cosgrove and Gavin Quinn.[12] Though not entirely unique to Pan Pan, this model of artistic directorship being shared by a designer (Cosgrove) and a director (Quinn) speaks to both an ambition and care for the role of design materials in the work produced, and it seems impossible to comment on the synaesthetic experience for the audience without also noting the collaborative process of its creation.

This volume extends conversations on the creativity of lighting designers and the creative practice of light through chapters that examine design practice in depth – such as those by Jennifer Tipton and Michael Breiner. Katharine Williams' chapter explores lighting design as a feminist practice, drawing specifically on their collaboration with RashDash. Meanwhile, in a discipline that has been dominated by Western practices, Psyche Chui's chapter makes a valuable contribution by exploring her intercultural practice, drawing on aesthetics from Chinese opera. Kelli Zezulka's chapter provides rich insight into the usually hidden labour of lighting design processes. Her research explores the way collaboration unfolds in technical rehearsals, using detailed linguistic analysis to examine the ways in which lighting designers, directors and programmers communicate in the moment of creation. Taken in combination, all of the chapters in this section speak to the value of light as a creative medium, acknowledging the role of light and lighting designers in the making of performance and the potential of light's qualities (colour, intensity, movement, rhythm, directionality, texture, shadow and so on) in the visual, temporal and experiential composition of performance.

Meaning

Theatre and performance offer a privileged space for the construction and exploration of meaning, and so, in these contexts, light operates in a complex system of meaning-making. This volume proposes to examine light's relationship to the production of meaning in relation to both the qualities of light as a creative material and the manifold operation of light as a material of encounter. Elsewhere, meaning in light has been considered principally in relation to a semiotic coding of the readable stage (see, e.g. Abulafia, 2016; Fischer-Lichte, 1992). While we acknowledge the value of that work, this volume positions meaning-making processes in relation to the generative capacities of material light in the moment of encounter. The ongoing expansion of research on light has begun to suggest significant ways in which light might both condition and shape our understanding of the world around us. As Zerdy and Schweitzer argue, 'in approaching a performance of light, we must contend with light's conditioning of our experience' (2016, p.6). Greater attentiveness to the layering of meaning-making in performance in general (as in, e.g. Lehmann, 2006) and scenography in particular (McKinney and Butterworth, 2009; McKinney and Palmer, 2017; Hann, 2019) points to complex polysemic modes of thinking and being occasioned through performance. Explorations in this volume contribute to these expanded understandings by considering closely what is occasioned by light in performance and related practices. The affective and dynamic meaning-making potential of light is borne out in the ways that light enables unique modes of encounter and generates both substantive events in performance and material conditions in which performance is experienced.

In Pan Pan's *All That Fall*, the process of meaning-making in light exceeds an indexical relationship to imagined storytelling details to comprise a generative encounter in which meaning can be produced. Light, in this performance, becomes a generative material; in sensory terms, in pushing the piece beyond representation, and the ways that it plays with theatrical convention, the light here generates meanings and terms of encounter that are at the core of the meaning-making encounter with the work. Here, light is an integral dramaturgical material; it is a leading element in the way this performance is composed to *make sense* (in intertwined cognitive and embodied ways) for its audience. Light affords a particular kind of engagement with the performance, expanding possibilities of meaning-making through its operation as a distinct language of performance that is continually and productively in relationship with all other elements.

As may be evident from the image on our cover, this production presents a distinct and spectacular image of light and space. For Abulafia, the signification of this kind of image lies in the 'sensation of light itself' (2016, p.111). In his account, the principal qualities of signification through the sensation of light are 'spectacularity' – the aesthetic pleasure derived from light itself and a sense of the virtuosity of its craft – and 'hypermediacy' – the explicit and active presence of technology in our reading of an image (Abulafia, 2016, p.111). Yet, neither of these seem to *fully* account for the signification of light in this case, nor for the meaning-making capacities of performance light more generally. Certainly, the ebb and flow of light is a source of aesthetic pleasure in this production, and the exposure of the lanterns and bulbs in the space would seem to indicate an explicit engagement with technology. Furthermore, as Abulafia correctly points out, light, when used as a material in itself, can display a performative autonomy, creating elements of performance independent of the text, and multiple meanings that need to be negotiated through performance (Abulafia, 2016, p.112). This example shows that, in addition to spectacularity and hypermediacy, there is a third important quality in experiencing light itself, that of the phenomenal encounter. As we have already discussed, this phenomenal encounter relates to the bodily and affective experience of light and dark but, significantly, the distinct material encounter with light also becomes a site for the generation of meaning.

The meaning-making capacities of light are thus deeply entwined with its materiality. In *All That Fall*, light does not serve to cast light onto something else but is instead the subject of its own illumination. Significantly, for our purposes, the shifting flow of light does not illustrate or support discrete meanings defined elsewhere in the production, nor does it 'suggest a figurative or real-world alignment' (Johnson and Heron, 2020, p.49). This does not, however, suggest an absence of meaning; rather – and excitingly – this production points to the manifold production and operation of meaning in performance. Meaning, here, is something that emerges productively and substantively in the multiplicity of performance languages, including a distinct offering from light. Light swells and fades in tandem with the sound but without corresponding exactly; light seems to exist separately, following a distinct rhythm or logic. Shapes or structures of light sometimes emerge as we hear the central character encounter a new person or event on her journey, but changes in light also begin to occur before or after these moments. This sense, of co-existence rather than correspondence, creates a sense of a multilayered sensual experience, one that is evocative without being representational. In the slippages that begin to seep in between the aural and visual chapters of the action, light seems to suggest itself as a proxy for the material bodies of the characters, and then to resist this elision. In resisting, the light performs not only as a commentary on the action but also as a body in the space, one whose impactful presence shapes the ways in which the audience understands the work.

Accordingly, the consideration of meaning-making in light offers an expanded view of performance aesthetics, positioning the operation of light as a dynamic and consequential language of performance. Through this focus on meaning, this volume is able to consider the material, cultural and ethical operation of light in a range of performance contexts. This framing extends ideas of light in the field of performance, examining the dramaturgical, meaning-making capacity of light as a material and its capacity to influence and generate meaning within performance.

In this book, Katherine Graham's chapter examines the scenographic action of light, and the multiple ways that this can co-compose meaning in performance. Lighting designer Paule Constable explores the ways in which she uses light as a storytelling tool in her practice. She argues for the importance of rigour in the lighting design process, examining how light articulates and shapes meaning in performance, and how she approaches this with a collaborative sensibility and an awareness of how light intersects with other aspects of theatre practice. Constable's reflections on her practice connect the materiality of light (its muscularity and 'smell' (p.182, 189), this volume) to dramaturgy and storytelling.

Elsewhere in this section, Nick Hunt and Hansjörg Schmidt connect the materiality of light to a sited encounter with practices of seeing. Their chapter reflects on their interactive light installation, *Traces,* which asks its audience to explore their own engagement with light, manipulating reflective panels to catch light, and in so doing, to catch their own contingent experience of seeing and playing with light. Christopher Baugh's chapter theorizes perceptions of light more broadly, arguing that the perception of light is 'socially and culturally constructed' (p.201, this volume). Through this understanding that light is contingent on both physiological and sociological factors, it becomes possible to view the action of manipulated light in performance in terms of its wider significance. Each of these chapters, and indeed in the chapters elsewhere in this volume, makes clear that light constructs transformative possibilities that are indivisible from the meanings and structures of the performances, thus verifying, and extending, Crisafulli's assertion that light is 'structural, constructive, poetic, and dramaturgic' (2013, p.18).

Focusing on light

This volume is the first to bring together international practitioners and academics of performance light and, in so doing, aims to celebrate the depth and diversity of making and thinking with light today. Where other accounts of the evolution of stage lighting have tended to focus on the work of specific (almost exclusively male) practitioners – namely, usually, Adolphe Appia, Edward Gordon Craig, Josef Svoboda and Robert Wilson – in aiming to focus on light and lighting practices, this volume has been able to take a wider view. Here, we have included a variety of voices, including scholars, practitioners and scholar–practitioners, writing about light in and beyond performance from international perspectives, thus moving away from the notion of the single artist and towards a more diverse engagement with the stuff and substance of light itself. Significantly, contributors in this book reflect on light not only from different perspectives but also in different ways, enabling us to interrogate the multiple ways in which light is used as a creative material. What emerges, cumulatively, is a picture of light that is never static, but is shifting, heterogenous and contingent. Light is thus shown to be a material that is more intricately embedded in aesthetic, dramaturgical and expressive processes than has previously been accounted for in subject literature.

The multiplicity of voices included here also addresses the significant difficulties in articulating an ephemeral material and its temporal qualities on the stage in written form. Issues associated with the documentation of the contribution of light to performance have also impacted on theatre scholarship (see Palmer, 2013, pp.xiv–xv). Historical research has to rely upon contemporary writings, reviews and artists' impressions. Sketches, paintings and engravings were often designed to represent spectacular moments on stage as a way of publicizing the event to a prospective audience. They are often impressionistic rather than an accurate documentation of a moment on stage (e.g. see Figure 1 on p.31 and Plate 31). Despite their importance to our understanding of past performance, it is important to be equally cautious of graphic illustration and photographs as of written sources in providing definitive evidence of how stage lighting may have appeared at a particular moment in history. Acknowledging the problematics associated with attempting to analyse light when it has not been experienced at first hand in performance is also important in understanding the context of research in this field. In this book, light is documented in several ways including recollection; evocation of detail; exploration of creative decisions in the process; examination of wider social, cultural, or philosophical connections; and by reference to illustrative images. This is in part because, as Moran points out, light is 'context-dependent' and does not leave artefacts after performance in the ways that set and costume might (2017, p.26), nor is it reproducible after the event in the ways that even other ephemeral materials, like sound, might be. Through presenting this range of approaches to articulating light, we hope this book contributes to yet further expansion of analysis in the field and that the inclusion of new voices here paves the way for further diversification of the field of light research.

The analysis of light here is framed by the key themes outlined earlier: experience, creativity and meaning. These themes are reflected in the three main sections of the book, in each of which contributions have been grouped in ways that initiate or expand conversations around these integral ideas. It is important to note, however, that these are not rigid divisions, and these principles are in evidence throughout the book. Scott Palmer's chapter, for instance, examines felt encounters with light in ways that attend to experience, but also points to the creative capacities of light, in its ability to forge new connections. Jesper Kongshaug's chapter positions valuable material about the measurable ways in which light shapes experience and directly affects behaviour but also speaks to creative processes through which the detail of technical care is translated into an aesthetic experience. David Shearing and Lucy Carter's chapters each speak across themes of experience, creativity and meaning in their entwining of aesthetic, ethical and dramaturgical thinking. Yaron Shyldkrot's contribution directly addresses the experiential, processual and uncertain modes of experiencing extreme levels of light or dark, and his analysis also contributes to understandings of the meaning-making potential of encounters with light and darkness.

Through a linguistic ethnographic approach, Kelli Zezulka's chapter explicates the hidden mechanisms of collaboration and underlying structures of agency, power and hierarchy that characterize technical rehearsals, contributing to an understanding of how lighting designers and programmers work and bringing to light the 'unseen work' (Essin, 2015) that is integral to theatre production, which is fundamental to how light is created on stage and connects to wider ideas of experience-making and authorship. Both Katharine Williams and Psyche Chui connect their artistic practice with light to wider meaning-making contexts – for Williams, through the lens of feminist practice and, for Chui, from her unique positionality as a lighting designer working across cultural and artistic traditions from both East and West.

In different sections of the book, both Paule Constable and Michael Breiner speak about the thinking that underpins their design work, advocating for a clear framework that connects the materiality of light with its dramaturgical role. Katherine Graham's chapter explores the meaning-making possibilities of the aesthetic encounter with light, in ways that are reflective of the experiential qualities of such encounters. Chapters from Christopher Baugh and Nick Hunt and Hansjörg Schmidt note the contingency of perception and are positioned here in relation to the ways that performance invites its audience to construct meanings, but this material also connects with wider ideas of experience and creativity discussed elsewhere in the volume.

This cross-pollination emphasizes the richness of field, as well as the depths of each of the themes that we have posited as integral to the analysis of light. As a result, each of the chapters that follow can be read independently, but this book can also be read thematically – with each of the contributions in a single section in productive conversation with each other, and with the volume as a whole. The insights about light that emerge in this book extend conversations about the significance of light in new directions, asking deeper questions of its position in artistic practice, illustrating the myriad possibilities of light as a material and the infinite possibilities it holds for performance practice.

Notes

1 See, for example, volumes by Palmer (2013), Baugh (2013), Crisafulli (2013), Abulafia (2016), Moran (2017), and Humalisto, Karjunen, and Kilpelainen (2019), and discussion later in this chapter.

2. 'General cover' and 'specials' are terms used in stage lighting to denote, respectively, washes of light that illuminate the acting area, and lights that are rigged to serve a specific purpose. (See Moran, 2018, pp.121–2 and Pilbrow, 1997, pp.11–30.)
3. 'Experience economy' is a term coined by Pine and Gilmore (1998) to recognise the value of memorable experiences to customers.
4. See www.luciassociation.org/about-luci/.
5. A summary of this collaboration can be viewed at: https://webarchive.nationalarchives.gov.uk/ukgwa/20210802104942/https://ahrc.ukri.org/research/case-study-archives/dance-and-digital-arts/.
6. Scandlight is organized by Ulf Nielsen and Anders Larsson every three years on behalf of the Association of Swedish Lighting Designers (SLF) and OISTAT's international lighting design group.
7. The volume has also been shaped in a more general sense by annual meetings of the scenography working groups of both IFTR and TaPRA, successive iterations of the Prague Quadrennial, Showlight, and the work of OISTAT and the Association for Lighting Production and Design (ALPD).
8. These include texts by Bentham (1950 and 1968), Essig (2002 and 2005), Fraser (2002 and 2003), Moran (2007 and 2018), Pilbrow (2010 and earlier editions) and Reid (2001 and earlier editions), among others.
9. Now the Association for Lighting Production and Design (ALPD). This masterclass is also discussed in Nick Hunt and Hansjörg Schmidt's chapter in this volume.
10. This phenomenon can be seen more widely in criticism, marketing and publicity generally, as well as in the use of the hashtag #CreditTheCreatives on social media, which aims to encourage theatres and performance companies to include the entire creative team alongside production photography, in particular.
11. See also Kevin Dreyer's *Dance and Light* (2020).
12. Cosgrove discusses her work with Beckett in Crawley (2016).

SECTION 1

Experience

1

Theatrical atmospheres and the experience of light

Scott Palmer

May 2019 – I am standing alone, ankle-deep in water in the darkness of a disused underground water tank underneath Søndermarken park in Copenhagen. I have walked several miles through an unfamiliar city to get here and have exchanged my shoes for Wellington boots to navigate this strange labyrinth. I am tentatively moving through the water, guided by selectively positioned shafts of light and enveloped in darkness that is underscored by a disconcerting, deconstructed futurist soundscape of Justin Timberlake's *Cry Me a River*.

What has brought me here to Superflex's art installation *It Is Not the End of the World* (2019) is the promise of a theatrical experience defined through light. I am not disappointed – it is a multisensory immersive experience, unlike anything I have encountered before. Light guides my underground journey and allows me, on occasion, to glimpse some of the other participants, whose shadowy forms appear as performers in this theatricalized space. As participants in this world, we are cast as 'archaeologists of the future' (Superflex, 2019), and the work invites us to explore built structures and artefacts submerged in the cavernous spaces of the Cisternerne, a nineteenth-century reservoir now used as a subterranean exhibition space that has been re-flooded for this event.

The spaces of the Cisternerne are unnerving both in their scale and in the fact that I am being asked to navigate them in low light while wading through water to do so. I can't see clearly what is under the water and the lack of light seems to intensify the physical sensation of wading through the water. The combination of the darkness, the resistance of the water and the cool air both highlight the uncanny nature of this environment and serve to heighten my sensory awareness. Soon, I encounter a doorway, slightly ajar, with light spilling from beyond it and reflecting on the surface of the water. Beyond, I am able to glimpse a strange parallel world, illuminated by stark white recessed spotlights. This hyper-realistic structure is a genuine surprise. I later discover that it is an exact replica of the executive toilets from a United Nations climate conference that are now eerily abandoned and flooded. I am able to walk around and look into this space from different perspectives through partially open doorways and narrow windows. The contrast in the quality of light from the theatrically low-lit darkness of my surroundings in the vaults to the brightly lit interiors of the rooms I am peering into is analogous to the experience of viewing an illuminated stage from a darkened auditorium. The light reflected in the water helps to create an uncanny atmosphere and a feeling of dystopia reminiscent of Tarkovsky's film *Stalker*. In witnessing this abandoned space I am looking into the past, and also into our possible futures, asked to contemplate the failure of human consumption and of our global struggles to counteract the climate emergency.

Further on, at the far end of the linked chambers, a mesmerizing blue light seems to attract the audience towards it. Silhouetted figures wade carefully through the floodwater towards a space that contains a large LED sign, reminiscent of neon advertising hoardings that are found atop city-centre buildings (see Plate 4). The light 'repurposes the aesthetics of commercial signage to rebrand the end of humanity' (Superflex, 2019). It reminds us of a past focused on consumerism but also spells out a clear message of the title of the installation. However, through partial glimpses of the words between the columns of the Cisternerne, I am also able to discern alternative readings of the illuminated lettering as both a prophetic 'THE END OF THE WORLD' and a defiant yet hopeful 'IT IS NOT THE END', which offers a literal glimmer of light reflecting in the water (see Plate 4). This illuminated object also perhaps references, and certainly illustrates, Walter Benjamin's observation of the power of illuminated advertising which lies not so much in the message spelt out by the neon sign but in 'the fiery pool reflecting in the asphalt' (1997, p.476).

The use of light in Superflex's piece is highly theatricalized not only in terms of the revelation of the final illuminated sign but also in the way in which light creates atmosphere through framing the entire environment, creating a pathway and revealing and concealing both the architecture of the Cisternerne and the surface of the water that we are moving through. In the denouement of this work, we are being asked to stand in the water, enveloped in darkness and bathed in its blue light to consider the provocation that this may be the end of humanity but not necessarily the end of the world: 'The planet will probably do just fine without us' (Superflex, 2019). I linger at this point, rapt by the reflections of light rippling in the water and enjoying the experience of the other-worldly blue luminescence, while at the same time trying to make sense of what I am experiencing. I watch other audience members arrive, observe, ponder and then depart, their movements creating ripples and reflections of light on the surface of the water. Some of these shadowy human forms stop to take photographs of the extraordinary space and light, just as I have done. It is at this moment at the end of the caverns that we are asked to pause and to reflect on what we might need to change to prevent this dystopian vision of a post-anthropocene world, before retracing our steps back to terra firma, daylight and our everyday lives. Is there actually light at the end of the tunnel?

In this chapter I focus on the *experience* of both light and its absence, darkness, from the perspective of the audience. With a particular emphasis on postdramatic, relational performance environments, I will draw on specific examples of performances and practitioners to explore the implications for both designers and audiences about the ways in which the material of light performs.

All of the materials in Superflex's installation are performing, but light, in particular, with darkness, works on multiple levels to frame the entire experience, helping to establish an atmosphere that, like the darkened theatre, is set apart from everyday experience. On entering a theatre, audiences are asked to cross a threshold, often marked by a light lobby that provides acoustic separation and a clear physical division between the space of the auditorium and the outside world. The threshold in Superflex's installation is even more extreme as the audience leaves the daylight and descends from grassland in a public park into a dark, industrial, underground space. As soon as this threshold is crossed, artificial light both works to guide the audience members on their journey and, where it is absent or at a low level, serves to directly accentuate the nature of the experience, because darkness foregrounds our other senses, haptic experience and 'residual proprioception' (Gibson, 1966, p.303), when sight is compromised. In Superflex's dark world, light conditions human movement, controlling how the audience moves through an environment in which light also becomes central to the process of meaning-making, providing specific points of focus, allowing meanings to emerge and both literally and metaphorically providing light in the darkness.

The use of theatrical light and its antithesis, darkness, has been increasingly employed as a design strategy in performance and especially in performances in which the audience is placed at the centre, or offered the opportunity to be active participants as co-creators in the work. As I will discuss later in this chapter, light and its absence provide an affordance in relational performance and are critical in establishing both atmosphere and particular conditions for a shared audience experience. In Superflex's piece, the other co-experiencers are glimpsed in the shadows, never fully visible, but observed as dark shapes that are backlit, moving through the caverns. The bodies are those of strangers and, although never overtly acknowledged, the work points to a communal experience that represents humanity and reminds us that 'we are all in this together'.

The impact of light

In his chapter 'What in the world is light?', Tim Ingold neatly problematizes the issues with our experience of light as a material:

> Light is among the fundamental constituents of our universe; but it also lies at the heart of human experience. It is both so near that it invades our being, and yet so far that beside it our human presence pales into insignificance. We know a great deal about it, and yet we do not know what it is. (2022, 85)

Physicists, psychologists and philosophers continue to debate the precise nature of the strange substance that is light and our relationship to and with it (e.g. Merleau-Ponty, 1968; Levinas, 1978; Gibson, 1979; Böhme, 2017; Ingold 2022). We see things in light, but the light itself is invisible – it needs to strike another material, such as particles of smoke or dust in the air, for it to be seen.

However, *It Is Not the End of the World* also reveals the limitations of light to convey complex meanings on its own, and in choosing to recount my experience of light in this chapter I am faced with a significant challenge. I remember both trying to make sense of the work at the time and also processing the experience immediately after the event. In attempting to describe this in writing after a period of two years has elapsed, how can I make sense of my own experience of light? How do I describe it in the hope of conveying to others what was a highly subjective experience? The ephemeral and temporal nature of light as a material complicates matters further, and this exercise foregrounds the significant challenges in describing the qualities of a substance which seems to elude attempts to fix it on the page. How can we hope to communicate the very particular qualities of light that we experience especially when the actual experience of light might not align precisely with the meaning-making that the Superflex website and notes are guiding me towards? What is clear, however, in this example and in others in this chapter, is that something profound happens to spectating bodies in and through light and that the phenomenological experience of light is a fundamentally unstable one. Light creates an atmosphere that is fluid – a constant transformation that is always in the process of becoming (Deleuze and Guattari, 1988).

Spectacular light

Theatre critics have faced the difficulties of describing light on the stage and as we note in our introduction have largely avoided references to light in their reviews of performances. Writing about light is difficult and where it has been mentioned in relation to performance these examples overwhelmingly focus on specific lighting moments and spectacular dramatic effects – where light draws attention to itself and is overtly experienced or noticed by the audience. In theatre history, the famous moment of 'The Vision of Queen Katherine' from Charles Kean's production of *Henry VIII* in 1855 at the Princess's Theatre, for example, has been preserved for posterity because of its overwhelming impact on the audience and the need for newspapers of the time to represent this in illustrations (see Figure 1). Kean's astonishing light effect used the bright new light of the electric carbon arc technology to recreate the transcendental image of angels suspended in air and bathed in heavenly light from William Blake's illustrations to Shakespeare (1783–90) and Henry Fuseli's 1781 painting of the same scene.[1] In the theatre, the intense beam of light, created by a hidden

FIGURE 1 Interpretation of 'The Vision of Queen Katherine' from Charles Kean's *Henry VIII*. Princess's Theatre, London, 1855.

source high offstage, had a quality and intensity that had never been witnessed previously on stage and both the power of the light and the live re-creation of this familiar pictorial image astonished. It is because of the spectacular scenographic image and its direct impact on audiences that this light moment became the defining image of a production that otherwise would probably have long been forgotten. This example reveals how the performance of light evades linguistic description and the need to attempt to represent the remarkable moment on stage through pictorial means. In Kean's production and in many other theatrical experiences throughout the nineteenth century, the very technologies of light were used as an overt marketing tool focused on highlighting the new and the innovative (irrespective of artistic merit), and the 'spectacular' experiences they afforded. The website that promoted Superflex's installation could be seen to be offering something similar for contemporary audiences – the promise of an experiential encounter with spectacular light which can then also provide an appropriately striking image to post on social media.

There are many other examples of spectacular moments both from historical performances and indeed more recent work, where light plays a significant or central role in creating a memorable moment on stage. These instances could be seen as scenographic outliers that reveal little about the general role or overall contribution of light in the rest of the performance and are noticed precisely because theatrical light rarely draws attention to itself in creating a singular light-based image. Instead, light more often works on a subliminal level through subtle shifts that are experienced by performers and audience alike and, just like the ever-changing qualities of daylight, are rarely consciously perceived.

The lighting designer Max Keller summarizes what this means for the designer:

> The eye is able to register: differences in brightness, colour differences, shapes, movements and distances. Lighting is intended to make it easier for the eye to fulfil these functions, or even make it possible in the first place. A certain minimum illumination is needed for seeing, perceiving and recognising. Perception is an individual process, invoking a sensation, triggered by the psychological and physical effect of the five points mentioned above. (Keller, 1999, p.25)

We notice light when our eyes are drawn to differentiation in illumination levels; we notice stars against the backdrop of a dark sky even though they appear to be tiny pinpricks of light, and we are conscious of the change in the quality of light as a cloud passes in front of the sun. Reflections of light from bright surfaces draw our attention and especially if the light appears to move – reflections on water or dappled light through foliage, for example. Our 'reptilian brains' (Di Benedetto, 2010 p.65) are drawn to observe the light sources themselves: the streetlamp, the flames of the fire and, of course, the sun and its reflected light from the moon.

Our eyes are subconsciously drawn to the brightest areas of our field of vision, a principle called 'selective visibility',[2] which lighting designers can harness to focus an audience's attention to parts of the stage. This can be critical to the reception of performance and fulfils a similar role to that of the close-up in film. At its most obvious this effect is observable in the followspot – a bright shaft of moving light that is manually manipulated to highlight one body or area on stage above all of the others. Light centres our attention and the followspot operator ensures that the audience's gaze remains focused. It is precisely from this effect that the term of 'being in the limelight' has evolved – of one element being highlighted above everything else. On a more subtle level, lighting designers can use this physiological phenomenon of 'selective visibility' and shift the relative illumination of different parts of the stage to attract our eyes subliminally and to guide attention. This process is also used by magicians in reverse – to deliberately obscure and mislead an audience's gaze.[3]

The physical movement of light sources through space, such as car headlights or fireworks, also draws our attention involuntarily. The fairground exploits this phenomenon through moving and flashing lights which, when augmented by vibrant colour combinations, appear seductively thrilling, especially when combined with exaggerated physical movements such as the turning of the big wheel or carousel. These dynamic qualities of light – colour, movement and intensity – are used for a very different purpose on emergency vehicles to draw our attention, and the same qualities were exploited by Italian Futurists in their artworks and light plays.[4]

In Superflex's work, light served to subconsciously direct and also attract the experiencer towards the denouement of the illuminated sign which then became animated through reflections in the rippling water. Here light was the focal point of the work and at the same time created ambient spaces bathed in light that were conducive to contemplation. McKinney (2018), drawing on Barad (2007), helps to explain the complex, felt experience of the materiality of light and meaning-making in performance: 'Embodied spectatorship recognises that the event of experiencing scenography is a dynamic and iterative process of intra-action between the materiality of human and non-human where "knowing and being . . . are mutually implicated"' (2018, p.115).

Subliminal light

Our experience of overt lighting effects such as a distinct shaft of light, a lightning flash or a sudden change in levels of illumination or colour, is at first pre-reflective and experienced involuntarily. Such sudden shifts are then consciously comprehended as the body attends to them, and in the theatre, the impact of these moments may stay in the memory long after the immediate experience of the performance. This in part explains the prevalence of the spectacular visual moment in the documentation of performance noted earlier.

More gradual shifts of light through time, which are fundamental to the experience of the theatrical event, will not be so readily perceived and cannot be captured in a single image. This temporal aspect of dramatic light, first theorized by Adolphe Appia and defined in musical terms as a 'score' is rarely acknowledged or comprehended even though it is at the very heart of what a lighting designer does.

The subliminal experience of transitions of light plays a critical role in the reception of theatre, from the moment that the audience crosses the threshold and enters the space demarked for performance. Auditoria are usually illuminated by special 'houselights' in order to create a welcoming atmosphere, and the moment when these lights fade out and the auditorium descends into darkness marks another important threshold moment in which light – or rather its absence – prepares the bodies of the theatre audience members for what is to come.[5]

It is important to note the shift from a focus on the individual light moment, cue or lighting state to an acknowledgement of the essential nature of the temporal experience of light throughout the entire performance. In relating the qualities of postmodern lighting design for the stage with the qualities of light found in urban space, rock concerts and electronic media, Aronson observes:

> Light may emphasize juxtaposition and contrast rather than organic unity. Light, in fact, is no longer about unity but about transition. *How* we get from one place or moment to the next has become more important than what it looks like when we are there. (2005, p.35 italics in original)

In relational work where the audience shares the same space as the performers this temporal experience of light becomes even more critical since they are not separated, sitting in the darkness, but rather 'on stage', immersed in the same light. This relationship would appear to amplify further Di Benedetto's view of the importance of the designer: 'A scenographer is a god of sorts creating the world through the shaping of the lighting, the objects, the colours and movements' (2013, p.190) in order to focus experience and guide the audience to better comprehend what is happening on stage. This observation is also a reminder of the deeper biological and neurological levels of scenographic processes that are key to our understanding of the visible, spatial and temporal world both on stage and off.[6] The phenomenological impact of light is only partially understood. The director, Dieter Dorn, notes that

> The success of the visual effect also depends on the individual's emotional state. Fortunately there is no generally valid reaction to lighting effects. Light, like music, is a particularly subjective sphere. Sensuous perception of light is seldom a conscious practice. Perhaps it is precisely because its emotional effect is unconscious that it affects our sensibilities so incisively. (quoted in Keller, 1999, p.11)

Light's profound psychological and physiological effect on the human body is certainly recognized in its centrality in the Western scopic regime and is surely responsible for its employment as a metaphorical term to signify life, hope, truth and the banishment of death. In religious ceremonies of all faiths, light plays a pivotal role and is foregrounded in specific events such as the Hindu festival of Diwali. In religious iconography blinding light is employed to represent God, sacred power and the afterlife, while light is also linked closely to our primordial sense of safety, just as its antithesis, darkness, represents danger and all that is unknown (Hensey and Dowd, 2016).

It is this duality that offers such a rich opportunity for theatre-makers. The effect of light on our bodies and minds has also provided a rich area of investigation in the fine arts – as Levinas observes: 'It is the very intelligibility of light that is astonishing' (1978, p.22).

The work of light artist James Turrell, for example, has focused on creating spaces defined with diffused light for audiences to experience. In some of his gallery installations, these rooms offer a total immersion in an other-worldly saturated diffused light experience. In his *Ganzfeld* series the light cycles imperceptibly appear to fluctuate the temperature of the air in the space, while *Bindu Shards* (2010), in contrast, offers an extreme solo experience of light within what Turrell calls a 'perceptual cell'. This isolation tank is akin to an MRI scanner but appears to be presented at the level of a psychological experiment. White-coated laboratory attendants with clipboards usher participants onto a gurney which then slides into the cell. Once inside the structure the participant is bombarded with rapidly changing, bright, flashing coloured light to trigger the mind's eye through exploiting the phenomenon of the Purkinje effect, in which the perception of colour changes according to the different levels of illumination and wavelengths of light.[7] One critic observed: 'you don't know what is inside and outside of your head [. . .]. The whole of space seems compressed into your skull' (Jones, 2010, n.p.).

Light's profound psychological and physiological effect on human bodies conditions our entire experience of the world and the way in which we think and feel (de Kort and Veitch, 2014). We see through light, we witness the effects of light, and we feel light. Light is therefore of primary importance in shaping audiences' experience of theatre since 'by opening our eyes we open ourselves to feeling as well as to light' (Ingold, 2005, p.100). And so, even in the most simply lit of performances, light is never only illuminating the stage or making things visible but operating on both physiological and phenomenological levels.

Postdramatic light

As we note in our introduction to this volume, throughout most of the twentieth century, theatre lighting practice followed the problematic mantra that light should not consciously draw attention to itself and generally should not be noticed by an audience. In postdramatic theatre, light is not bound to the potential restrictions and requirements of the naturalistic stage, and indeed the absence of light has also become a key expressive element in shaping audience experience. Aronson notes: 'We are, historically, in a period of political and social transition, and lighting design inevitably reflects that sense of instability. It is light that ebbs and flows, startles and surprises. What we don't see becomes as important as what we do see' (2005, p.36).

The collapse of traditional hierarchies and an explicit acknowledgement of the potential power of light, in tandem with other materials of the stage, offers new aesthetic possibilities in theatre-making. As Hans-Thies Lehmann helpfully concludes: 'By regarding the theatre text as an independent poetic dimension and simultaneously considering the "poetry" of the stage uncoupled from the text as an independent atmospheric poetry of space and light, a new theatrical disposition becomes possible' (2006, p.59).

Erika Fischer-Lichte attempts to explain the particular experience of light on audiences in the postdramatic theatre of director/designer Robert Wilson. She attributes the sensation in part to the use of hundreds of cues in his performances that create a constant shifting of light colour and intensity:

> The atmosphere changes simultaneously. Due to their high frequency, these changes mostly occur at the threshold of conscious perception. Light is not only absorbed by the human eye but also by the skin. The human organism reacts particularly sensitively to light. Spectators exposed to continuous changes of light will find their disposition changing frequently and abruptly without being able to consciously register, even less control these swings. Wilson's productions lure the spectator under their influence because their atmosphere carries a strongly suggestive power, especially enhanced

through the deliberate slowness of the movements. The performative space here appears as a particularly atmospheric space. (2008, pp.118–19)

Fischer-Lichte, drawing on the work of Böhme, acknowledges both the role of light in creating atmosphere and the power of light experienced by audiences when sat in a darkened auditorium where the impact of light is dominated by the act of observing a brightly illuminated stage. Wilson prefers to work on a proscenium stage because the light can be more easily manipulated and precisely controlled with the audience viewing from a single direction only: 'I like the distance it creates between stage and audience. And I like what it lets me do with lights' (Wilson in Holmberg, 1996, p.124) The proscenium stage allows for complex compositions often with the assistance of a rear projection screen and the use of the stage floor as a further canvas for light.

> Light in Wilson's productions creates its own formal structure. At times, the structure runs parallel to the text without doubling it; at times, it contradicts the text; at rare times, it illustrates the text. Lights work subliminally on our feelings. They are one of the theatre's strongest weapons to create emotional climate. Wilson is a master of generating atmosphere through lights [. . .] Often in Wilson light expresses the unconscious – thoughts and feelings hiding just beneath the skin. These emotions can never be heaved into the mouth, language cannot speak them. Light whispers them. In sum, 'light' says Wilson, 'is the most important actor on stage'. (Holmberg, 1996, pp.127–8)

It is a testament to both Wilson's artistry and to the power of light in the theatre that the multiple feelings and complex sensations articulated by both Fischer-Lichte and Holmberg are possible even when viewing reflected light from a position of darkness and from a distance in the auditorium.

Atmosphere and immersion

In a work in which the audience share the same space as the performers, there is no possibility or indeed need to paint beautiful images with light on stage as Wilson does; rather, light is liberated to take on a new role. Contemporary 'immersive theatre' or 'environmental performance' (Aronson, 2018) is predicated on relational encounters and a collapse of physical distance both between performer and spectator and between spectator and the scenographic environment. The design and control of light, therefore, become fundamental to the creation and success of such work when staged in indoor spaces. Lighting needs to accommodate the needs of a moving audience, with multiple points of view, who are often invited to take part in the action as co-creators rather than as seated spectators. Although work in this genre does not preclude evocative or spectacular lighting (e.g. see Plates 5–10), light can be centred on the creation of atmosphere for the whole space and focused on bodily experience. Rather than a composition designed to be viewed remotely, audience members in relational performances are immersed in the same theatrical light and environment as the performers, and this offers the opportunity to foreground the phenomenological impact of the experience of being in the light. Furthermore, just as in the conventional theatre space, where there is a fundamental dialectic between light and darkness that is critical in shaping the audience experience,[8] 'immersive' work frequently relies upon the overt employment of darkness as a dramaturgical strategy that establishes a distinct atmosphere that frames the quality of the whole audience experience. I will return to this idea later, in analysing the work of Punchdrunk as follows.

The terms 'atmosphere' and 'mood' are widely and often interchangeably used in describing theatrical light. Katherine Graham (2020b) helpfully critiques the overuse of these generalizations and analyses the complexities behind these terms. Gernot Böhme has repeatedly drawn directly on stage lighting in combination with setting as a central paradigm to account for an aesthetics of atmosphere (e.g. 1993, 2011, 2013). Focused theatrical light in the indoor theatre automatically creates what Böhme terms a 'tuned space' – it is an atmosphere that excludes daylight and is created by sources that provide a distinctly different quality of light than that experienced in domestic or everyday spaces. Like the houselights discussed earlier, the special quality of theatrical light also makes us feel differently and serves to mark the threshold moment of being in an aesthetic, fluid space that is denoted as separate from the outside world. Inside the theatre, focused theatrical light also defines the edges of the performance area/theatrical world and is often crucial in rendering the walls and paraphernalia of the building less visible in the surrounding darkness. Böhme recognizes the vital importance of the quality and levels of light in creating the liminal 'in-between existence' and fluid experience of the theatre space (2017). This fluidity is especially apparent and amplified in relational performances where the strict boundaries between stage and auditorium no longer exist.

In relational work such as Fix & Foxy's *Ungdom* [*Youth*] (2015), the demarcation created by light was central to the creation of a 'tuned space' and consequently to the quality of the audience experience. A theatrical representation of a festival campsite was created as the environment for the action where audience and performers mixed together over a period of two-and-a-half hours in a world of tents complete with sand, trees, and a forest lake (see Plate 5): 'Together they experience a "theatrical day" where everything can happen, and the phenomenon of youth is explored' (Fix & Foxy n.d.).

Michael Breiner's lighting design worked both symbolically and representationally, framing the dramaturgy into eight separate moods staged across afternoon, evening, sunset and night, and finally culminating with the sunrise of a new day (see Plate 6). Despite the apparent realism of the setting and the notional diurnal and nocturnal experience of light that was offered, the stage lighting did not attempt to be naturalistic but operated on multiple levels, working in tandem with the sound to provide specific cues for the performers and to establish a festival-like atmosphere that allowed audience members to not only recognize the highly theatrical environment but also create the conditions in which immersion in the world might occur. Haze introduced into the space played a crucial role in the creation of this 'tuned space' through foregrounding the felt, material experience of light (see Plate 6). The air appears thicker in haze and the light becomes tangible, and it is this interaction of light with other scenographic elements that emphasizes 'the sense we have of being in a significant wordly situation that is not of our own making' (Ratcliffe, 2013, p.160).

In *Ungdom*, focused light, haze and surrounding darkness brought strangers together in an atmosphere that promoted the sharing of stories and ultimately a common feeling of well-being. During the night-time sequence, for example, lights inside each tent provided an invitation for audiences to dwell and to attend to the intimate thoughts of young people. Strong xenon strobe lights created periodic pulses of light that had a dual function. These provided a signal for the performers to move to the next part of the performance and at the same time created a repeating light motif that emphasized the passing of time: 'Many older audiences described it as the passing from one age to the next, every time something was lost, but not forgotten' (Breiner, 2021, personal correspondence). The pulsing light therefore not only worked dramaturgically to mark the beginning and ending of scenes but the quality of light also instilled a feeling of nostalgia as the repetition came to denote both the immediate passing of time and a more profound change – of youth giving way to adulthood.

Combinations of different light sources and colours were used to help underscore the different moods of each scene, with LED light bulbs in tents, fluorescent objects and ultraviolet lighting for the party scene, HMI light sources for the moon, and fibre optics for the stars. The sunrise in the final section of the performance was created with a rectangular wall of 120 Parcans, where the physical experience of the heat felt on the body was as important as the blazing visual effect (see Plate 6). The most significant aspect of the lighting design

> was the fact that the lighting had to be experienced from the performers' point of view. So I was working partly as a theatre designer, but also as an architectural designer. The light was creating rooms within the room and

at the same time driving the atmosphere, together with the sound design to provide rhythm and phase to the performance. (Breiner, 2021, personal correspondence)

Darkness and the collapse of distance

I have already noted the critical importance of darkness in framing the experience of theatre audiences and in the creation of atmosphere. Architect Juhani Pallasmaa, drawing on Japanese philosopher Tanazaki, reminds us of the significance and affective qualities of the shadow, which all performance-makers should be aware of and lighting designers specifically should attend to. The affective qualities of lower levels of light relate directly to the 'tuned space' of *Ungdom* and many other examples of relational theatre:

> The imagination and daydreaming are stimulated by dim light and shadow. In order to think clearly, the sharpness of vision has to be suppressed, for thoughts travel with an absent-minded and unfocussed gaze. Homogeneous bright light paralyses the imagination in the same way that homogenisation of space weakens the experience of being, and wipes away the sense of place.
>
> The human eye is most perfectly tuned for twilight rather than bright daylight.
>
> Mist and twilight awaken the imagination by making visual images unclear and ambiguous. (Pallasmaa, 2005, p.46)

Martin Welton (2012, 2013 and 2017) has also explored the phenomenological impact of light in relation to darkness for the audience experience: 'the visual experience of light is one of proximity. It is right there in front of you, and the pleasures and terrors of the dark surely rest on the collapse of distance as a result' (Welton, 2013, p.5). The withdrawal of light of course immediately removes the primacy of the optical in the audience's experience and therefore foregrounds a reconsideration of the other senses in theatrical meaning-making. This chimes with the wider field of academic study where the embodied and phenomenal aspects of performance work are now acknowledged more widely (e.g. McKinney, 2015). There has been a postdramatic and scenographic turn away from the primacy of the written and spoken word and from what is seen to what is felt.

The German director and composer Heiner Goebbels exemplifies this approach in this articulation of his own practice:

> I am interested in inventing a theatre where all the means that make up theatre do not just illustrate and duplicate each other but instead all

maintain their own forces but act together, and where one does not just rely on the conventional hierarchy of means. That means, for example, where a light can be so strong that you suddenly only watch the light and forget the text, where a costume speaks its own language or where there is a distance between speaker and text and a tension between music and text. I experience theatre as exciting whenever you can sense distances on stage that I as a spectator can then cross. (quoted in Lehmann, 2006, p.86)

The acknowledgement that scenographic elements, including light, can create the potential for a collapsing of distance is further exemplified in relational 'immersive' performances that are designed to encourage spectators to make this 'crossing' physically as well as metaphorically. The final examples of audience experience of light in this chapter reveal how darkness is used as a scenographic and dramaturgical strategy to shape audience experience in a different way to the darkness that was employed as an enveloping force, with light as a guide, that was evident in the opening account of Superflex's work. I will concentrate on two separate 'immersive' productions by Punchdrunk, both of which I experienced as an audience member.

Punchdrunk is a company that has consciously sought to make work in which the felt atmosphere is central to the performance. Its artistic director, Felix Barrett, has acknowledged his own inspiration, which stems from an embodied experience of theatrical light and darkness through learning about Edward Gordon Craig at school: 'It's remarkable how his vision has shaped everything we see today; for me it is entirely formative I just wanted to submerge myself in Craig's stylised, total world. That's why I started Punchdrunk' (Barrett, 2014).

It Felt Like A Kiss (2009) was staged in a disused city-centre office space once belonging to the National Probation Service but transformed into a six-floor theatrical environment in which daylight had been totally expunged. Controlling light ingress was therefore the underlying practical and aesthetic concern in creating a performative space of darkness for this work to be experienced. The audience entered this environment via a lift but soon found themselves jettisoned into a seemingly pitch-black space. This deliberate disorientation through darkness is a frequent trope of Punchdrunk's work, which draws directly on our physiology as eyes need to adjust to the blackness of the corridor space.

Loosely based on Buchner's fragmentary unfinished play *Woyzeck, – The Drowned Man: A Hollywood Fable* (2013–14) used a similar approach in re-appropriating a disused building – the post office sorting depot adjacent to Paddington station. This work takes the form of a looped ludic structure that unfolded across four floors for over three hours. Audiences wearing white masks were asked to navigate a space that had been transformed into a dark playground that held secrets that could be discovered through an engagement with the objects and materials located within it and the characters that also inhabited it. Layers of light and shadow in both performances stimulate sensorial perception which Machon argues requires 'a new taxonomy for holistic appreciation in immersive theatres' (2013, p.80).

It Felt Like A Kiss presented a multitude of performance spaces across several floors of the building and was navigated almost entirely without the presence of performers. The audience were invited in small groups to explore the artefacts and environments in each space, and our innate fear of the dark was used to underscore the failure of 'The American Dream' and, towards the end of the three-hour experience, to create a heightened visceral experience.

The dramaturgical use of darkness from the outset deliberately disoriented the audience in an experience that also foregrounded the ending of the performance. The audience were required to navigate a seemingly endless labyrinth of rooms full of artefacts, and the gradual descent into the basement culminated in audience groups of eight being chased through corridors by a chainsaw-wielding figure. Despite being told explicitly that the audience group *must* stay together at all times for our safety, in the final moments of the performance we experienced a forced separation through a series of turnstiles in which we were reduced to a group of four, then two and finally each audience member found themselves alone in a narrow corridor and in total darkness.

Darkness in *It Felt Like A Kiss* was used as a practical strategy, as metaphor and as overt subject of the performance. Echoing narratives of Hollywood horror films where characters get picked off one by one, the audience were asked explicitly to confront their individual fears of the dark in the final narrow corridor space. Barrett in his programme notes acknowledges his love of ghost trains and haunted houses and the urge to blur fiction and reality and darkness is clearly used as a conditioning agent to assist this aim and has become a design trope in many of Punchdrunk's productions.

The much larger industrial service lift in *The Drowned Man* was first reached through a dimly lit audience waiting area and corridor described by one online reviewer as 'impossibly dark' – it is here where we were given verbal instructions and the licence to explore the spaces. It is interesting to note in this case that the corridor was not actually dark but instead lit with purple fluorescent tubes – providing the suggestion of darkness – but this threshold space served both as a waiting room for the lift and a space to prepare us to don our white masks. Once inside the lift some privileged audience members, who had paid for VIP tickets, were ejected into their own private experience of a very dark basement space. Those of us who remained in the lift looked at each other with a tangible sense of relief that we had not been instructed to get out on that floor, but this experience of darkness also served to provoke a very real sense of trepidation about what terrors might be awaiting us on our particular journey.

In fact, when the lift doors opened on an upper floor, we encountered what appeared to be night-time, theatrical reconstruction of a 1950s townscape complete with a bar, shops and a central fountain – a 'film setting' that was part of the theatrical conceit that we had entered a forgotten Hollywood film production facility. The National Theatre's programme notes state:

> Lines between space, performer and spectator are constantly shifting. Audiences are invited to rediscover the childlike excitement and anticipation of exploring the unknown and experience a real sense of adventure. Free to encounter the installed environment in an individual imaginative journey, the choice of what to watch and where to go is theirs alone. (National Theatre, 2013, p.16)

Although there are some significant issues relating to the extent that the audience in Punchdrunk shows really has agency, the design of their worlds certainly fosters an invitation to explore. An experience of light is integral to instilling an appropriate atmosphere to facilitate playful discovery. In *It Felt Like A Kiss* the journey was a linear one, each space leading to the next. In *The Drowned Man*, in addition to the key scenographic environments on each floor, there were a number of other spaces seeded throughout. These secret passageways, hidden rooms and objects offered the possibility of individual one-to-one encounters with characters in the drama. While we might feel that there is safety in light, we are provoked: Do you dare to explore beyond the light? For the most intrepid audience members there is another world waiting in the darkness, behind 'secret' doors, through costume rails or in one case accessed by crawling through a very dark tunnel.

The audience in Punchdrunk's work are often invited to 'play in the dark' and if you are prepared to seek out the hidden spaces in *The Drowned Man* you might be rewarded by an individual encounter. These heightened one-to-one experiences can leave profound impressions on the individuals who are fortunate to encounter or willing to uncover them (e.g. see Westling 2020). Aspects of light and darkness are also employed explicitly in these private performance encounters.

In one, a clown leads you through a series of secret spaces in darkness with a torch. You must follow the light and look at what is revealed through it. In another, the 'Dust Witch' takes you into a private room where your mask is removed and you are blindfolded. The removal of sight is disconcerting and as your body is manipulated you are disoriented. You are told a story of the Sandman – a tale about seeing and light – and, although you cannot see it, an actual light source is placed in close proximity to your face and you feel its warmth through your skin. In these one-to-one encounters, the characters are showing you the light both physically as well as metaphorically and offering you a private insight into their individual stories. Darkness frames these intimate exchanges and micro-scenes where light and its absence are employed overtly as both metaphors and for phenomenological affect.

In contrast to more typical theatrical practices the lighting transitions in *The Drowned Man* were automated and changed in relation to the soundscape which in tandem provided the cues to guide the performers. Shifts in the levels of intensity of light provided the audience members with clues about which areas of the vast performance area were about to be populated with performers and which areas might offer less focus at particular moments of the performance. Whereas it is sound in *The Drowned Man* that structures the narrative through guiding the performers, it is light that guides the audience through structuring the space.

Punchdrunk operates a deliberate strategy of disorientation, and this is achieved primarily through darkness. The strict control of light from the very beginning of these performances, therefore, establishes it as a material for making strange. In both of these Punchdrunk productions that are centred on the experience of a moving audience, light – and, specifically, its absence – is used to define the separate scenographic spaces of encounter while also masking the utilitarian characters of the building itself.

In creating a space for 'active immersion', an atmosphere of darkness underpins the company's approach to making work, promoting feelings of disorientation and dislocation and offering a heightened sensory experience while simultaneously providing agency for masked participants to wander anonymously, as ghostlike figures through the multiple scenographic environments (see Plate 7).

The low levels of light used as an affective, aesthetic force are a contemporary response to Appia and Craig's advocacy for light, mood and atmosphere to become central to theatrical experience:

> What Craig realised was that every single theatrical element – the scenography, the music, the state of the mind of the audience, the auditorium itself – should be about creating the atmosphere, or *Stimmung*, of that work. (Barrett, 2014)

Both the conventional black box theatre space of *Ungdom* and the blacked-out buildings of Punchdrunk are immersive environments that are defined through light and focused on the creation of atmosphere. When the audience are asked to enter them, they understand that they are entering a theatrical reality that is signified by the absence of daylight. In such spaces, whether purpose-built or adapted to exclude daylight, postdramatic lighting is less about making visible, but in making invisible, thereby creating a visceral response in the audience and guiding bodies from one encounter to the next. We might observe therefore that it is the specific employment of theatrical light (and its absence) that is the primary material that assists in the transformation from what Appia termed the framed illusionary theatre space of 'art' into the 'immersive' postdramatic space of action, experience and encounter.

Notes

1 See https://collections.vam.ac.uk/item/O134509/the-dream-of-queen-katherine-oil-painting-fuseli-henry/
2 A concept emerging from stage lighting practice and acknowledged increasingly by lighting designers in the 1950s and 1960s (e.g. see Dunham, 2019, p.4; Palmer, R.H., 1994, p.8).
3 See Di Benedetto (2010 and 2017), Pringle, T. (2002).
4 See Palmer, (2013, pp.162–72).
5 For further analysis of this moment, see Palmer (2017).
6 See, for example, McKinney, (2013) and (2018).
7 The Purkinje phenomenon can be observed in the natural world. The human perception of colour is compromised at night when the red wavelengths of light are missing – a red flower with green leaves, for example, may be perceived as a black flower with grey leaves as daylight fades.
8 See Palmer (2017) and Alston and Welton (2017)

2

Felt dramaturgies of light

David Shearing

An atmospheric sense

This chapter outlines how the felt experience of light can be used to craft an atmospheric reception of performance. I explore how light can contextualize audience experience and shape felt dramaturgies. I question how our emotional capacities and the performance text might fuse through an embodied experience, and how our multiple subjective memories of light commingle in atmospheric reception. Juhani Pallasmaa outlines the case for the value of an 'atmospheric sense' (2019, p.130). Of emotions, he contests that 'love, happiness and hate, for instance, are not objects; they are relations, moods and states of mind', further suggesting that 'we many never intellectually "understand" a work of art, but it can convey an ineffable influence throughout our lives' (2019, p.127). I am interested in the emotional significance of light to shape experience. I am writing here in the context of environmental and immersive experiences in which the audience inhabits the performance space, where light is used as part of the theatrical medium, and where light does not just illuminate actors or the set but is the dramaturgical vehicle for meaning and sense-making. I am interested in the ways light is used as a medium in which to craft an audience experience, where audiences are central to its reception.

I grew up in the 1980s in the suburbs of outer East London and Essex. My own personal felt encounters with light from childhood have shaped my thinking as an artist and fed into an embodied sense of lighting design rather than as a technical craft. Concrete streetlamps lit the pebble-dashed roads of my youth. At dusk, the streetlamps would flicker on, a burnt red, slowly turning into a dark amber and finally a monochromic yellow, the light frequency flattening the tonal depth, inhibiting the reception of colour – sepia roads and lime trees linger in my memory: November nights, fallen leaves and autumn mist. I distinctly remember the thick autumn air, filled with the smell of bonfires and the sharp aroma of what I would later understand to be the by-product of Romford Brewery. I remember long car journeys to family friends, half asleep, watching the sodium lamps trail for miles like golden snakes around the motorways. I remember late night laying on my parent's sheepskin rug, soft to the touch, the light from the streetlamps streaming in through the windows and net curtains casting long amber shadows on the wall. This wasn't just one experience of light; it is multiple, saturated in my memory, formed through numerous encounters – a multisensory engagement with the world from the flattened spatial/temporal perspective of childhood. My understanding and experience of light come deeply infused with my being; it is an ongoing relational encounter of memories formed through my physical and imaginative participation with the world. Many of us share these encounters, even if we are not fully conscious of them. We store moments, like reference points, structures of atmosphere. As a scenographer I look for ways to orientate audiences to an attunement of our inner 'atmospheric sense' (Pallasmaa, 2019, p.130), to build subjective relational encounters between participants and the performance environment. My hope is that those moments of performance might become infused in the subjective memories of the audience, allowing space for participants to bring their own experiences, to form their own relational encounter with the performance world. Light in participatory and immersive experiences has the potential to guide our atmospheric sense to specific moments of dramaturgical attention, and to saturate us within general feelings of space and time. Like the memories of my youth, I see the experience of light in performance as fluid, interwoven with our individual and shared understandings. The felt experience of light is bound up with our multisensory impressions of previous encounters with it. Light is foundational to our immersion in the world – we are light. How we come to know it and receive it in performance has often been the domain of an ocular-centric position, but in this chapter, I explore how light can be felt as part of an embodied reception of performance.

Beyond the illumination of a stage, I am interested in light as part of the medium in which we perceive the world, specifically I am referring to the 'air'. I prefer the use of the term 'medium' over air as it offers us a way to consider how a medium acts as a carrier for odour, sound, temperature, light and sense-making. In everyday life our different sense modalities are fused in the medium in which we inhabit the world, so much so it is almost impossible to separate individual experiences of them. We therefore cannot assess the full potential of light without considering its embodied scenographic sensibilities. In performance, we can shape and manipulate the medium to direct meaning and craft felt dramaturgies of light. The air is a carrier, a medium in which we might shape experiences of light. I want to build a more productive discourse around the reception of light in performance, not as an object of perception but as a relational and ecological encounter. Yaron Shyldkrot suggests that relational encounters with atmospheres are

> the result of a constellation, assemblage or encounters between things (whether human or non-human, material or immaterial), which can lead to various sensations, feelings and affects either when we notice them or as they unfold over time. (Shyldkrot, 2019, p.162)

He considers the conditions in which atmosphere might emerge, working with Gernot Böhme's relationality of 'atmospheric things', contesting that they 'do not form the atmosphere – or a representation of an atmosphere for that matter. Rather, they create "tuned" spaces and set up the conditions for atmospheres to appear' (Shyldkrot, 2019, p.152). He goes on to suggest that 'the composition of atmosphere is an invitation that seeks to enhance or shift the tone, the general character of a space, or intensify its experiential qualities as a result of particular material circumstances' (ibid.). These ongoing concerns around the development of atmospheres in performance are useful in articulating often marginalized receptions of scenography. However, there is a need for a more precise understanding of the given nature of materials in performance at a particular time or moment, that are constructed and orchestrated within dramaturgical frames and not just installation art. The weather, for me, has been a useful way to conceptualize the specific, rather than prevailing atmospheric conditions of performance. First, I will build a theoretical framework around light as part of a weather-world to further contextualize my thinking within an ecological framework. My aim in this chapter is to offer a critical frame for understanding light as a mode of making through directorial applications of light and its scenographic reception. I will predominantly draw on my own practice as a designer, where I deploy light as a tool for crafting the audience's felt experience of performance. I am compelled by light's potential to saturate our consciousness and how, through the air, light becomes a locus for our multisensory experience of performance. Much has been written of the potential of sound to craft deep spatial experiences, in part to decentre ocular-centric understandings of the world (Pallasmaa, 1996; Blesser, 2007). This chapter seeks to articulate how visual reception can embrace light as part of a multisensory experience and explore light's power to tap into latent emotional potentials.

As light as air

To consider how light can be experienced as an atmospheric phenomenon, which, as Martin Welton suggests, is acted upon and within the body (2012, p.131), I first want to conceptualize the experience of scenography through the fluxes and flows of the air – the medium that fills space. As humans our medium of existence is the air, just as water is that of fish. We breathe air, we hear through vibrations in the air, we feel the air on our skin, light refracts and disperses in air. It might seem trivial, but often the potential of light as experienced through the air is marginalized in lighting design, both its application in performance, from an artistic point of view, and in our understanding of an audience's reception of it. Air functions as part of our wider climate and atmosphere, with temperature shifts or by carrying water vapour in the form of fog. I am reminded of the artworks of Tomas Saraceno, whose material inventions often draw attention to the air's presence. In *Cosmos of the Breath*, (2007), Saraceno created a large solar dome made of lightweight iridescent foil with a diameter of around 60 metres. At dawn, the material was anchored to the ground, and as the sun rose over Gunpower Park, Essex, UK, the air underneath the foil began to heat, lifting the material into the air in a large fluttering dome-like shape. The shiny foil reflected the sky and earth and shimmered in the morning light. The sculpture became a compound of air light and material each mutually dependent. The project not only drew attention to the medium of air through its continuous fluctuation but also to our climate and wider ecology, reminding us that light is energy. Light supports all life on earth. Experientially, light from the sun is more than illumination; it is the foundation for our very being, providing us with the warmth and energy to survive. Light seeps into every aspect of our lives, whether we see it or not.

In my own environmental artworks, the medium or air of a space is the condition for experiencing design elements; the participants are in sound, in fog and in light. The medium of air, as outlined by American psychologist James Jerome Gibson, is what facilitates how an animal moves through a space (1979, pp.16–32), and movement provides significant sensory information about their environment to the subject. Gibson writes:

> Animal locomotion is not usually aimless but is guided or controlled – by light if the animal can see, by sound if the animal can hear, and by odour if the animal can smell. The medium thus contains information about things that reflect light, vibrate, or are volatile. By detecting this information, the animal guides and controls locomotion. (Gibson, 1979, p.17)

The environment around us provides clues that guide and control our actions. It is easy to take for granted that the air that fills space is simply there, but it is in fact the very conditioning of our reception of the world. Our experience of the world is never static and is predicated on the movement of a subject in order to provide a sense of orientation and spatial depth. The environment is made up of surfaces and objects, and the medium is gases and fluids. Light interacts with surfaces directly. The medium (air or water) diffuses, bends and manipulates light. Traditional approaches to scenographic analysis have tended to focus more on objects of perception; however, our reception of light is a compound experience of how it relates with surfaces and interacts with the medium. In theatre, a movement of light against objects will reveal spatial depth. The turn-of-the-century-scenographic pioneers such as Edward Gordon Craig (1872–1966) and Adolphe Appia (1862–1928) understood this potential well; to create drama and mood, the dynamic interplay of the movement of light, architecture and the body was paramount. However, the rise of immersive and participatory experiences over the past two decades, both in and outside theatre spaces, has reconfigured our understanding and use of light for affective potential. I prefer the term *environmental performance* over *immersive theatre* to delineate a spatial reception in which all elements that make up performance contribute to its reception. As Richard Schechner writes, '[a]n environmental performance is one in which *all the elements or parts* making up the performance are recognized as alive' (Schechner, 1994, p.10, emphasis in original). In environmental performance the audience, performers and scenographic materials might coexist in the same dramatic space; here, the air and light are brought to the foreground *as* the conditions through which we perceive the event. In non-environmental performance, light is at a distance, illuminating the stage space – light is predominantly read and understood visually, separate from the audience's body. In environmental performance, we might engage directly with light, other materials and the performance text, which might further produce relational and immersive experiences for audiences. In environmental performance, light and the absence of light (darkness) are felt experiences and can be deployed as tools to shift and direct attention where quite literally the medium/air becomes the message. Conceptualizing the medium as a scenographic axis of reception offers a useful frame for performance reception analysis. It offers a way to consider scenography's potential to craft experience in that the phenomena of design – light, sound, odour and touch (felt sensations on the skin) – are carried by and combined within the air through time. The medium of air is scenographic.

In examining the experience of light, it is essential to consider it as part of an entwined experience for the participant. Anthropologist Tim Ingold develops Gibson's framework of the medium of air and considers this perceptual approach by proposing human existence as part of a 'weather-world' (Ingold, 2011, pp.115–39). Ingold furthers Gibson's visual/motor action approach by articulating an entwined connection between the air and body. He suggests that in open space the body and medium mingle:

> To feel the air and walk on the ground is not to make external, tactile contact with our surroundings but to mingle with them. In this mingling, as

we live and breathe, the wind, light and moisture of the sky bind with the substances of the earth in the continual forging of a way through the tangle of lifelines that comprise the land. (Ingold, 2011, p.115)

Ingold's observations offer a profound way for us to consider audience experience within environmental performance, where we come into direct contact with the performance world. In environmental performance, audiences are often invited to roam or move around the physical space; we, therefore, encounter the materials of light, haze and sound in more subtle, intimate and embodied ways. Ingold presents a subject bound up in the material elements of the air, light, wind, moisture and breath, a multisensory immersion in a weather-world that is both the 'essence of perception and the essence of what is perceived' (2011, p.117). The experience of weather 'is just as much auditory, haptic and olfactory as it is visual; indeed in most practical circumstances these sensory modalities cooperate so closely that it is impossible to disentangle their respective contributions' (Ingold, 2005, p.97). Depending on the phenomena in question – the temperature of a room, the wind brushing against the skin or the sound of rain at night – we can attune to these various conditions, which activate self-awareness (Shearing, 2017), thus drawing attention to our immersion in the world. When we enter a low-lit space, we might feel the weight of the darkness, or if we encounter sunbeams that catch the dust through a window, we see the lightness and delicateness of the air. Our sense-making is fused with our embodied reception – the light looks delicate, so I feel delicate. Light in environmental performance is foundational to conditioning audience reception. There is a reciprocity between what we see and feel, and how this affects us. In relation to weather, Welton suggests how changes in the weather are neither wholly subjective nor objective:

In noticing a change in the weather, we notice also a corresponding change in ourselves: it has grown colder, because I have grown colder. Sensing (rather than instrumentally measuring) it to be thus is neither to make a wholly objective judgement, nor an entirely subjective claim; rather, it falls somewhere in between the two as a feeling of a change (a movement) in the atmosphere. (Welton, 2012, p.150)

I use the phrase 'scenographic weather', as it situates Ingold's thinking within a scenographic and performance context. In the time-based medium of the theatre, a change in the medium can be felt by a participant; unlike the general theorization around atmosphere, this is a direct and orchestrated design decision rather than the conditioning atmospherics Shyldkrot (2019) identifies. Welton also cites Böhme, who suggests that atmospheres constitute the 'in-between' of environmental qualities and human sensibilities (quoted in Welton, 2012, p.150). If we are to consider the subjective experiences of light in performance, then the weather, or fluxes in the air, provides an essential link between the objective and subjective experience of light; in this way, perception and feeling, and environment and individual, are intrinsically connected. The conception of a 'scenographic weather' is a direct call to action, an invitation for the participant to be aware of the shifting felt dramaturgy of performance. It is this internal–external cycling of felt experience and dramatic action that interests me in this chapter, and how light can drive and shape this conditioning. I now want to offer a more precise understanding of two different modes of experiencing felt dramaturgies as part of a weather-world of performance.

and it all comes down to this . . .

To illustrate my thinking, I turn to my own work to outline how dramaturgical and scenographic compositions might create moments of aesthetic fulfilment, drawing attention to the reception of what I term '*this* light', the general ambience to shape a sense of feeling and place to condition reception, and what I call '*that* light', where a participant is made aware of a particular dramaturgical use of light. I have applied my thinking to my performance installation *and it all comes down to this . . .* performed at stage@leeds in 2012. In this installation I specifically attempted to draw the audience's awareness to light as a condition for performance reception and in its dramaturgical experience, both through the design and narrative.

The performance was a forty-five-minute event designed for twelve participants and staged without performers. The space was designed to operate as a total environment that aimed to consider the different hemispheres of experience, that of the ground (surfaces) and sky (air), binding the audience within an evolving scenographic ecology. The terrain was shaped using 2,500 glass vessels composed of jars and wine glasses (see Plate 8). Surrounding the space were eight loudspeakers on stands; two further speakers were placed in the gantry for the playback of birdsong. At the centre of the space were twelve deckchairs, each with a low-hanging pendant filament light bulb close enough to touch; on the chairs were headphones placed on top of a handmade book (Figure 2).

Three large portrait screens (see Plate 9) were suspended from the gantry that divided the space; each projection was one-third of a larger 16:9 landscape image. The aim was to position the audience inside the image rather than present a single pictorial perspective. Three birdhouses were positioned into openings of the glass terrain with an adjacent hanging bird box. The hanging boxes acted as mini lighthouses, each illuminated by a bulb inside to signal the arrival of spoken text in the box. The freestanding birdhouse structures

FIGURE 2 *and it all comes down to this* . . . David Shearing, 2012. The space without participants (David Shearing). Photograph by David Shearing.

each contained a large glass jar. Inside the jar was a miniature world depicting a scene from the text, drowned in murky water. Nested in the roof of the birdhouses were speakers that emitted spoken words.

Above the central space were over 1,000 paper birds, made from pages of old books, suspended in mid-flight. Towards the end of the piece, the birds were lit from above, causing the light to pass through the paper onto the audience below (see Plate 10). Through this effect I aimed to create a dynamic space that used the movement of the haze to create shafts of dappled light upon the audience and space below.

The structure of the performance was designed around a series of temperaments, or moods. Each section aimed to encourage different modes of physical and imaginative engagement, thereby creating shifts in experience to take the audience on an imaginative journey in one singular environment. Light and darkness were used to craft the audience experience by inviting engagement with specific moments of light, or by directing attention around the space.

The content of the piece was based on an original story written by Kamal Kaan about a boy and his kite. At first, the story was fragmented and presented in the space via spoken word emanating from the birdhouses and through hidden pages of text nested in the glass jars. As the performance progressed, the audience was taken on an audio journey through the headphones, with the handmade book as a guide. The text aimed to be dynamic, continuously being rewritten; language was crossed out and reordered so that there was a gradual switching between third- and first-person perspectives. The multidimensional phenomenon of light was explored in the written text, exposing the scientific and poetic potentials of light and its relation to time and our own temporality. Light, at times, was both the subject and object in question which is evidenced in some of these excerpts from the script:

> If there's *no light,* there can be *no time* –
> There's always time.
> Each second isn't just a fleeting ticking on the face of the watch tied to your wrist.
> If there's *no time,* there *can* be no light.
> But knowing the speed of light can determine where it began.
> Light can be a time machine into the past
> using a telescope, we can see what it all looked like before our existence.
> Light travels at 186,000 miles per second.
> A photon of light is possibly the fastest thing in the universe because nothing can travel faster than light.
> A photon: a drop of life on the brink of your eyelash.
> *We* couldn't travel faster than light because if we could, we would be in a time that hasn't yet happened.
> We would be *ahead* of time and we can't be in a time that hasn't yet occurred because we would begin traveling backwards in time.
> (If you were a particle of light, you would have travelled 18,600,000 miles by the time you get to this full stop.)
> So the faster you travel, the more time slows down *for* the traveller . . .
> . . . So,
> Just
> Slow down.
> (Script extracts 'Mood 3 – Reflection' from *and it all comes down to this . . .* (2012), text by Kamal Kaan. See also, Shearing (2015) pp. 86–91)

Ultimately, the intention was to include the audience as part of the dramaturgy, so that the story of the boy became the embodied story of the participant, who was gradually taken on an experience of contemplation, acceptance and release. Furthermore, incorporating the physics and poetics of light into the text was a method to engage the audience in both an imaginative and felt experience of light as it happened around them – light was conceived as an experiential phenomenon to be questioned, not just as illumination of the space.

In developing a structured journey for the audience, I initially mapped an emotional outline of the performance. Each mood sought to take the audience through different feelings and temperaments:

- Mood 1 – **Discovery**: confusion and the physical exploration of the space. Low-level lighting was used. Small light fixtures illuminated the glass vessels on the floor, and the audience was invited to explore the space with a sense of disorientation. There were video projections of waves crashing on the three large screens. The bird boxes were illuminated to signal the arrival of new sound and to direct attention – tuning the audience into the logic of light being the dramaturgical and physical guide for the piece. The use of mirrors on the floor sought to give the space a rippling effect, like sunlight dancing on the waves of the sea as the audience moved through the space.

- Mood 2 – **Maelstrom**: dilemma, darkness and introspection. In this section the audience was plunged into a near-darkness, allowing the focus to turn inwards. The darkness was used as a dramaturgical tool, and the narrative focused on a power cut, allowing the audience to contemplate their existence through its absence.

- Mood 3 – **Reflection**: light, distance and contemplation. This section focused on the description of light as energy and as time (see the extract of text earlier). Light bulbs were used to guide the audience's attention around the space; tiny individual stars became a full constellation. Shades of blue were used to create a sense of distance. On the screens, a small boat was projected, moving slowly between them.

- Mood 4 – **Release**: looking up, moving the body and connecting with light. The end sequence used 1,000 paper birds. As the haze pumped into the space it delicately moved the paper birds. One large 5-kilowatt lamp with a split gel was used to create the impression of the sun; shafts of light through the haze on birds rained down on the audience below. The aim was to provide a cathartic release, inviting the audience to reach out to touch and feel the light at that moment. The final image used every light that had been used throughout the performance, each set to 100 per cent – the brilliant white light exposed the full space and its construction; dramaturgically it exposed the journey of light, totally saturating the audience.

The journey was intended to be emotionally and perceptually engaging, with design decisions aimed to alter sensory engagement throughout. My aim was to structure the event through dramaturgical feelings, with each section allowing participants to bring their own emotional and subjective emotions and feelings into the piece. The piece was designed so that each mood shifted the feeling of the space, while using the same set of design materials throughout. At times, the light was used to condition and contextualize the audience in a performance world; at other times light and darkness were used as part of the poetic text and dramaturgy of the piece.

This light

Edward Gordon Craig, whose writing and designs have inspired much of my own practice, has enabled me to conceive of a theatre 'without the written play, without the use of actors' (quoted in Palmer, 2013, p.100). Craig's understanding of light combined with movement to create architectonic scenes inspired me to consider the interplay of materials to create different moods. For Craig, light could be used to shift the emotional tone and feeling of space, to communicate and express beyond words. It is a rare occurrence in a theatrical context to be guided and conditioned purely by the means of design material, not least to be in and among the material orchestrations. The subtle interplay of light, sound, projection and objects in my practice all cooperate to build a sense of feeling or mood. I value the creation of mood *as* experience, which holds value in and of itself. I use the term '*this* light' to conceptualize the general ambience, a contextual light that locates felt experience, where significance is open to subjective interpretation, and where the audience is saturated within the light. This means considering light as a part of an ecology of performance design, a total felt environment.

In the creation process of *and it all . . .*, I was captivated by Edward Hopper's painting *People in the Sun* (1960). This work served as one of the main inspirations for the piece. I was fascinated by the overriding sense of solitude that permeates the image; the sense of loneliness while in the company of others; how the position of the chairs affects the posture of its inhabitants; and the engrossed view of the front row and the inattentive but absorbed figure at the back.

The construction of distance, crafted out of an interplay between figure, environment and light, is apparent in many of Hopper's paintings and sketches. He creates a depth of space that I wanted to explore with my audience. Hopper skilfully composes the land, sky and figures into a total world-like ecology, a unified spatial composition. Ingold notes that the success of landscape painting is often dependent on this ecology: 'the painter depicting a world of both earth and sky, recognising full well that in the play of colour, light and shade, one could not exist without the other' (Ingold 2011, p.127). I was intrigued as to how the 'hemispheres' (Gibson, 1979, p.66), as Gibson puts it, of earth and sky cooperate in the experience of scenography. I am interested in the way light can be used to build a world and contextual space for an audience, to situate them in a particular feeling of mood.

An example of providing a contextual '*this* light' space can be seen in my explorations of using the colour blue and its subsequent feeling and significance. In *A Field Guide to Getting Lost* (2006), Rebecca Solnit discusses the perceptual ambiguity of the colour blue, on ageing and on the surfaces and distance inherent in our environments. She constructs an analogy around the distance gained as a child matures into adulthood, of our bodily relationship with distance, environment, and the blue of the sky:

> There is no distance in childhood: for a baby, a mother in the other room is gone forever, for a child the time until a birthday is endless. Whatever is absent is impossible, irretrievable, unreachable. Their mental landscape is like that of medieval paintings: a foreground full of vivid things and then a wall. The blue of distance comes with time, with the discovery of melancholy, of loss, the textures of longing, of the complexity of the terrain we traverse and with the years of travel. (Solnit, 2006, p.39)

In the experience of *and it all . . .* I played with shifting perspectives and scale. Clouds and blue skies switched from being filmed vertically (looking up) to horizontally (looking across). Miniature scenes were presented in the birdboxes for participants to contemplate. I did not want to locate my audience *in* a particular place but to give the impression and flattened experience of an *emotion* of a place. Solnit further exposes a deep melancholy within the blue light of the horizon; blue is the light, the colour that is forever dispersing and fragmenting. The light at the blue end of the spectrum disperses among the molecules of air and water (2006, p.26) where the light travelling from the horizon does not make it the whole distance; 'it is the light that gets lost' (2006, p.29), she proclaims. As I created the experience, I filmed my surroundings: horizon lines, water, clouds and skies. I was mindful of this philosophy and how the experience of distance could be captured and felt via the use of colour and its associations with distance.

In Hopper's painting *People in the Sun* (1960), the horizon line appears a vivid blue that conceals the texture of the mountains, creating a sense of distance. Hopper brings about solitude not only through the representation of people but also through a composition of environment, space and colour. Distance here is also partly represented through the ageing of figures, with the most elderly looking out into the distance, while the more youthful remain caught up in their own immediate experience. However, through the composition of the painted figures and the blue of the horizon, a melancholy unfolds in the gulf between the figure and the ground. The aesthetic intention of *and it all* . . . was to explore distance through colour, reflection, and duration, drawing on the participants' subjective experiences of light and using an individual's 'atmospheric sense' – a general feeling and impression, in this case of melancholy and distance. In crafting *Mood 3 – Reflection*, I explored the blue for the glass vessels, using a small fixture with different tones of blue and projected images of the sea and sky (see Plate 9). Overall, the light was diffused; a small amount of haze filled the space, there was no set focal point. I constructed an ecology of light. I wanted to saturate the audience in subtle tones, creating a simultaneous feeling of expanse and introspection.

The use of haze produced a diffused light, slightly clouding vision, where blue hues saturated the air. There is an atmospheric circling of light through haze, and an emotional melancholic involvement – a 'scenographic weather' that provides the foundation of the concept of '*this* light'. Environmental philosopher David Macauley reminds us that, in life, '[w]ith our heads immersed in the thickness of the atmosphere or our lungs and limbs engaged with the swirling winds, we repeatedly breathe, think and dream in the regions of the air' (Macauley, 2005, p.307) not 'on the fixed surfaces of the landscape but in the swirling midst of the weather-world' (Ingold, 2011, p.135). I used floor lighting, colour, haze and projected light to make us conscious of the air, to enable the audience to breathe, think and dream in this space, to produce a productive reverie.

Maurice Merleau-Ponty in his phenomenological account of perceiving the sky asserts how our bodies are not cages for the mind and articulates an understanding where the body and environment are entwined:

> As I contemplate the blue of the sky I am not set over against it as an acosmic subject; I do not possess it in thought, or spread out towards it some idea of blue such as might reveal the secret of it, I abandon myself to it and plunge into this mystery, it 'thinks itself within me', I am the sky itself as it is drawn together and unified, and as it begins to exist for itself; my consciousness is saturated with this limitless blue. (Merleau-Ponty, 2002, p.249)

This light is a sense of oneness, a totality of a lit environment. I wanted light to saturate my audience, not in an abundant way, but where they abandon themselves to it, for it to be saturated within their consciousness. This is different from locating an audience in a place or location; it is an embodied feeling, of memory and time – it is a philosophical and felt reception. In *and it all* . . . the audience is part of light's composition; they are bound up in *this* light. Light is the condition for emotional contemplation – I am the sky as it unfolds to me.

That light

In contrast to the conditioning ambience of *this* light, I now consider how specific moments of light can act as part of a felt dramaturgical reception. Henry David Thoreau (1886) offers profound ways to conceive of the rich experience of everyday life, and for me, a potential mode of engagement for scenographic reception. Thoreau states:

> we are in danger of forgetting the language which all things and events speak without metaphor, which alone is copious and standard. Much is published, but little printed. The rays which stream through the shutter will be no longer remembered when the shutter is wholly removed. (1886, p.109)

Thoreau notes how *a* particular moment – the experience of light – becomes fused in our consciousness and awakens us and we become attuned to its momentary presence; it stands out from our usual engagement with the world. The rays that stream through the shutters are of *that* light, in *that* time, in *that* air, culminating in our recognizing it as *a* moment as distinct from the usual continuation of experience. I am sure most of us can attest to a moment like this, the golden hour, as light streams through the window, catching dust motes in the air. Thoreau reminds us of the qualitative experience of light, one that cannot be documented, only experienced, in *that* moment, and these experiences are abundant if we attune ourselves to their emergence.

For Böhme, 'the ecstasies of things indicate the ways in which things radiate outwards into space, make a certain impression on us, and thus contribute to the formation of an atmosphere' (Böhme, 2017, p.5). The constellation of materials, temporary and fleeting, is recognizable as a distinct moment, and we may or may not notice their affective potentials to change our mood. Our noticing of experience is important, however, particularly in performance. In our noticing of a shift in mood, it stands out to us and becomes what Martin Heidegger terms as a 'deficient' mode of our usual concern with the world (Leder, 1990, p.19). This deficiency, as performance scholar Anna Fenemore notes, 'implies not a hierarchy, but an extra-ordinary mode of embodiment such that absence is the norm and presence the "deficiency" from that norm' (Fenemore, 2001, pp.78–9). In my practice, I work to draw attention towards these extraordinary moments of embodiment. Brilliant white haze might seep underneath the audience, inviting them to reach out and touch or swirl it around. You might be invited to hold your hand close to a filament light bulb and contemplate the burning tungsten inside, or feel the affective heat radiate from a series of Parcans as they create the effect of the sun. The cycling of affect (feeling of the light) and dramaturgical effect (significance and meaning of light) is one tool I use to immerse an audience (see Shearing, 2017). In these examples, the participants are invited to engage with light as an embodied experience, which stands out from our usual engagement with it – light becomes a moment of felt signification. I use light to shift experience, so we are continuously made aware of light's presence in the unfolding dramatic action. The moment we recognize the experience of light it invites a temporal–spatial adjustment of self and the performance world.

The nature of our experience in the natural world is that it is always running continuously; to further consider how we come to recognize 'a moment', I turn to American philosopher John Dewey, whose writing on experience explores this question. Dewey outlines how ourselves and our world are implicated together and how we quantify experience with emotion:

> Experience occurs continuously, because the interaction of live creature and environing conditions is involved in the very process of living. Under conditions of resistance and conflict, aspects and elements of the self and the world that are implicated in this interaction qualify experience with emotions and ideas so that conscious intent emerges. (1958, p.35)

He goes on to suggest that '[a]n experience has a unity that gives it its name, *that* meal, *that* storm, *that* rupture of friendship' (Dewey, 1958, p.37, emphasis added). A series of processes fold into each other and compound to become a unity of an experience. We are continuously in the flow and reciprocity of the world, material and self. What is useful as a frame for performance studies and environmental performance is how a certain moment of experience might be brought to a fulfilment, a conclusion that can be recognized as a significant moment by an audience:

> The experience, like that of watching a storm reach its height and gradually subside, is one of continuous movement of subject-matters. Like the ocean in the storm, there are a series of waves; suggestions reaching out and being broken in a clash, or being carried onwards by a cooperative wave. If a conclusion is reached, it is that of a movement of anticipation and cumulation, one that finally comes to completion. A 'conclusion' is no separate and independent thing; it is the consummation of a movement. (Dewey, 1958, p.38)

In performance we might recognize the passing of light, like waves, forming sequences of light moments. Dewey further suggests that 'an experience has pattern and structure, because it is not just doing and undergoing in alternation but consists of them in relationship [. . .] to put one's hand in the fire that consumes it is not necessarily to have an experience' (1958, p.44).

My argument here is that to experience 'a moment' of light in performance, as a distinct 'moment', is to be placed at a threshold that is hinged between the felt material presence and its recognizable dramaturgical purpose in a succession of events.

In my practice, I actively craft the integration of haze and light as part of the design composition. I believe that theatrical haze, smoke and fog can be seen as part of an overall construction of mood, rhythm and pace that might aid in the conditioning of audience experience as part of a 'scenographic weather'. Haze does not only provide a substance to the air but it also helps draw attention to light by creating a three-dimensionality as light passes through the mist particles. The haze deployed in *and it all . . .* was used in different sections of the production, as one might with any other scenographic element, to create perceptual shifts in clarity and to obscure visual perception of the space in the moments of discovery. Haze makes the air and light active as conjoined elements. In experiencing haze, we come to move it, taste it and smell it, which makes us mindful of our bodies in the space. More than just giving light a materiality, haze draws attention towards the medium of air, that medium in which we inhabit and experience the performance. Haze helps visualize the concept of 'scenographic weather' and supports the creation of a micro-climate of performance.

In the final sequence of the performance, *Mood 4 – Release*, the perception of air was further foregrounded as fans pushed haze upward, causing the air and paper birds above to slowly move. As the light passed through the birds it created subtle moving beams of light, a 'material solidity' (Baugh, 2005, p.120) that pierced through the gaps and onto the audience and floor below. Crucially, this moment took place in the dramatic climax of the piece. The light through the haze and the movement of the birds was a representation of release that was intended to be felt as a moment of performance. This can be considered as what Josef Svoboda termed a 'psycho-plastic' space (Svoboda quoted in Burian, 1971, p.31). Svoboda's concept emphasizes the intangible forces of time, space and movement, to create a scenographic 'dynamism' (Burian, 1971, p.31). The scenographic dynamism seeks to transform space in response to the 'psychic pulse of the dramatic action' (Burian, 1971, 31). Svoboda's concept is principally developed through the experience of end-on theatre in which movement is predominantly registered optically. I adapt this concept and bring it within the framework of an embodied and felt experience as part of the dramaturgy of the event, where the participant – in this case sat in deck chairs enveloped in the haze and light – become bound up with the 'psychic pulse' of the dramatic action (see Plate 10).

The bird sequence at the end of the piece was intended to produce a cathartic release for the audience that I hoped would encourage a feeling of 'letting go'. The intention was that the movement of the light in the haze would inspire the audience to move, to look up and to explore the space with their bodies; some reached out while others seemed to enjoy being bathed in the light. The material of light invited a playful physical engagement, as audience members touched the moving beams of light. The scenography invited bodily participation; the light beams extended bodily connection with the space. The expanded touch of light bound the audience into the dramaturgy of *that* moment, *that* release – the psychic pulse of the dramatic action.

This returns me to Thoreau, whose earlier statement reminds us not only of the qualitative experience of light but also of the power of light as a living thing that has a temporality that can only be experienced in that moment. The conclusion of *and it all . . .* was part of a dramaturgical journey, the fulfilment of the performance event – light was composed as part of an experiential journey. The entwined nature of the participant in the scenographic materials (haze and light), develops Svoboda's concept of psycho-plastic space. When the audience is bound up through a dynamic movement of scenography, through the dramatic action (in this case, the moment of cathartic release, the feeling of letting go), there is a psycho-dynamic commingling of audience body, design material (haze, light, sound and birds) and performance text.

As an 'attendant' (Di Benedetto, 2010, p.158) to the experience, we are able to distinguish a pattern and shape of the event that culminates in an aesthetic moment of fulfilment. This extends notions of attunement of light towards its purposeful signification and reception; I define this here as '*that* light'. To structure light dramaturgically is to create a journey in the continuous flow of the performance text towards fulfilment – becoming a moment of significance – of felt light.

Fulfilment

I have sought to explore the complex, multidimensional experience of light in performance as it is acted within and through the body. I have explained how the medium of air is an axis of experience, a comingling of light, sound, odour, touch and breath with the dramatic action. Light here is seen as part of a weather-world and more specifically for design as part of a 'scenographic weather'. The air is the medium for theatrical reception in which the participant is central. I have built a framework that extends what Pallasmaa calls our 'atmospheric sense' (2019, p.130), as an attunement to our environment, towards its potential dramaturgical use in performance. To offer a more precise understanding of the role and function of light, not just to create an ambience or mood, I have considered the ways in which light can be practised as part of felt dramaturgies. I have positioned my thinking around light as part of a 'scenographic weather', a twofold conception of audience experience, an environmental comingling of the senses, and the felt experience of the dramatic action. I have attempted to not separate light from our other sense modalities and offer two specific felt dramaturgies for audience-centred and environmental performance practice. I have done this via the general conditioning and attunement of audience experience via '*this* light' and specific dramaturgical moments of felt light conceived of as '*that* light'.

This light accounts for the generalized and often preconscious reception of light, where memories are forged through the fluxes and flows of a body commingling with performance material. Past, present and future reside here, an imaginative space where latent potential receptions are brought to the foreground through wider atmospheric and dramaturgical strategies of engagement. Light is used to condition the audience, to open up possibilities of emotional involvement. *This* light saturates us and is a felt attunement of participant, environment and dramaturgical mood. I used the example of the colour blue to consider how it might imbue the subject with a sense of environmental totality in which we inhabit and forge emotional resonances.

That light foregrounds the intentional applications and uses of light that puncture or stand out from everyday experience. I used the dust motes as an example to outline a moment of rupture that foregrounds light. I draw this concept into a performance setting considering how '*that* light' moments can be used for dramatic affect as part of fulfilment of an experience. Like the waves crashing in the sea, fulfilment does not just have to occur at the end of a performance, but as part of a continuation of experience where it can be recognized as *that* light. I used the example of the last section of the performance in which the haze, materialized the beams of light through the movement of the birds, completed the performance text as a felt dramaturgy. The audience feels *that* light as significant, a moment, as part of a dramaturgical journey – it is a part of the psychic pulse of the dramatic action that is embodied through the participant.

3

Transforming visitor experience through light
Tivoli Gardens: A case study

Jesper Kongshaug

I think that the theatre format is changing as well as lighting design. We are moving theatre out of traditional theatre spaces. We are also moving the theatrical thinking; lighting design for storytelling is also moving out of theatre stages and moving into architecture. It's moving into public space and people are welcoming that. People like to feel that somebody designed something intentionally that has an impact on their mood or their behaviour. They might not be fully aware of how that is done, but they like the fact that they have been taken by hand through a building, through a square, through a street, through a city or through an evening. Tivoli is a kind of a playground for me in that sense, because I've been working a lot in theatrical spaces, in Denmark and internationally. The understanding and appreciation of lighting from the theatre has come to be a gift in working in Tivoli because we have guests coming from all over the world.

The composition of the audience at Tivoli depends on the season. Walking around, listening to the languages being spoken, we find a lot of people from southern Europe and from China. It is true that tourists may not know that the place is spectacular in the evening unless they're going for dinner. In the winter season, the evening audience is often mainly composed of Danes, who come to experience the artificial lighting. Tivoli's northern geographical location provides an extended period of twilight. This lasts two or three hours in the summertime, and people have a high awareness of this fading daylight.

The fact that light comes from one horizontal angle during those hours also is part of a cultural understanding of light. It's visible in our design tradition that we have many hours of more horizontal lighting than in southern latitudes. When you look at our design tradition in the north of Europe, it's clear that it is influenced by natural lighting. All of our design schools, for example, have big open windows, so when the students are being taught and when they're practising, they have a high intake of horizontal lighting into the modelling rooms and the teaching rooms.

The importance of this long period of twilight is also reflected in our audience. Our biggest increase in customers is not at the weekend; it is actually after sunset, at dusk hours. This tendency is evident throughout the seasons, and this variation has to do with the sunset so people will arrive later in the brighter seasons and earlier in the darker parts of the year. That means that we can see that the transformation provided by light is the attraction.

I had the feeling that this pattern was not only because people visited after finishing work but that it also had to do with the lighting. I asked the statistics department to look at variations, and they were more striking than we had thought. There's a group of people consistently arriving around the dusk hours, around sunset (see Plate 11). We have a marked increase of people who arrive at that moment, to experience the curiosity of sitting around in the dark or semi-dark hours. The times when you have this mixture of daylight and artificial lighting it's really difficult to find a seat as there are so many people sitting enjoying themselves and experiencing the light. This opportunity to experience light has become an attraction in itself (see Plate 12). This has commercial value, so we have developed that further and we have all kinds of settings now for artificial lighting. We can give the garden a crisp feeling or a poetic feeling in different contexts, and there are a range of settings that depend on the time of the year and respond to the time of the day (see Plate 13).

Outside of twilight hours, we have found out that we can make a grey day more lively by turning on some of these Tivoli lights along the buildings, for example, so that you get this change that takes the greyness out of the day. Previously, we had a tendency to only take publicity pictures of the gardens on sunny days, and the reality in Copenhagen is that we have a lot of grey days. By taking that realization into the lighting control we can use the comparable conditions of gloomy weather to evoke the transitional experience of the garden lights appearing while daylight fades. This has made it a more appealing experience to come here on grey days, when kids can still play in the water and adults can observe the lighting, even though we're not even close to sunset.

As well as paying attention to the value of this transitional moment of twilight, I have tried to see how little light is needed in storytelling more generally. I have tried to see how little intensity is actually needed and how that affects people. This is an important part of how we curate the journey through Tivoli Gardens and also connects with lighting for theatrical space. In Tivoli, each lamp has its own little story. The combination of all these lamps creates this space, which you can navigate and experience through time. There's no lighting for the pathways. All the lighting in Tivoli Gardens is created by lamps that seem to have another function, but actually combine to provide illumination of spaces and indirectly light the pathways. This fairy tale, you could say, is used to keep people safe. We can see that people actually prefer to inhabit the darker spaces and to look into the brighter spaces from the darker zones.

We have a lot of regulations on how to light up areas for public access. We can see that if you can look, in an effortless way, out of your space, into the light, you can actually see and navigate very, very comfortably. If we have made a small space with more lighting, people will tend to use the darker areas around it, rather than dwelling in those bright zones. This contradicts the common perception of needing more and more light in public spaces. From my experience, what people actually mean when they say, 'we need more light' is that 'I want to see better', which is an important distinction to make.

This experience gave me the opportunity to investigate glare. One season, I went around with an assistant to examine about sixty or seventy spots in the gardens, in order to eliminate the glare. We refocused each spotlight, or turned them so that the glare was directed away from the viewer. The immediate response – which we gathered through an exit poll – was that people thought Tivoli had become brighter! I knew that I had actually made the place darker, but by protecting people's eyes, their eyes can open more, so they perceive the place as being brighter. That is quite an interesting observation, because in public spaces, we see more and more LED lighting that is uncontrolled optically. This has contributed to the public feeling that it's challenging to see. It's not related to the lighting intensity, but it happens because the lighting is preventing you from seeing.

I have also observed this phenomenon outside of Tivoli. The charts shown in Figure 3 follow an investigation I did in the city of Roskilde, where I hoped to prove my point that people generally have a tendency to walk in the darker zone more than in the brighter one. This graph shows that people prefer to walk in a darker spot if they have the choice. Two streets in Roskilde were observed at the same hours. We used a GoPro camera, and we also interviewed some of the visitors to hear why they chose to walk in an area where there was only one lamp every 100 feet or so. Respondents reported that they felt more comfortable. As the research was held in a city space it was not a controlled situation. If you're in a controlled situation, like Tivoli, you feel safe because there's a fence that separates the gardens

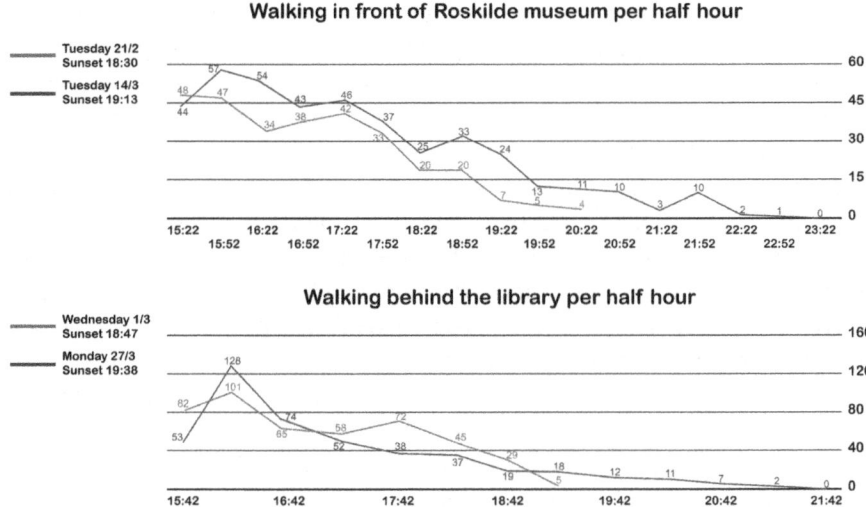

FIGURE 3 *Roskilde street lighting.* Data tracking footfall through brighter and darker areas.

from the city space, so it could be seen as an entirely artificial situation. The study in Roskilde, however, reveals that same behaviour, of dwelling in the darker spaces, in an open urban environment. It certainly proves what a lot of people don't know or don't trust: that lighting is extremely important (Figure 3).

In the northern part of Europe, we tend to prefer a warmer colour temperature (low Kelvin value) in the artificial lighting for interiors and exteriors. I think this is because the sun brings comfort and liveability in most months of the year, and actually is needed for our survival. The direct low sun is very comfortable for Scandinavians most of the year, and therefore this warm spectrum is preferred. In the countries south of the Alps, the cooler shadow is preferred in the daytime, where the colour spectrum of light is also cool or even blue. This tint reminds us of the comfort of being in the shadow of the daylight, which results in a preference for cooler lighting (higher Kelvin values).

In Tivoli we tend to use more saturated, primary colours on our performance stages, but when we're working with the garden in general, we use secondary colours. This is for me about the hierarchy between natural and artificial lighting. It could be that, living in northern latitudes, we don't want to show the performance of the lighting. We want to show the lighting in connection with nature. If we're paying attention to colour saturation, then we still have a natural balance between nature and our contribution, and I think that's quite important. Therefore, there is a direct relationship between the pigmentation of the building surface and the colours of the lighting. For example, if a fabric or a building surface is green, I will use green, turquoise or orange lighting. If it is blue I will use blue, turquoise or lavender lighting. If it is red, I will use orange, lavender or pink. Red lighting on red pigments will tend to make the colour seem white. In this way it is the building that is lit, rather than the lighting being important. This priority comes from my work on the performers on stage, giving them focus, rather than taking focus from them through lighting.

We have also worked to ensure uniformity of the colour white, which has been a technical challenge in the move from incandescent to LED sources. We have had to put a lot of effort into defining this white colour in collaboration with the lamp manufacturers. Colour temperature can tend towards either pink or green, and this shift is much more noticeable at lower intensities so we need to take great care when specifying lighting colours. Even though we started with a specific Kelvin, when we measured the lamps we still found some that were a little green, or a little lavender, so we realized we needed to specify the curve more exactly. If we have any variation we make sure that the lamps tend towards lavender, rather than green, which is a risk with warm LEDs, but the result is that we see a more uniform definition of the white colour. We have more than 1.2 million lights and we need to coordinate the whiteness to maintain aesthetic coherence throughout the visitor experience.

This technical care has allowed us to go further, to create all of these pictures of optimism and beauty in the dark months. The winter wonderland Christmas season, which is dominated by white light, has now been refined technically and aesthetically so that we can replicate it every year, and reuse a lot of the same bulbs because they have been specified so precisely. This partnership with the manufacturer has resulted in LEDs that last longer, and a more sustainable and conscious approach to lighting in Tivoli than we had before I started. The lighting is more coordinated now and very carefully choreographed. We have a clear framework to follow, and, as a result, we can see that people are attracted more and more to the experience offered through light.

An interesting example of how the use of colour has directly affected the audience experience in Tivoli relates to the red silk lamps in what's called the Chinese area. Traditionally, red has a specific meaning in China, being the colour of happiness and good luck. We put energy-saving equipment inside, but they produced a red colour that looked slightly green or grey. It was an area of the park that was threatened because of limited income and very few people staying there after sunset. I changed the LED to one that enhanced the colour of the paper lanterns, which immediately started to look more vibrant because the new sources were able to accentuate the red (see Plate 13). We looked into the statistics for the transactions in that area, which were corrected for the weather and the different number of guests in the garden. As you can see in Figure 4, after changing the light, there was a significant increase in visitor numbers. I had expected it to be around 5–10 per cent[1] but in the Chinese area in Tivoli we had 16 per cent more visitors between 9 and 10 pm and 62 per cent more guests after sunset. Astonishingly, when it was completely dark, the number of guests increased by 77 per cent. Moreover people showed a different behaviour: they would, first of all, stay longer to experience the area, but also they would choose to socialize and get a drink in that area before leaving Tivoli (See Figure 4). As a result, the Chinese area,

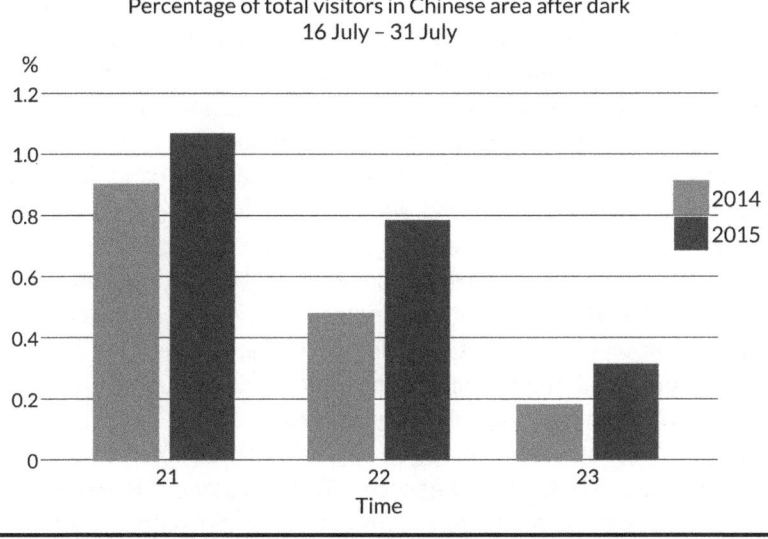

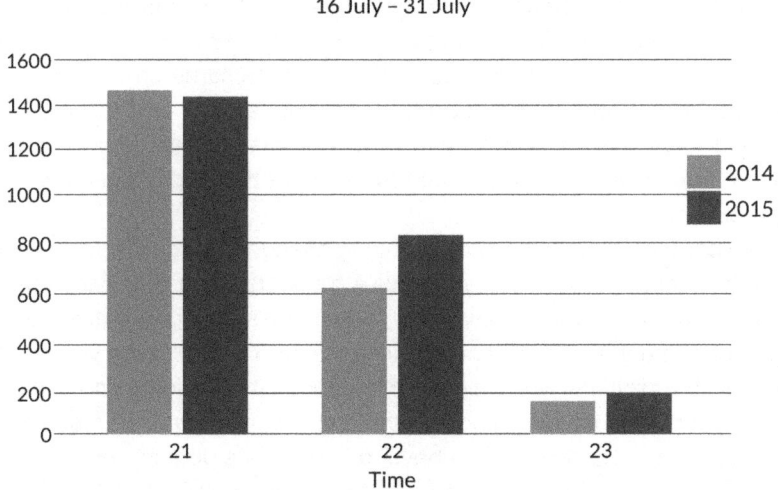

FIGURE 4 Tivoli Gardens. Guest data, tracking visitors to the Chinese area before and after lighting change.

which had been in danger of closure on economic grounds, remains a thriving part of Tivoli. That means that this design approach, of keeping a coherence between a material and the lighting colour, actually has a commercial value. It's surprising how much visitor behaviour has been impacted by attention to detail in the lighting design. The numbers are quite stunning. This coordinated approach to design actually had a measurable economic impact. You can see that more people are staying later after dark, when the red light begins to predominate (Figure 4).

Another part of what I do at Tivoli involves a more analogue approach to coloured lighting. We still use glass shades to manually change the colour of some of our lighting (see Plate 13). This seems quite unique to Tivoli that we still actually change the thousands of kuppels – the coloured glass shades that adorn lamps on buildings and walkways. In the summer season the kuppels have many different colours and they are all changed by hand. Most of them provide quite subtle colouring and we use them to change the colour of the light produced, of course, but also to change the colour of the instruments in the daytime because we have so many hours then with the sunlight being present. They are all changed by hand instead of using LEDs. You could change the colour that way but then it wouldn't be changed when the sun is there. It's quite important that the sunlight also affects this colouring. This is why it's not an option to change it digitally because we would not get this colouring in the daylight. This is quite an analogue approach, and we can see that people really appreciate this kind of presence. Tivoli's history, this extremely long history of 178 years, is reflected in some of our lighting choices. At the same time, we try to renew ourselves by having more modern things too. I think this contrast between bringing something new and keeping the old is quite important, especially for local visitors, many of whom came here in childhood and want to relive those memories, and then at the same time they want to get a high level of entertainment. I think that quite early on I realized that if I just modernize this place, then there's no contrast – it won't work. I had to respect where it came from and learn more about that and make the renewal a more conscious process.

When people have seen a building being changed by lighting, it's changed forever for them. The fact that you have a transformation of a place that you already know, or think you know, and suddenly it's changed in front of you, that will become a quality of that building forever. The next time you see that building in the daylight, you will still think about this building as having this quality. That comes from lighting and the fact that light can come and go like a bird. An example of this – from beyond Tivoli – is a project I did at Kolding castle. The building had burned down 200 years ago and I was asked if I could make it burn again, to mark the anniversary. I made this 27-minute event with the lighting spreading through the windows and making it look like the building was burning. The first thing I told the Kolding municipality when we wanted to do this project was if they wanted to recreate something from 200 years ago, they would have to turn off all the lights in the city of Kolding first, because that's the biggest change, that we had darkness back then. And they said, 'Are you crazy?' No, I'm not crazy. There's not going to be any problem if we have half an hour of darkness. We called the fire authorities, and they agreed. So we made this event and the fact that the city was dark was actually the most valuable thing. This was some years ago but I can still ask people, 'Were you there that night?' It was only a short moment in people's lives but the people who saw it remember it vividly; it's an amazingly strong memory people have of something that went on for such a short period of time. About 35,000 people came to see these stones suddenly come alive, and what is really interesting is that the memory around this change is so strong. I think the impact of putting lighting onto something that people think they know and transforming it is probably the most powerful lighting tool because it doesn't affect the building at all. It only affects our perception of the building. As a professional you know it's only some lamps and some power, but for them it's new; it's become a different building. We have put it into the dark and brought it alive through light.

Notes

1 Measured against typical changes in Las Vegas, where a successful design change might attract an increase in visitors of around 10 per cent.

4

Narratives, choreographies and felt experiences of light

Lucy Carter

Having grown up creatively around choreographers and observed them working by being present and active in the creative process and in the rehearsal room as much as possible, I have developed a lighting design practice that is heavily influenced by and draws upon the choreographic methods used to create dance. This has naturally built upon my own study of choreography at university and from my professional career, which began with an immersion in contemporary dance, almost exclusively, for five to seven years.

The body and choreography are my inspiration, and I find that observing the choreographic process is the most creatively inspiring and idea and concept-generating experience I have. In reflecting on my lighting design practice while writing this chapter, I have come to realize that my creative practice at present is focused around and involves light as the core and leading element in a performative artwork. This has evolved because of and from my career-long involvement in creating lighting designs for dance and ballet. A constant lack of any type of set design, mostly due to programming and budget constraints, meant that I was often designing light for empty stages, open spaces that were waiting to be populated with visual environments and bodies. This led me to develop a practice in which I sculpt spaces, help portray themes and stories, create context, provide semiotic cues, direct the audience's eye, expose bodies and the choreographic object variously, and enforce or create the rhythm, flow, pace and the dynamics of a work, as well as ensuring that the feeling and emotion of the work reaches and affects the audience. In contemporary dance, lighting is used as a fully integral part of the performance, in a bold and conscious way, with all creative elements working together symbiotically to create the work. This is very much the way in which I have consistently worked with the choreographer Wayne McGregor, resident choreographer of the Royal Ballet, with whom I have collaborated for the whole of my career.

Wayne McGregor's production of *Woolf Works* is an example that I think truly illustrates the multiple functions that a lighting design can fulfil for a live dance/ballet performance, and how all the creative elements of a production work together to create the whole. *Woolf Works* for the Royal Ballet premiered in 2015 at the Royal Opera House in Covent Garden, London (see Plates 14 and 15). The ballet is in three parts, and each part explored and used as its source material one of Virginia Woolf's novels. Act one, *I now, I then*, was taken from her novel *Mrs. Dalloway* and depicted essences of the narrative, the characters and the dramatic themes from the novel, which were explored through the choreography. The lighting design worked alongside the story and action, and in partnership with the set, designed by Ciguë, evoking a sense of time and place, using the emotional colours of the story beats to enforce and make explicit the meaning and thread of the narrative, choreography and direction. In act two, *Becomings*, a stunning set design by WeNotI created an infinite reflective and physical void, and I created a light installation world inside which the choreography wound its magic. This second part of the ballet was inspired by *Orlando*, Woolf's novel that spans 300 years of history and sees the protagonist transform from male to female. It has fantasy and time travel at its core, with a somewhat cosmic gaze, but it also has a great deal of period detail. The novel has a sense of 'time and space incessantly and endlessly reconfiguring' (Hamed, 2015, p.11) and the main character continually shape shifts. Uzma Hamed, the production's dramaturg, writes in the programme notes for the production: 'The novel is a breathless, virtuoso dash, reminiscent of Woolf's famous comparison of life to "being blown through the Tube at fifty miles an hour"' (2015, p.11). It was these elements we wanted to draw upon to create the visual and physical context for this section of ballet to exist in and to evoke the sensation of time travel. With sculpted beams of light and strong spatial isolation, the ballet begins with a historical artefact-like image of dancers dressed in abstracted period costumes in highly reflective and gold-coloured fabric (designed by Moritz Jung), searched out by a single beam of light scouring the space for the characters of the narrative, the dancers who will participate in the mad dash through time that is about to come. Numerous sections within act two follow, where laser lights construct and deconstruct physically present, abstract and cosmic environments in the air for the choreography to exist in, like constructing worlds from the ether: shifting the sculptural design of the space through light every few minutes (see Plate 15). The idea of threads of history stretching back from every one of us, which Woolf describes in the novel, found form through the threads of laser lines scratching through the darkness above and around the dancers, and finally penetrating into the auditorium to connect every member of the audience to the threads of their history. This was light functioning on many levels, to enforce the conceptual theme of the work, to sculpt and enforce the physical space, to create an emotional context for the choreography, and to evoke sensation and connection with the audience. This is not light working solely on its own but as part of the whole collaborative, visual, choreographic and aural worlds, following a non-linear dynamic taken from Woolf's stretched-out linear narrative. Act three, *Tuesday*, was from Woolf's novel, *The Waves*. While choreographically, this third part of the ballet plurally, explored the narrative and thematic threads from the novel and Woolf's own personal biographical story in an abstracted and non-linear way, the lighting design worked in close conjunction with the video designs, by Ravi Deepres, to explore thematic ideas and dynamic expressions of the novel and choreography. Expressing loss and isolation through an enveloping terrain of repetitive waves, tumbling, falling, rippling, continuous and unrelenting. Light environments quietly evolved and flowed around the dancers and the choreography. In this instance light is not theatrically telling a story, evoking a place or time of day, but employing a theme, a core element; in this case, water and its qualities, as inspiration for an ever-shifting and subtly visceral visual layer, supporting and immersing the choreography and the themes that the work is exploring.

Using the repetitive kinetic of waves, the light rolls down the stage and recedes back, the energy of a constant ebb and flow from the light and video, stimulating a sense of surging waves and of life cycles and of being swept along unable to stop the inevitable. Taking the temporal shimmering reflections of moonlight on water and sunlight reflecting off hot sand and create a visceral sensation of a summer's day on the beach or a calm moonlit night through light, where mystery and adventure seem possible. As the ballet ends, the dancer who embodies the character of Woolf, is laid to the floor and as the waves of light recede, evaporate and cease into darkness, so too does Virginia's life end. Giving herself and her life up to the water and the light, just as Virginia Woolf does, committing suicide at the end of her life.

In writing this chapter I am reminded of how incredibly hard it is to talk about light. Light is a feeling, a sensation, an emotion. I have always reasoned that that was why I find it hard to portray to a director or choreographer what I was intending, hard to explain what I could see in my head. Really, though, it isn't because it is a visual picture in my head, which I could somehow manage, even with my limited skill, to draw or sketch or use imagery to show them; it is actually because it isn't an image in my head at all, but a feeling in my body that I want to create, a sensation.

Perhaps that is why, despite brilliant photography of beautiful shows that can impress and excite people into wanting to go and see a production, the emotion of something, the impression or effect of the production is not adequately captured by the photograph. Perhaps that is good publicity, a visual taster, but it is not the full experience. It explains why seeing a live-streamed cinema performance of a stage production goes partway in giving the audience the live experience, but if the atmosphere of the theatre, the visceral experience of the sound and lighting, and the tension of the performance are absent, then the truly felt and embodied experience of being in the theatre is missing: the warmth and comfort of the heat of warm sunny lights, the desolate coolness of stark and icy lights, the frightening darkness of the shadows, the vibrations or the quiet distance of the sound.

A generally perceived notion that a good lighting design should be invisible and not draw attention to itself can partially be backed up by the suggestion that lighting is a feeling and a felt expression of ideas, moods, locations and signals. My personal feeling is that a truly well-balanced lighting design is one in which the lighting has a powerful presence, can portray themes and ideas, evoke the emotional bed of the work and enforce narratives and structures, without overtly calling attention to how it is technically being achieved. A lighting design also needs to ensure that it is not just a visually stunning decoration, without feeling. The desire is not to purely stimulate the eye but to make the experience visually and emotionally felt. To truly experience something, we need to be immersed and transported, by which I mean the sensation and effect the lighting has on the viewer should be the overriding experience and that the method by which the lighting state is being achieved, the type of equipment or the cleverness of the technology used, is not overpowering or does not become the sole aspect the viewer is attentive to.

To ensure my designs are fully embedded into the work and are addressing all these elements, I often consider and draw upon many choreographic structuring tools and provocations when I create my designs, evolved through my extensive design practice, from my education and training and from working exhaustively in dance, and through my long-term collaboration with Wayne McGregor. For example, five overriding factors that can be considered when creating dance choreography are body, action, time, space and energy. These have become reference points for me when I create my lighting designs. I have, somewhat intuitively adapted some choreographic provocations to stimulate my thinking during every step of my lighting design process.

- Body: How light can reveal the body or obscure it, how to reveal not just the dancers' bodies but also the choreographic object – the intention of the movement and the idea behind it.

- Action: How light can enforce the action – the feeling and the type of movement, with the relevant feeling and quality of light? Light can reinforce the action, the narrative of the story, or theme of the work.

- Time: Consider the time – when you change lighting states, how, with what tempo and rhythm, and with what intention.

- Space: Light needs to sculpt not just the space the choreography occupies but also the surrounding space and its relationship to, or perhaps its symbolic meaning for, the choreography. Light creates the environment within the performance space and the auditorium or the space the audience occupies.

- Energy: Light is energy. The electrical current of light produces energy that performers can feel and respond to, but audiences can also feel and respond to the light; subconsciously, they are affected and moved by the lighting textures. Energy is emotion.

What I am trying to explain is that every lighting choice needs a motivation or reason to be present in the design for that particular production. There is no formula that I apply to my thinking in order to produce my designs, but I ask myself some of these questions, almost subconsciously now, in order to adequately enforce and serve the conceptual ideas of the work. This is surely the lighting designer's brief: to make the choreography seen, not just by illuminating, but also by making the concepts, themes and emotions truly visible, felt and experienced. This is the dramaturgy of light in my mind, and this can further be developed to enforce the choreographic motivations and increase the clarity of content.

To engage in this deeper development, I further draw upon other choreographic tools and provocations:

Do I need a lighting **motif**? Should there be a **beginning, middle, and end** to the lighting design? Where will I create a **climax**? Should the light work in **unison** with the choreography or in **contrast** or as **counterpoint** to it? Am I providing enough visual and contextual **variety**? How might the lighting **sequence**, **repeat**, and **flow**.

When I am polishing and finalizing a lighting composition, I often consider ways in which I can manipulate the lighting in choreographic terms – **repetition, retrograde, inversion, size** – to **condense** or **expand**, **vary** the **tempo** or **rhythm**, enforce **effort** qualities, or use the idea of body part **impetus** to inform the light language. For example, where does the impetus for a lighting state physically come from; how much **force** does a lighting state arrive with or leave with; can light adopt an attitude of **canon** or **fragmentation**; and can light create changing **planes** of sight and **levels** within the space? Again, these are choreographic tools that can be used to create movement motifs, applied to the qualities of light.

In this way, the lighting becomes a score, like a piece of music, which integrally melds with the music and choreography to instruct, but more importantly to create a feeling, a sensation and a felt experience for the audience, an experience that provokes thought and contemplation.

Judith Mackrell, dance critic for the *Guardian* for many years, who has often written about lighting design for dance productions, said that dance lighting design has become 'a form of choreography in its own right [. . .] it is impossible to separate the movement from the light' (Mackrell, 2014, n.p.). But what if we take away the bodies and the choreographic object? Or what if the light becomes the body and the form? Light becomes the movement – the choreography – and provides the kinetic, the emotion and the sensation.

My installation and light art work is a clear and developed progression from my dance lighting designs, from my fascination with the dramaturgical abilities of light, and from a desire to create a powerful and a truly felt emotional experience in the viewer through light alone. I am aiming to find an expression of pure light that does all the above without the presence of a performative body. The light also then becomes the form, the kinetic interest and the sole provider of the embodied experience for the viewer or audience. Light *is* the performative medium. Audiences become part viewer/part performer when they are present in the installation environments. As light hits them or the space, the lighting atmospheres emote.

As I stated earlier, to truly experience and feel, audiences need to be immersed, transported and absorbed and so I equally believe that a lighting design for an installation or light art environment should not call attention to the way it is technically realized. It is not about technical prowess for technology's sake. Leaving things unsaid, creating mystery, and provoking thought lead to a continued consideration for the viewer even after they have left the lighting environment.

I have created light works that fully convey a narrative with the accompaniment of sound, pieces that portray a non-linear narrative – a journey and exploration of relationships – installations that purely convey an emotional experience, as well as fully abstract works that explore ideas and themes. Just as the work I have done in dance also includes working with those concepts, in both mediums the results are multilayered. For example, creating a design that portrays a narrative does not mean it solely does that; it also creates emotion and sensation and provokes thought and contains ideas. Lighting is multifunctional in a subliminal way.

My installation piece *Hidden*, which was created for Sadler's Wells, London, in 2016, was part of an event that invited creative collaborators in dance to produce installation pieces throughout the whole building. I created a triptych of work in collaboration with composer Jules Maxwell that evoked and exposed the atmospheres and creativity of the backstage teams and showcased some areas of the theatre that audiences rarely get to appreciate and see. *Hidden 1* told the story of and examined the working processes of the wardrobe and costume department, *Hidden 2* those of the sound and lighting teams, and *Hidden 3* was the story of the lights themselves – perhaps a personal, slightly romantic view of my relationship to light and the actual lanterns that create that light.

Hidden 3 told a narrative of what the lights do when left alone in the lighting store at the end of the day, when we all leave, through light and sound. We invited the audience into a room directly beneath the stage, a space they would not normally have access to, a privileged view of our backstage environments (see Plate 16), into an evocative world where sound and light tell the story together. A technician's workbench was lit and a radio was playing. Tools of the trade were scattered on the bench as if a lighting technician were working there. Magically the radio was then switched off, the light at the workbench was switched off, there was the sound of footsteps exiting the space and the door closed. There is darkness and silence. Then, a small indicator light buzzes and it goes quiet again, in darkness, then it repeats itself. Gradually the 200-plus lighting fixtures, mostly very old and vintage lanterns, slowly begin to join the youthful and small indicator light. They have conversations, they play chase, they develop into friendship groups and indulge in a playful dance that accumulates into the whole community of lighting fixtures surging light energy across the long and narrow space, in waves of light, heat and sound. They find joy together and, as their energy starts to become chaotic and climactic, the largest and oldest light calls a halt to the game, and then sings, lulls and spiritually calms everyone back down into a communal rest.

This is light and sound performing a narrative. It is providing sensation and emotion, a visceral experience that could be felt via the heat and energies of the lights and darkness. It was providing context, a consideration of the backstage teams and their creativity. It sculpted the space and provided the whole visual and physical world. It was the body, the action, the dance, the story and the idea. The lighting fixtures which were hung in groups by lantern type, pointed at the audience so that they fully experienced the sensations viscerally. The lights not only provided light energy but also a sound quality, the sounds of the power illuminating the light and then a surging sound energy as the lights played and coursed the light force around the room, developed and accentuated by the sound score. Each light had its own individual aural identity. The lights were not the technology but the characters in the story of the installation. The technology was the complex programming and syncing sound to light that remained invisible and unconsidered for the viewer.

Often, I have been tasked with creating an installation environment for live performance to exist within. So a lighting environment that sculpts and gives context to the air and void of a physical space, not just lighting that illuminates the actual space, room, theatre or location, and so on. That installation needs to and could exist without the live performance element and does not respond to or edit the physical action or choreography in the normal way we create lighting designs, that I outlined at the beginning of the chapter. With or without live bodies, installation light environments need to provide the full context and idea of the work, and in collaboration with the sound world, an audience can be invited to view or enter it to experience it from the inside.

F.LUX was a light and sound installation work I created for an art and music festival in Switzerland, for the Schlossmediale, Werdenberg, in 2014, with the composer and sound designer, Paul Corley (see Plate 17). The theme of the festival was 'the eternal female', and the installation was site specific. My main intention was to explore the theme of the female, and my response was a physical and structural design. I created four long steel poles that emitted light out of a slot along their entire length. They were approximately eight metres long and came out of holes in the walls of a cellar in the castle. The poles could rotate 360 degrees, reverse directions and revolve at any speed I wanted to programme them at. The holes and the castle became the inspiration for this work, as the last inhabitant of the castle had been a female recluse whose sister had committed suicide from the windows of the castle after falling pregnant out of wedlock, and both had lived under the rule of an oppressive father. I wanted to create something very feminine that came from the fabric of the building, and the holes in the walls of the cellar were an existing remnant from the construction of the castle itself. My identity as a woman was very much informed by and moulded through my relationship with my three elder sisters, and the final resident of the castle chose to be reclusive perhaps because of her elder sister's legacy, meaning that her life was shaped by their sibling associations. So, this light and sound piece became about four sisters or women and the relationship between them as it evolved over their lifetimes. The result was to evoke a feeling, an emotion, an overriding sensation, that a viewer could contemplate and experience to find an appreciation or a response and to provoke thought – just as any piece of art intends to do. It also sculpted and exposed and revealed the space; the space created the work – not just the room but also the whole castle. So multilayer motivations and inspirations were at play here once again. Paul Corley created the sound composition for the work and, although the inspiration came from a narrative and stories, we used them in an abstract way to create atmosphere, emotion and sensation that the viewer felt and experienced. The light came out of the steel poles and created sheets of light into the hazy atmosphere of the dark brick-walled cellar. In turn, the light traced and skimmed the walls and revealed and sculpted, not just the space but also the air of the space, as the poles rotated and interacted with each other in varying rhythms, speeds and changing dynamics, directions, qualities and intensities, as if the walls and the women were in discussion, whispering and gathering together. All the time the progression and emotions of the light poles and the qualities they emitted were supported, magnified and melded to the sound score, which evoked and purposefully played with abstract and human vocals to enmesh the ideas of the narrative coming from the fabric of the building and the female relational interaction within the core concept of the piece.

The Dream of Gerontius was a semi-staged opera production for English National Opera in 2017 at the Royal Festival Hall, London. I was commissioned to create the concept, designs and staging for this performance, for a full orchestra, three singers and a large chorus. What I imagined was to use light to create an additional layer of emotion and energy that supported and reflected the stories and power of the music. There was a lighting sculpture overhead that created detailed lighting textures playing above and across the orchestra, choir and singers to give the audience a visceral visual experience alongside the aural layer. The structure of the lighting rigged above was developed from the religious and spiritual connotations of the musical text. The shape and layout were taken from religious symbolism and classical religious art. The rig took the form of a three-layered triangle, in diminishing sizes, representing the Holy Trinity of the father, son and holy spirit. The light energies, while they were inspired by and reflect the narrative story of Gerontius and his journey through purgatory with an angel and to eventually meeting God, were abstract and suggestive of other-worldly and ethereal worlds of the protagonist's journeys, but the physical staging of the performers was static; it was the lighting that produced the energy of travel and movement. I was not trying to produce naturalism and reality but the mood, emotion and rhythms of the opera oratorio itself. It was a new way to realize the staging, to expose the intentions and signals from the stories of the work, by enforcing a subconscious sensation through light, producing a lighting work in which light is telling the stories themselves, mimicking the journeys and narrative from the musical score.

In a new light sculpture, created in 2020 for a light and literature festival in Macclesfield, Cheshire, I created a standalone artwork that was shown in the window of a closed bar. Commissioned to make a work in the middle of a pandemic, I wanted to use light and its ability to uplift and inspire to create a positive, forward-looking piece. Born out of the confusion of 2020, I asked the local community for words that represented their hopes for the future, and I instinctively selected seven words that resonated with me the most from the numerous ones submitted and sculpted those words out of warm white LED lights. The final piece, *Tangles*, was a mess of fairy lights that covered and enmeshed the words so that as the piece evolved and looped, over the duration of two and a half minutes, the words emerge from the confusion with clarity and positivity. It is like a mini dance of light, expressing hope and positivity.

It is interesting to note that in my recent installation pieces I have been exploring what I feel are lighting fixtures we use every day, without consideration, as the subject matter for the art piece. In some way, I am trying to expose to the viewer the qualities and functions the lighting fixtures provide in our lives other than purely to illuminate and give visibility. The emotional and felt experiences of light itself and what it contributes to our experiences. Calling attention to the lights themselves as the sculptural material, but leaving the technology, or the means by which the works are created as the unseen or unimportant element of the work. Challenging and inspiring the viewer to develop an opinion and to think about light as an emotive and evolving, ever-changing force that affects how we feel.

By explaining how light can be felt and can tell stories, portray ideas and create sensation, I have detailed collaborations that truthfully are not just lighting installations. From their conception, I nearly always had in my mind a musical or sound accompaniment or partnership. That is partly because, in my head, or in my embodied experience of the idea, there is sound energy as well as light. When I instigate the work and imagine light there is always music or sound; when I create for dance there is music to use and mine for inspiration. This speaks to my overriding passion and belief that art is always about collaboration – with other creatives and with spaces, or conversations with the ideas, or the movement or the bodies. This is an opinion that has been formed from my experience of working within the medium of dance because it is a deeply collaborative and collective process of creation. Jean Rosenthal in her book *The Magic of Light* talks about lighting for dance and writes: 'Dancers live in light as fish live in water. The stage space in which they move is their aquarium, their portion of the sea. Within translucent walls and above stage and floor, the lighting supports their flashing buoyancy or their arrested sculptural bodies' (1972, p.117). It is this, the mutual existence and the symbiotic and essential reliance of light and bodies, that keeps me creating and imagining new light worlds, for dancers, for audiences and for myself.

5

The unbearable brightness of beams
Light, darkness and obscure images

Yaron Shyldkrot

This chapter explores light and lighting design by means of visual obfuscation. Within the growing study of lighting practices, I examine the transformative role of light by looking at installations and performances which utilize light to confound or obstruct vision and generate experiences of not seeing clearly. Approaching light through its ability to unsettle or destabilize the clarity of what is seen, I turn to both ends of the intensity scale and reflect on the 'manipulation of light that is blinding either in its brightness or in its absence' (Öztürk, 2010, p.306). However, rather than contrasting light and darkness or simply suggesting that light can prevent one from seeing, this chapter considers dazzling and dim lighting in tandem, positing that both excessive lighting and lack thereof may pose a challenge to visual certainty. These lighting compositions, as I will argue, can produce altered forms of perception that do not rely on clear identification or recognition. Contesting 'an increasingly prevalent tradition of visual clarity' (Donger, 2012, p.14), I propose that not seeing clearly can break the habitual flow of perception, and thus resist ocular biases that tie vision to fixity and certainty. Thwarting fixity, such sensory experiences can reveal a variety of new or alternative interpretations of what is seen (or could be seen). These discernments might upset or even reject common and familiar understandings and thus hold the potential to bring different and novel views of what is perceived to light.

For many sighted people 'seeing is believing', and countless certainties come from being able to see. While traditionally, sight has been crowned 'the noblest and most comprehensive of the senses' (Descartes, 2002 [1637], p.116), more recent theses recognize how vision can, in fact, be fickle and unreliable. Not only can one be misled by what they see, but, following Maaike Bleeker, we can identify 'institutions of perspective': long-standing perceptual patterns that demonstrate 'how our senses are cultured to perceive certain privileged modes of representation as more natural, real, objective, or convincing than others', borne out of the discourses that mediate what we think we see (2008, p.13). The presumed definitiveness of sight lends itself to a deceptive impression of clarity, one which solidifies or neutralizes persistent normative and hegemonic perspectives. In response, I seek to trouble the notion that things are as they are because of how they are habitually seen and typically understood. Assuming that these institutions of perspective could be contested, modified or unlearned, this chapter attends to lighting compositions that, rather than clearly lighting *something*, instead aim to frustrate or dispel fixity and identification.

Focusing on moments of intensified 'vagueness', I depart from the examination of how light complements or 'supports' stage images through illustrative depictions and representations. Instead, I examine states of extreme brightness and dimness to consider how artists and designers have carefully utilized artificial lighting – employing both glares and glimmers – to profoundly alter the appearance of what is seen, generating perceptual uncertainty. Light, as Katherine Graham notes, 'creates the conditions in which we encounter body, space, movement, and gesture, but also continually reconfigures those conditions' (2018b, p.208). Seen in this way, light does not merely 'embellish' what one sees but also influences and manipulates the means by which sense is made. Consequently, through obscure images and equivocal appearances, the compositions, artworks and designs discussed later question the reliability of sight to reveal its inconsistency.

That said, the emphasis on not seeing *clearly* is crucial. Notwithstanding the close terminology, when observing compositions in which viewers are 'being blinded by the lack of light and being blinded by its excess' (Donger, 2012, p.106), I do not wish to imply that these designs promote experiences of not seeing or of seeing nothing. Notably, despite the challenge to perception such works present, 'one's visual sense remains active even in conditions of total blackout' (Alston and Welton, 2017, p.18). The same applies to glaring light, where sighted viewers can still see, even if it is only brilliance itself. Distancing vision from its routine usage, the compositions discussed in this chapter deprive viewers of the ability to see (or perceive) *clearly* – both physically and more metaphorically – encouraging sensory recalibrations and fostering reconfigured perceptions. These experiences are more akin to seeing or making sense differently, as opposed to not seeing at all. I am wary of reinforcing stereotypes and the risk of conflating those experiences with blindness, as the two are not identical. While I concur with Alston and Welton that gloomy, hazy or blazing displays can 'invite one to experience the alterity of non-normative visual experiences' (Alston and Welton, 2017, p.25), I am mindful of the ethically problematic promises of a better understating of blindness or the experience of the visually impaired through darkness or dazzling light. Staring at blindness and darkness in disability-led performance, Amelia Cavallo and Maria Oshodi argue that

> in darkness no one has 'normal' vision, sighted or otherwise. It is because of this that blindness can escape negative stereotypes of incapability, lack and loss, becoming instead an example of how non-normative sensory make-ups can be catalysts for challenging assumed behaviour and identity constructs. (2017, p.173)

Though I share Cavallo and Oshodi's aim to disrupt 'the status quo of sighted dominance in society' (2017, p.172), I recognize that most of the modes of perception examined in this chapter still rely on varying degrees of seeing or physical acts of sight. Yet, presenting 'non-normative visual perspectives as a basis for creative potential and allow[ing] blindness to be conceptually explored on a sociopolitical and artistic level' (Cavallo and Oshodi, 2017, p.189) is still part of a greater ambition to emphasize the multiplicity of perspectives and perceptions that can critically extend to other sense modalities. Cavallo and Oshodi maintain that darkness 'can present blindness as an empowered identity while antagonizing and deconstructing normative, hierarchical values of ocular-centrism, and creating a communal need for access and inclusion, regardless of sensory make-up' (2017, p.170). Immediately, the attempt to explore not seeing clearly raises the question of what is clear to whom and from what point of view. However, as I propose, embracing the opportunity to modify the regime of clarity in an attempt to resist fixity and to undermine definite preconceptions, ideologies and privileged modes of looking might equally make room for more diverse ways of sense-making. Pluralizing these opportunities can be read – to borrow from Alston and Welton – as a means of 'dealing with the politics of perception that acknowledges how seeing or sensing darkness [. . .] can be bound up with other modes of looking and sensing', surpassing those that might be defined as 'ableist' (2017, p.25). Put differently, even though vision is centred in this chapter, by emphasizing not seeing clearly, I seek to promote the questioning of different modes of perception to unsettle those that have been set as 'normative' or prioritized as supposedly leading to certainty. The transformation of clarity, then, is not just a mode of theatrical expression, but a significant intervention in processes of sense-making, one that can actively hamper the risky and ocular-centric coupling of clarity and vision.

Continuing my ambition to resist a single understanding arising from one viewpoint, this chapter moves between perspectives and examines compositions of both light and darkness. I draw on direct experience as a practitioner–researcher, lighting designer and maker of theatre in the dark, situating my practice theoretically and as part of a longer artistic lineage. I begin with a critical framing of 'not seeing clearly' followed by an analysis of dazzling and cloudy compositions, discussing examples of work by other artists which are both notable in themselves and which have inspired and informed my practice research. To further evaluate the implications of 'not seeing clearly', I move on to discuss my own practice research. Specifically, I draw from insights emerging from the process of making *Overcast* (2017), a piece of performance in the dark, and focus specifically on dim and gloomy compositions as practical strategies for generating moments of visual obfuscation and disrupted clarity. This dual perspective affords a unique position from which to offer insights into the exploration of light and darkness. First, it enables a more nuanced account and argument for not seeing clearly by building on insights arising from studio experimentations and reflexive process in conjunction with analysis of relevant case studies. Second, it allows me to illuminate and articulate particular aspects of practice and process by addressing more than one approach to practice and moving from light to darkness (and vice versa). Indeed, as Graham asserts, 'darkness is a condition of light' and the practice of lighting design 'is as much about designing darkness as it is about designing light' (Graham, 2016, p.76). So, to advance the conceptualization of light, instead of sustaining a binary or opposition between light and darkness, I take darkness – understood here more broadly, by means of obstructed vision – as my main focus and thus frame a slightly altered interplay between light and darkness: one where varying intensities of light may also condition obfuscation or 'darkness'.

Not seeing clearly

The installation *J3RR1* (2018) dazzles viewers. Designed by Italian collective NONE and featured at the *24/7* exhibition in Somerset House in London (2019), it is comprised of two dozen bulbs (surrounded by mirrors) that pulse at varying paces and configurations, creating a harsh stunning effect (see Plate 18). When visitors face or pass by the large aluminium structure, as it hangs in the gallery space, they are confronted by an ongoing routine of glares, flickers and flashes. While viewers might need light to experience or see the work, it is the same light that makes it difficult to do so. *J3RR1* (subtitled *Programmed Torture*) is a productive example to begin elucidating how light does not simply facilitate the appearance of certain images; rather, it can also impact how these 'images' or objects of perception will be encountered. In other words, how things are seen tends to determine how they seem.

Unsettling perception through altered visibility is not a new artistic ambition. Simon Donger, for example, acknowledges that the history of scenography – culminating in the twentieth century with innovations in electric lighting – 'is punctuated by devices producing visual disturbances inasmuch as vision is attenuated and representation less than certain' (2012, p.13). Artworks and installations by artists such as Yayoi Kusama, Ann Veronica Janssens, Rafael Lozano-Hemmer, Carsten Holler, Liz West, James Turrell, Antony Gormley and Olafur Eliasson shape and utilize light and darkness (as well as colour, shadow and haze) to investigate the depths of perception as well as how the orchestration and interchange between these elements transform clarity and invite a reconsideration of viewers' senses and environment.

Notably, seeing is not an innocent sensory or physiological activity – it is an act of making sense (Welton, 2017, p.245). Thus, if light mediates what one sees, it is unsurprising that lighting design can impact how something might be grasped or understood. In that sense, light and sight are never neutral. This is why Hal Foster distinguishes between vision – the physical operation or mechanism of seeing – and visuality – the historical, social and discursive techniques, practices and determinations in which vision takes place (1988, p.ix). Akin to Bleeker's institutions of perspective noted earlier, the supposed priority of the brightest point or predication of focus exemplifies how viewers might attempt to 'make sense' of NONE's installation – even if it is physically demanding to do so. Yet these modes of looking also highlight an underlying and unnoticed perceptual hierarchy formed in and through visuality. Assigning value and judgement to objects of perception, visuality casts certain figures as more worthy of one's attention, more credible, truthful or significant. Examining visuality, then, not only exposes how certain images appear or are presented to viewers but it also defies 'the popular assumption that visual perception is a politically neutral, merely biological element of human experience' (Johnson, 2012, p.12). Foster proposes the notion of a 'scopic regime' to account for the complex interrelation between vision and visuality in a given time, place or culture where 'many social visualities' or manifestations of visual experiences turn into 'one essential vision' (1988, p.ix). Moreover, as Dominic Johnson explains, by 'disguising the social fact of visuality, scopic regimes naturalise the fiction of politically neutral vision, ordering contingent ways of seeing in an artificial hierarchy of visual styles' (2012, p.25). The origination of perspective in the fifteenth century, for instance, can be seen as an example for such 'ordering', constructing modes of looking that later became normalized and naturalized (Johnson, 2012, p.25). In a similar vein, in her critique of traditional divisions between sight and hearing, Lynne Kendrick alludes to 'the enduring visual bias that has rendered sight the dominant sense' along with 'the residual prejudice that assumes the world is reproduced for the eye' (2017, p.119). Kendrick clarifies that ocular-centrism – a perceptual disposition that prioritizes the visual – 'does not mean that the eye itself is dominant; rather swathes of historical and political discourses have made recourse to vision, cleaving apart the senses and forming a hierarchy of perceptual engagement' (2017, p.119). It is these discourses, ideologies and powers that establish and influence that (and what) visual faculties are considered important, determining what eyes should focus on.

Central to these scopic regimes is the promotion of fixity, distinct classification and identification, which results in different ocular (as well as racial, gendered, ableist, human-exceptionalist) biases propagated through the assumption that things (human or other-than-human) are as they are because of how they appear or are apprehended through vision. Crucially, Bleeker views the theatrical apparatus as a critical 'vision machine' (2008, p.60), recognizing theatre's capacity to produce 'visions', understood here as faculties of sight, imaginations and apparitions. Such a view is useful for my exploration of how *J3RR1* and other lighting compositions considered here disrupt the habitual flow of perception and tease or defy certain visual inclinations by instantiating experiences of not seeing clearly. Whether subtle or overwhelming, glaring or discreet, these compositions can be seen as 'a devastating critique of routine vision' (Bal, 2013, p.136), undermining dominant modes of looking by drawing attention to the process of perception itself. By producing obscure images, these works utilize light to unsettle the belief that objects of perception are knowable and determinate because of how they are normally seen or understood physically and therefore conceptually.

Not seeing clearly does not necessarily imply the elimination or rejection of clarity in its entirety. Rather, it denotes a perceptual stance where clarity is deferred or hindered. It is a challenge to the anticipated accuracy, fixity or decidedness of sight that may occur in moments where what is seen is/becomes ambiguous or not easily decipherable. For instance, the spectres, halos and after-images produced by retina burns caused by the brightness and direction of *J3RR1* impede clear vision. The dazzling installation does not negate vision, but radically transforms percepts by incising intense luminous shapes. Therefore, unlike a solitary state of not seeing, not seeing *clearly* provides a more processual and gradual understanding of perceptual uncertainty manifested through indeterminate and indistinct perceptions and referring to either the objects perceived or the act of perception itself. If clarity holds a strong affinity to brightness and coherence, its rejection might denote intangibility or vagueness and extend to other (not necessarily visual) perceptions and experiences. These might include the perception of space, its limits and the visitor's location within it; discernment of surface, distance and depth; the form/boundaries of the work and its relation to the visitor's body. Key to these indeterminate experiences and concrete experiments with 'ungraspability' (Bal, 2013, p.8) is that perception becomes undecided – it demands time and questioning as viewers and audiences end up recalibrating what they see and experience, and how. Accordingly, contra to just producing bright images with light, *J3RR1* can be seen as a site for reappraisal and negotiation of different perceptual and sensory modalities, enabling alternative modes of sense-making.

As such, by reconfiguring visuality, not seeing clearly can disrupt hegemonic status quos. If, by fixing certain modes of looking, various ideologies or scopic regimes enhance different ocular biases, and coerce/root notions of otherness and normativity, then not seeing clearly can begin to resist those worldviews that are established through visuality. Seen in generative terms, confronting visual perceptions not only holds the capacity to bring certain objects of sight to the foreground, deeming them more significant or deserving of attention; beyond this, by interrupting the customary course of perception, the deference of clarity can unshackle visual dispositions and biases from their expected or anticipated meanings. Encouraging viewers to see differently allows alternative and multiple interpretations to take shape. So, rather than underscoring lack or loss, as I carry on my discussion of visual obfuscation, I argue for the creative and generative potential imbued in not seeing clearly, conceived as the transformation of clarity fostered through the modulation of habitual patterns of perception.

Hazy vision(s)

As clarity tends to denote brightness, translucency and lucidity, I continue to consider what happens when illumination is pushed to the extreme: how the intensification of light might conversely lead to the attenuation of clarity. Amid the flourishing creative and engagements with light design, artists and makers have increasingly used the striking potential of bright light to generate different effects. Performances such as Pan Pan Theatre's *All That Fall* (2011) (directed by Gavin Quinn with lighting design by Aedín Cosgrove), Christopher Brett Bailey's *This is How We Die* (2014) (lighting design by Sherry Coenen), Lucy Carter's *Hidden* (2016) (specifically *Hidden 3: Light Store*[1]) and Fye and Foul's *Cathedral* (2016) incorporate extreme brightness, shining brilliantly on viewers at different points in the performance. Producing destabilized images and uncomfortable brilliance, these compositions continuously defy the hackneyed 'maxim of the lighting industry' which suggests, as Gernot Böhme affirms, that 'light sources should be designed to prevent blinding glare' to the maximum extent (2017, p.195). More than idle curiosities or novelty-seeking compositions, the inclusion of glare in performance designs often draws attention to the lanterns or light itself. They do not merely accentuate certain details of the stage image, paint the stage, or set up a general 'atmospheric background' (Böhme, 2017, p.30). Rather, by reducing the distinctiveness, sharpness or veracity of what is seen, these designs conjure up alternative encounters with the visual, demonstrating how light can inhibit seeing clearly and entice seeing beyond recognition.

Staring at *J3RR1*, for instance, the large structure illuminates primarily those who face it. As viewers are confronted by an intensified sequence of flashes and glares, the main visual offering is the hues, shapes and halos produced by the light emitted. The prominent distinguishable objects in sight are the machine and bulbs themselves, and deciphering them behind a striking wall of light proves to be rather challenging. Indeed, these excessive degrees of brightness tend to be, as Böhme maintains, 'unbearable for human beings' (2017, p.199). However, despite such observation (and the slightly hyperbolic title of this chapter), I do not mean to imply that these compositions are primarily intended to cause discomfort or aggressively assault viewers. Carefully sidestepping their often-negative connotations, I propose that these dazzling lights can also elicit other modes of looking, puncturing the clarity of vision. As a piece of light art, *J3RR1* does not attempt to light something (object, faces or a background). Instead, following the installation makers, '[i]n front of *J3RR1* we feel heat, energy and the clarity of an order that cannot be disobeyed' (NONE, n.p.). Despite connoting adherence to clarity, it seems that this is an ordering of a different kind; certainly, the intensity of light dominates the image and can hardly be avoided or ignored, even when closing one's eyes or looking away. Yet, the actual visual faculties produced by *J3RR1* are not necessarily clear, at least in the sense of sharp or easily comprehensible. Being overpowered by such extreme intensity can prompt 'a kind of unintentional vision', hindering the possibility of 'objectifying' what is seen (Böhme, 2017, p.196). Put differently, the work can be seen as eliciting a mode of looking which moves beyond fixed visual distinctions or clear identification of what is in sight. Instead, it offers viewers the opportunity to yield to light's power and revaluate their 'obedience' to orders of vision, as perception breaks free from the rigidity of making sense by seeing clearly.

Moreover, looking at the fierce brightness, light presses against the retina, leaving its trace in the form of an after-image. As Erin Hurley expands, '[h]overing for a moment before fading, belatedly, into obscurity, the apparition burned onto the retina captures the outline of what had previously been lit. Put differently, one "sees" phantoms' (2004, p.207). Much like moving away from looking directly at the blazing sun, these 'phantoms' or (after-) images produced are a collection of indeterminate visions that do not set as a clear and decipherable object. Similarly, when *J3RR1* flashes off, or viewers look away, it becomes hard to distinguish whether the gloaming glow is the dimming fixture or an after-image, a figure of the imagination or the edge of vision. These flashing harsh intensities, to borrow from Donger's explanation, formulate 'an in-between experience in perceptual terms'; they suspend visual processing, as 'visual content has not yet taken shape as such but still occurs as flickering abstract particles that are remnants of past perception (2012, pp.78–9). In other words, *J3RR1* does not simply eliminate seeing but renders visual faculties more abstract, indistinct and fuzzy. The percepts generated by the work seem to resist strict interpretation as clarity and lucidity of vision are obstructed.

Significantly, trying to make sense of abstract(ed) or vague perceptions can open the prospect to think about and embrace what is perceived anew. Vagueness denotes fuzziness, imprecision or indistinctness. Ascribed to instances and perceptions that are uncertain or missing the clarity of definition, when something appears to be vague – or possessing equivocal properties – it is understood as not entirely definite, hazily bordered – physically or conceptually. However, rather than sketching vagueness as a deficiency or something lacking, I approach it through openness. If clarity implies distinct and precise entities perceived through recognition or identification, vagueness tends towards change and movement. It can be understood as a gesture that 'resists categories, boundaries, calculations and identities' (Carney and Miller, 2009, p.35) and, in that sense, vagueness can help to account for the different ways through which destabilized perceptions can reveal the possibility to encounter what is seen – even if it is abstracted or obstructed – in unexpected ways. Reviewing *J3RR1* again, as glare counters the consistency of vision and the eyes adjust, the work invites an encounter with different spectre-like glowing percepts that hover but never set, producing new/other possibilities for interpretation and appraisal.

Extending the intensification of light further, what happens when it transfixes viewers by dominating the entire field of vision? Fascinated with isolating the physical and psychological conditions of vision, mid-twentieth-century investigations into sensory deprivation sought to better grasp the total field of perception/vision, also known as Ganzfeld. While several researchers experimented with homogeneous retinal images or stimulation, they often studied impressions obtained in/through total darkness or with closed eyes as opposed to dazzling brightness. For psychologists James J. Gibson and Dickens Waddell, a homogeneous image is 'ordinarily obtained only by looking at the cloudless sky, or by being in a wholly dark room or by closing the eyes' (1952, p.263). For the image to be differentiated – in the sense of sharp and clear – there is a need for shifts between relative degrees or regions of light and dark. Thus researchers set out to compare the effects of homogeneous (or undifferentiated) images with that of differentiated ones: 'images' constituting a uniform degree of light striking the retina in contrast with those comprised of changes in gradients of luminosity or different regions of light and dark. Given my focus on brightness, I linger here on the former, when viewers were drowned in a 'sea of light' (Gibson and Waddell, 1952, p.267). Reviewing their findings, Gibson and Waddell noted participant responses that included: 'Like a fog coming up to my eyes'; 'A white that you could go into'; 'Levels of nothingness'; 'Clouds . . . very thick . . . endless' (1952, p.267). They concluded that the impressions emerging when looking at a homogeneous field of vision 'are indefinite, unspecific, and ambiguous' (1952, p.270). Unable to distinguish between the different aspects or properties of visual faculties – through shadow or size – the ability to decipher or construe percepts as 'objects' is once again compromised. Participants experiencing 'pure vision' reported an extraordinary difficulty to articulate or 'express what they saw. [. . .] After prolonged exposure (ten to twenty minutes) subjects would even report difficulty sensing whether their eyes were open or closed. Vision would "blank out"' (Massumi, 2002, p.145). By undergoing, as Brian Massumi notes, a 'visual experience of the visually unexperienceable', viewers found themselves 'lost' in vision (2002, p.147). Whether subjects reported a perception of a dense whiteout or a foggy blackout, by missing a steady identifiable or recognizable object, focus or differentiated faculties, the Ganzfeld experiments cultivated structurally unstructured experiences. Paradoxically, the apparent fixity of gradients of luminous intensity unfixed vision from its usual operation as viewers practised an uncommon mode of perception or manifestation of the visual – even if it ultimately resulted in the appearance of hallucinations and apparitions.

The 'pure vision' experiments resonate with James Turrell's *Ganzfeld* installations (1988–), where visitors encounter a visual field comprised of the same brightness and colour. As viewers step into spaces of coloured light almost 'tangible in density', they struggle to determine their coordinates in, and outlines of the room that they are in, and even unable to differentiate if the colours and shapes they see, derive from their own imagination or actually radiate in space (Bishop, 2005, pp.84–5). Reducing, heightening or stretching the field of vision frustrates conventional sensory experiences, to the point where, as Claire Bishop suggests, Turrell's installations

> are spaces of withdrawal that suspend time and orphan us from the world. [. . .] Turrell describes the works as situations where 'imaginative

seeing and outside seeing meet, where it becomes difficult to differentiate between seeing from the inside and seeing from the outside'. (2005, p.85)

In other words, instead of producing experiences where the viewer sees herself seeing, which arguably draws attention to perception itself, for Bishop, the extreme effects elicited by these expansive brightly coloured spaces actually upset the ability to reflect on one's perception (2005, p.87). That said, even if not fully provoking conscious reflection on what is in sight or the questioning of how one sees, *Ganzfeld* still expands or modifies the visual faculties from which sense – including frustrated or disrupted sense – is made. To borrow from Massumi, '[t]he eyes, astrain in the fog, took the leap of producing its own variations from the endogenous (self-caused) retinal firings' (2002, p.149). Visions (including imaginative and hallucinatory ones) can at once emerge and dissolve, take form and disappear, shift and reform as they establish new and alternative perceptions despite, or precisely because of, the inability to see clearly. Thus, Turrell's coloured spaces can also be seen as vague since one cannot distinguish *exactly* where things begin and end. While some of their properties or qualities can be perceived but not fully grasped, the *Ganzfeld* installations confound conventional perceptual clarity. Moreover, hovering between different understandings, seeing and unseeing, the installations echo the movement of vagueness – not a movement towards determinate vision but a movement-between: between the concrete light meeting the retina and the blanking-out of vision; the challenge to habitual modes of perception; and the emergence of alternative ways of making sense borne of obstructed clarity.

Such a movement is also evident in Ann Veronica Janssens' *Mist Rooms* (2001–), in which visitors are not only disoriented in light but also bewildered by fog as they enter illuminated spaces filled with dense colourful mist. In *Blue, Red and Yellow* (2001–), for example, as viewers meander through the haze-filled pavilion, different coloured light shifts the shade of fog from yellow to blue to red, obfuscating clarity. Janssens' installations seek to transform perception 'by slowing it down' (Bal, 2013, p.135). As viewers encounter an obscure space produced by mist and different coloured light, the habitual flow of perception is suspended: fog obstructs reference points and diminishes conventional perceptions of spatial relations by defying clear focus, precision, orientation and sensibility. However, in these moments of contumacious visibility, sight is not damaged, broken or no longer useful. As the eye takes time to (re) adjust when deciphering what appears before it, perception is delayed and stretched, and 'cannot just happen in an instant; instead it must emerge' (Bal, 2013, p.39), demanding more time to make (any kind of) sense of what is seen. So while overwhelming onlookers, clarity is unsettled but not entirely lost. As shimmering fog disrupts the acuity of vision, Janssens establishes moments of visual instability, 'reduced to the barest essence of seeing below the threshold of representation' (Bal, 2013, p.104; see Welton, 2017). Again, light does not necessarily illuminate *something* or direct vision, nor is it an attempt to represent or capture natural phenomena. In lieu, Janssens offers an invitation to marvel, wander through and make sense of arrangements of light, shade and suspended droplets. Rather than fixed and fully formed objects of perception, viewers encounter images or apparitions in their making, constantly suspended and in formation. Counter to the 'blanking-out' of vision produced through *Ganzfeld*, visitors are not stranded in a total field of vision. When peering through the blurring mist, shapes – and, occasionally, fellow visitors – are still somewhat decipherable. However, beyond a thick 'filter' of colourful smog, they are not seen clearly. Elucidating her motivation, Janssens explains how 'sometimes you have to erase reality – erase what's visible – in order to see something else. To make the invisible visible in fact' (2020, n.p.). In this vein, Janssens' work can be seen as an attempt to offset visuality in favour of a return to vision (in Foster's terms). By means of opaque and foggy entities, she calls for a revision of what is seen, advocating for a broader understanding of vision, which adopts more creative and imaginative engagements. As gradients of luminosity shift and the air fills and moves around the room, perceptions and images are continuously morphing: in the midst of mist, both visions and water droplets are in perpetual suspension, constantly shapeshifting, forming and reforming as light illuminates beyond clear recognition.

Critically, vagueness 'cannot be resolved'; it inhibits 'any final and decisive conclusion, offering, at best, a tentative or potential interpretation' (Sørensen, 2016, p.748). In that sense, and through their perceptual obscurity and sensory manipulation, the blurry mist rooms, *Ganzfeld* installations and the dazzling design of *J3RR1* can dismantle existing perceptions, as vision is unable to clearly determine what is seen. In the absence of clear focus, or concrete formation and identification of objects in sight, nothing takes precedence. Notwithstanding their brightness, these works are not bound by fixity and therefore extend the opportunity to break free from the dominance (or assumed legitimacy) of clarity and vision. Disrupting hierarchical systems or scopic regimes that appear to maintain the status quo formed by 'one essential vision', these light compositions challenge the privilege of a single, stable or constant point of view. Emphasizing the multiplicity of experiences, the indeterminacy of not seeing clearly can produce hazy visions that invite viewers to pause, reassess or even reform their typical mode of (visual) perception, revealing in its place a plurality of ways in which objects of sight could be encountered and new perspectives adopted.

Light, but dim

From glaring and foggy visions, I turn to the lower end of the intensity scale as this part of the chapter moves on to reflect on the use of low lighting within my own practice research. Informed by the examples examined earlier, to enhance the study of visual obfuscation, I evaluate the insights emerging from my process of devising *Overcast* (2017) and my experimentation and making of theatre in the dark using light. *Overcast* utilized darkness, haze and various lighting compositions to simulate the 'creation' and emergence of clouds as well as to attempt to emulate experiences of being immersed in or looking through mist – vague experiences of thwarted clarity.[2] By reflecting on the partial/obscure images generated in *Overcast*, I am able to focus on fleeting and indistinct occurrences for which I (as a performance maker) set out the stimuli for. These 'unbearably' dim compositions were set as an invitation to see with/through lack of precision or distinctness. Continuing to resist fixity and clear recognition, and delineating the significance of these compositions, I suggest that dimness or near-darkness might unsettle or reorientate different sensory encounters with the world. Rather than affirming that in such meagre lighting viewers do not see or see nothing, I argue that such designs can once again elicit alternative perceptions that do not rely on predetermined or set identifications. As darkness and gloom alternately bring forward and withdraw visual opportunities, they can equally destabilize persistent ocular illusions stemming from clarity, and thus resist the dominance of the visual (and other similar biases) through theatre practice and design.

Accordingly, I propose low lighting and partial images as practical strategies to generate obscure impressions leading to the questioning of vision's reliability. These performative tactics are intrinsically linked, yet as low light might imply a broader state of diffuse illumination, I also name partial images as a performative device, where light sources (bright or otherwise) pierce through darkness but only reveal part of the object in sight, producing incomplete or indefinite impressions. Performances such as Ad Infinitum's *Light* (2016), Ultimate Dancer and Robbie Thomson's *YAYAYA AYAYAY* (2017) and Darkfield's *Flight* (2018) used various degrees of low and diffused lighting to create blurry or undecided percepts drowning and resurfacing from the umbra. In a similar vein, *Overcast* sought to destabilize the appearance of one audience member to another, using low lights as undependable sources that shift and alter how one looks and what one sees.

Overcast hosts four audience members around a table. On it is a bowl of water, along with white floury powder which is scattered to create random shapes and constellations. As audience members enter the (fairly large) space, two bright beams of light help them find their way. Albeit in shadows, the table is still visible, concentrated in the middle of the space, and framed by four lighting 'booms', one behind each chair. Once the audience is seated, the beams begin to gently fade and, halfway through the fade, light suddenly cuts out. In darkness, different voices begin to describe unclear images (blended descriptions of three Turner paintings). Unexpectedly, the loud pulsing sound of a smoke machine fills the space. It is followed by a gentle brush of air and the sound of rippling water, which softly fades in. Then, extremely dim or hazy 'images' begin to emerge, playing with the tone and volume of murk and gloom. First, a low frosty beam slowly appears. As this becomes brighter, or as the audience is more accustomed to its very low intensity, both light and the blurry image begin to solidify: they appear somewhat sharper, more discernible. It is the water bowl, and the light reflects the water on the ceiling. Second, a strip of warm-orange light above the audience's head shines through the slowly moving haze, encouraging viewers to look up. Light then directs attention to the table, which suddenly seems to glow in the dark. Finally, an extended composition of white and blue lighting emerges above and behind the audience, creating multiple vague and hallucinatory silhouettes, outlines and distorted images. The haze shapeshifts around the space and dips in and out of light to simulate the experience of being immersed in fog. As with the bright designs discussed in the previous section, light in *Overcast* was designed to draw attention to itself (whether source, beam or colour) and to the subtle and often unnoticed movements of air and haze, seeking to alter the visitors' sense of space and, crucially, the appearance of fellow audience members sitting around the table.

Experimenting with thresholds of visibility and luminosity and entangling light and darkness, the lighting compositions in *Overcast* were given time to unfold and get accustomed to, but not enough intensity to fix visions. As low lighting faded in and out it recreated the coordinates of space, shifting its edges and what was decipherable in it. In such low lighting, the perception of accurate detail was arguably removed; fellow viewers and objects were reduced to ambiguous figures. The outlines of what was visible became almost fluid, as physical or solid forms lost their expected definition. For example, the angle and level of light altered the bowl's appearance, to the point where its shape and presence were rendered fuzzy (see Plate 19). Confounding vision and clarity (in the performance and documentation image alike), the narrow beams that illuminated the translucent bowl suspended its materiality. This faint beam facilitated the slow re-emergence of the image as it indicated that there is something to see. Yet, attempting to deliberately confound clarity, its intensity hindered the appearance of the image as a distinguishable one. As such, it offered a more flexible view of the object. Similarly, when light appeared behind the audience, silhouettes took time to form as the thick haze extended and re-formed people's outlines, features and shadows, emphasizing light's ability to mediate and modulate (objects of) perception. Such a constellation of haze and dimness attempted to generate moments where one was unable 'to see the image clearly', but also an image that 'may be perceived as unclear due to its vague boundaries' (Sørensen, 2016, p.747). As gloom thickened, under the cover of haze the limits of the body grew indistinct, merging bodies and surroundings. In this vein, familiar perceptions of fellow audience members were deferred and suspended, making room for new or alternative apprehensions. For me, in such low intensities, light appeared as thick brushstrokes, and haze seemed denser and more impenetrable. While it slowly faded in, light became more noticeable, almost tangible (as light hit the haze/dust particles), but as it remained dim and faint, light turned out to be fleeting and ungraspable. Ultimately, *Overcast* sought to create a state of fuzzy vision, which simultaneously revealed and concealed. Unable to clearly decide or make sense through vision, light obscured clarity from what one can see, while inviting (re-) envisioning of what/how one might see. In that sense, the images gave up their optical clarity in favour of their material presence, but even this was deliberately made hard to establish.

Unlike most of the examples discussed earlier, partial images still rely on light to illuminate *something*. Nevertheless, light does not passively support the display of certain entities. Accordingly, dimness manifests itself through a dance of revelation, manipulation and occlusion. In such low intensities, by (partially) illuminating particular 'scenes', light draws attention to itself as an object of mediation, underscoring its capacity to influence, transform or distort visual faculties and apprehensions through vision. Notably, as Welton asserts, 'the darkness suggested by 'gloom' is one that is hard – but not impossible – to see into' (2017, p.246). As opposed to the removal of all light sources, which breeds the unique visual modality of *seeing darkness*, the murky state of gloom still retains some (visual) reference points that intermingle with darkness. Both darkness and gloom are able to eschew clarity and disrupt one's spatial sensibility, leaving viewers to ponder on their own engagements with their surroundings. However, in contrast with a total absence of illuminated visual cues, by setting specific points of focus in space through (relative) brightness partial images punctuate darkness and produce an altered perceptual experience. Avoiding the reductive interpretation of negated vision, as visual faculties are not entirely removed, dim and incomplete images can still direct the eye while hindering perception by rendering uncertain what might appear and emerge from the shadows.

As discussed, in *Overcast*, I attempted to create palpable yet unstable images, heightened by the blurry boundaries of mist. Moreover, the performance was framed as simulating the experience of being immersed in clouds but by no means attempted direct representation of that experience. Investigating indeterminate and diffuse entities and vague phenomena such as clouds and fog and their presence in low lighting, I attempted to undermine the audience's ability to determine what they see, questioning the appearance and credibility of visual faculties: whether it is the shape of a cloud or the subtle passage of air, a radiant silhouette of the person sitting across the table, or a figure of their imagination. These intentionally muffled images sought to go beyond clear recognition, definitiveness or classification, shifting perspectives (sometimes literally) and offering multiple possible meanings, interpretations and affective resonances.

Barbra Erwine affirms that '[t]he brightest node is usually perceived as the most important' (2017, p.65). 'Since people are phototropic (tending to move toward the light)', she notes, 'a pool of light with darker space surrounding it focuses attention' (Erwine, 2017, p.65). When clarifying this physiological trait, Erwine alludes to Foster's scopic regimes and Bleeker's institutions of perspective, both of which deem certain visions as more significant, valuable or worthy of being seen. Yet in *Overcast*, the cloudiness of/in both dimness and mist turned objects in/of sight unstable by rendering those focal points obscure, *clearly indistinct*. In contrast to traditionally 'well-lit' images, the murky images that invited the audience to look through haze did not seek to verify, define or pin down any facts. Though low lighting may have helped with an initial orientation in the dark by retaining points of concentration, or indeed directing the eye to brighter entities, the dimness of lights tried to unfix and destabilize the images formed: in this way the work resisted a single firm interpretation, continuously challenging the nature of its encounter, generating a mode of seeing unclearly, where one cannot 'conclude' what or who is in sight.

Consequently, I suggest that (low) lighting design and the composition of gloomy states can be understood as a strategy to break the habitual flow of visual perception. In *Overcast*, despite the invitation to see things (clouds, silhouettes, shadows, shapes) the images do not champion or prioritize one particular view but encourage looking through multiple perspectives. Looking, for instance, at the water bowl as it is lit from different angles altered its appearance rendering the object unfamiliar. However, this is not only a process of estrangement or de-familiarization. Rather, and recalling the hover of vagueness, in much the same way as the 'clouds' in *Overcast* shifted and moved, moulded and dissipated, so did the images produced. Restlessly transforming, due to their constant reconfiguration and interaction with light, objects in sight became indefinite and unclear, as eyes could not resolve what they encountered. Such a view(ing) offers an unusual way of looking, which can liberate the eye from the implicit political desire 'to fix us with its deadening stare' (Bal, 2013, p.265). As low lighting dims the definiteness of vision – through, for example, making depth, distance and boundaries unclear or illuminating half the object – it renders the relationship with visual faculties continuously in formation. These cloudy images destabilize the definiteness of vision and encourage a constant sense of reviewing, wandering between diverse interpretations or perspectives, where meaning does not persist. As Graham explains, light invites 'the audience to see the space and bodies in its path *in a certain way*', and this call to see 'in a certain way' can determine 'the seer's initial engagement with the work' (Graham, 2018a, p.126, emphasis in original). This can be understood as either seeing unequivocally or in one of many available ways of encountering the visual. Attempting to escape the regime of clarity, I have tried to emphasize the latter, doing so by inviting audiences to see *in an uncertain way*. In the dimness, the invitation to constantly re-assemble objects of sight might facilitate a new encounter that does not stem from usual and predetermined recognition. Instead of prioritizing one singular view, perceptions become more plural as gloom makes room for the inclusion of different and novel points of view.

Lighting beyond recognition

Sitting opposite each other, across a table outcropping from the mist, we catch glimpses of obscure appearances of materials, phenomena and fellow audience members (see Plate 19). Manifesting as shadows, silhouettes or murky displays, the fuzzy impressions produced in *Overcast* and the other case studies explored in this chapter elucidate how the wax and wane of light and darkness might generate instances of not seeing clearly. Looking at these vague images – whether live or recorded, through equally confounding pieces of documentation that seek to (accurately) capture unstable moments of challenged visibility – one is left to decipher clearly indistinct illuminations. Rather than attempting to render objects visibly clear, the different lighting compositions I discussed, aimed to reveal and reclaim 'many visualities', countering and critiquing perceptions and biases ironed by 'one essential vision'. Obviously, the perceptual uncertainty produced by these designs is not limited to visual experiences and can extend to other sense modalities. Yet, as light can shape perception and influence how things are seen and understood, in my endeavour to disturb the relentless regime of clarity, and trouble different predispositions that result from the alleged certainty accompanying vision, light becomes a significant instrument to interrupt expected encounters with the visible. Recognizing the discursive and historical shaping of vision that is still at play in the background, the shaping of vision that I dealt with here is a compositional–dramaturgical one, which tackles visuality by attempting to evoke altered perceptual and sensory encounters, where the different arrangements and orchestrations of light render objects of perception fuzzy or indistinct. I acknowledge that the ocular focus of this chapter might appear to reinforce a (false) priority of vision. However, by turning to both ends of the intensity scale, I have argued that light can actually upset fixity and suspend preconceptions and, in turn, reveal the plurality of ways in which objects of sight could be apprehended. By hindering clear and distinct recognitions and identifications of visual faculties, these glares and glimmers potentially resist expected and privileged points of view, breaking the habitual flow of perception. Consequently, the vagueness emerging from these low and dazzling lights can suggest new modes of sense-making, shifting understandings within the politics of perception.

Critically, in my own practice research and in this chapter, I have shown how light and darkness can introduce a variety of encounters and understandings of what is seen, pushing viewers to contemplate what they see, or choose to see. These multiple possible exchanges might be eliminated through apparent clarity, but in gloom, murk or extreme brilliance, they may coexist simultaneously, without adhering to a single interpretation. Continuously hovering between different states, these critical visions highlight the pluralization of perception, working to undermine the certainty which seeing tricks us into, 'a false sense that the world is as it is: not changeable and subject to change' (Kendrick, 2017, p.128). While certain institutions of perspective fix habitual modes of looking, thereby fostering the notion that this is the only way the world is or can be, other views might reveal that things are not always as they seem. By encouraging not seeing clearly and moving between the literal and metaphorical, lighting design can, as I have proposed, move us to look beyond recognition. Whether around the table of *Overcast*, in colourful mist or vibrant *Ganzfeld*, light challenges or suspends typical apprehensions, revealing different possibilities for seeing and being with others. In other words, and seen in generative terms, not seeing clearly introduces new vantage points and invites viewers to look in other directions, apply alternative focuses, practise more diverse perspectives, adopt new outlooks and conceive more inclusive views that do not prioritize a singular or fixed vision.

Notes

1 See Chapter 4 by Lucy Carter, pp.72–81.
2 *Overcast* was a solo project as part of my PhD research, which was informed by and built on my work with Fye and Foul.

SECTION 2

Creativity

6

Language, creativity and collaboration

Kelli Zezulka

Light occupies a unique position in the dramaturgy of live performance: it is the only visual design element that can only be seen when in situ, being reliant on the articulation of both space and time. Although light is a visual design element, it is not solely image based (as can be seen from contributions elsewhere in this volume). As a performance material, it is dynamic and fluid, and the process of creating light on stage is equally dynamic and fluid. Lighting designers (as well as lighting programmers) are required to complete their work on site in theatre spaces during technical rehearsals[1] and are thus subject to an exceptional set of spatial and temporal constraints that differentiate their creative working practices from those involved in other scenographic processes. Technical rehearsals[2] are at the start of what is called the 'production week' and mark the first time that the entire company (cast, creative team and production team) is in the theatre together. For the lighting designer, the technical rehearsals are often very 'expos[ing] – "like standing naked on a table and asking 'what do you think?'", as [lighting designer] Mark Jonathan puts it' (Moran, 2017, p.27). I am specifically interested in technical rehearsals as they are 'a period of often intense activity' (Moran, 2017, p.27) and 'intense creativity but also of anxiety and strain' (Hunt, 2015, p.1). Lighting designer Lizzie Powell describes the start of a technical rehearsal as a 'horrible feeling because it's the first time ever you're showing people your thoughts' (Powell in Fisher, 2021, p.12). Therefore, as Nick Hunt argues, 'a conception of lighting design not as object, pre-made for reproduction, but as process – a continuous act up to and through the moment of performance

– might prove to be a better fit with the immediacy with which theatre is made and experienced' (quoted in Palmer, 2013, p.240). To further interrogate this provocation, I want to examine two ways in which the creativity of the lighting designer – and the interwoven work of the lighting programmer – can be made visible: through performance installation (and light itself) and ethnography. In the first half of this chapter, I will provide some context for my study of technical rehearsals, including why they are a crucial part of the theatre production process and how an understanding of the hidden process that occurs during this period is essential for a fuller comprehension of the ways in which performance is made (and, by extension, what performance *is*). The second half of the chapter draws on naturally occurring examples of language and interaction from technical rehearsals, taken from my doctoral fieldwork, in order to explicate this further.

Lighting designer Lucy Carter's triptych, *Hidden*, at Sadler's Wells in 2016 as part of *No Body*, was a promenade experience constructed specifically around light and sound as performance materials. *No Body* was conceived as an immersive, interactive experience – a 'dance' show without the physical presence of dancers, a clear departure from Sadler's Wells' usual programming. The first piece was *LightSpace* by lighting designer Michael Hulls, who since 2009 has been an associate artist at Sadler's Wells and is the first non-choreographer to fulfil this role. This performance took place on the stage at Sadler's Wells and fully immersed the audience in light and sound through an exploration of and homage to the power of tungsten light. Audiences were free to wander around the stage, between clusters of bare tungsten light bulbs and through the beams of light from large banks of Parcans overhead. In *Indelible*, composer Nitin Sawhney then took audiences on a historical tour of Sadler's Wells through the building's foyer and public spaces using a combination of projection, binaural sound effects and original compositions. *The Running Tongue* and *Kairos* were films by choreographers Siobhan Davies and Russell Maliphant, respectively. In different ways, both films sought to envelop the audience in a series of dramatic visual moments, focusing on bodies in motion in light. Finally, Carter's *Hidden* showcased the backstage areas of Sadler's Wells, places and spaces audiences were not usually privy to.[3]

In all three pieces of this lighting triptych, Carter showcased a hidden world, full of hidden people and their hidden creativity. According to Carter, *Hidden* was 'an opportunity to show audiences all the work, all the massive creativity, that goes on backstage' (Sadler's Wells Theatre, 2016, 0:12–0:22). Paradoxically, it was 'a performance with no bodies, and I was interested in how I could represent these creative people backstage but without them being there' (Sadler's Wells Theatre, 2016, 0:27–0:38). The installation was divided into three sections, each showing a different backstage area and the work of the people who usually inhabit these spaces. *Wardrobe and Wigs* (Hidden 1) took audiences through the costume workshop, full of costume rails and wig heads, and a looped soundtrack that accompanied LED-lit interiors of washing machines, giving the impression of a busy team in the middle of their work. In *Control Room* (Hidden 2), the audience was invited into the lighting and sound control rooms, a space usually hidden at the back of the auditorium behind thick panes of glass. The sound of the performance along with the deputy stage manager calling the show could be heard in both control rooms. On the lighting side, a lighting control desk was set up, complete with several monitors. On one monitor was the cue list, which moved on to the next cue with the deputy stage manager's 'go' command. Another monitor showed a 'magic sheet' – a diagrammatic view of the lighting plan, which highlighted the lights being used on stage in the cue that was currently live. While the actual lighting itself was not shown (as the stage was being used for Michael Hulls' *LightSpace*), the process of its creation was on show. Here, the act of creation and reproduction was made visible, something Carter was keen to exhibit. The result was the feeling that you were witnessing the creation of a performance, that you were privy to something that was both 'a doing and a thing done' (Diamond, 1996, p.5) that captured the formation and dynamism of performance-making. In *Light Store* (Hidden 3), Carter created a lighting storage area underneath the Sadler's Wells stage in what is commonly the seat store (when the auditorium seats are removed to make space for the orchestra pit, this is where they are stored – see Plate 17). Here, Carter was particularly interested in showing the 'personalities' of the various lanterns used, in addition to representing the lighting technician who might work in that space. In each space, Carter included a large, transparent, glowing 'pebble', which served as a physical yet abstract representation of a body at work.

Individually, each section showcased a discrete area of backstage practice; taken as a whole, *Hidden* aimed to draw critical attention to the labour of backstage workers, theatricalizing and making visible both the people and the process of theatre-making. As backstage ethnographer Christin Essin notes, 'the complexity and significance' of this labour have historically been 'mostly overlooked, misunderstood, or deemed unworthy of examination' (2021, p.9). Like Carter and Essin, my aim in this chapter (and in my research more broadly) is to contribute to an understanding of the hidden, tacitly practised mechanisms that are integral to theatre-making, drawing out and unravelling the latent processes of creativity, agency and identity that characterize off- and backstage work. Unusually, however, in the study of scenographic processes, I use linguistic ethnography to do this, examining instances of naturally occurring dialogue at the production desk during technical rehearsals. This approach allows me to study the ways in which lighting designers and programmers, in particular, negotiate the creative hierarchies and personnel structures in which they work *while they are working*.

This chapter draws on my doctoral research and fieldwork, in which I observed lighting designers, lighting programmers, and directors at work during technical rehearsals (Zezulka, 2019). My interest is in how lighting designers and programmers, in particular, use language as part of the process of creation, as part of 'a reflective conversation with the situation' (Schön, 1991, p.76). I examine this through a concentrated focus on technical rehearsals, which occur just before the first public performance of a production. The technical rehearsal period is a fundamental part of the theatre production process but one that has been almost entirely overlooked in writing by both scholars and practitioners (the notable exception here being Nick Hunt's (2013a, 2013b, 2015) work). This has in turn led to an inadequate recognition of the skill and contribution of lighting professionals to the theatre production process, and their work, therefore, remains mostly unseen, unexamined and insufficiently understood. However, a detailed examination of technical rehearsals as a discrete and distinctive part of theatre-making is essential for understanding the integral and important contribution that both light and lighting designers make to a production. I have chosen to focus on technical rehearsals because both the environment and the work that takes place during this time are arguably challenging for lighting designers and programmers for a number of reasons: it is a creatively exposing time, the hours are long (usually 9.00 am to 10.00 pm, or a '10 out of 12' in the United States),[4] there is significant negotiation and constantly shifting power dynamics, and it is the time when the bulk of the physical work of the lighting designer and the lighting programmer happens.

The practices and processes of the technical rehearsal, for lighting designers and programmers, especially, are what Spencer Hazel describes as 'the kinds of practice that are most prevalent in our everyday affairs, but due to our having been so thoroughly socialized into them they can become challenging to describe' (Hazel, 2018, p.266). While the technical rehearsal may not seem like an 'everyday affair' to an outsider, for lighting professionals, it comprises a large and essential part of their working life. It is, in fact, one could argue, the most important part of the creative process for a lighting designer, and thus it is remarkable that the technical rehearsal has been largely neglected in scholarly research thus far, something my work seeks to address.

As freelance workers, theatre lighting designers and lighting programmers find themselves constantly having to navigate ever-changing workplace environments as they move between theatre venues and companies and are not tied to any one place. The nature of this movement means that there is limited time to build professional relationships and to integrate into a new or established workplace community. As McEntee-Atalianis posits,

> As we enter into any new setting, we are often confronted with patterns of behaviour that challenge our sociopragmatic and sociolinguistic frames of reference. In the workplace, integration into a new community of practice can be testing as we are confronted with an established community of professionals. (2019, p.98)

There is a process of assimilation that occurs with every production – this could be a freelance designer working with a new (also freelance) creative team; it could be a lighting designer working for the first time in a venue with locally employed, in-house staff; or it could be in a team that has worked together previously but not for some time.

In contrast to this environment, workplace discourse studies have primarily concentrated on an in-house, localized labour force rather than on freelance workers. It is perhaps easy to deduce the possible reasons for this: the relative stability and consistency of a permanent workforce, and the shared geography and proximity of workers. Theatre and live performance are industries in which 'freelance working has become deeply institutionalised' (Kitching, 2015, p.22), and therefore workplace studies in this area are few. As a lighting designer, working on more than one production simultaneously and often across different genres, approaches or traditions, and with different creative and production teams, requires an ability to concurrently develop shared languages within these varying teams and to adapt to variations in personal and professional relationships. Ultimately, the ability to assimilate into these teams impacts the process of theatre-making and creativity.

A historical look at agency and creativity

The agency afforded to the lighting designer and programmer is closely linked to the lighting profession's historic and continued marginalization, as can be demonstrated through a closer look at the language used to characterize the practices and processes of lighting and scenography. In the 1950s (in the UK), the move to a specialist lighting designer (a job role that had previously been undertaken by the director or chief electrician) brought about a corresponding change in the existing power relations of the creative and production teams. Rebellato (1999) maintains that this shift to professionalism and the related change in job titles – and, in some cases, responsibilities (e.g. from 'electrician' to 'lighting designer') – 'indicated much broader transformations' (p.83) in the industry. For lighting designers, this meant, among other things, vying for creative and authorial agency and input in a role that had traditionally been seen as 'technical – to make the lights work as required by the Producer and Designer' (Guthrie, 1952, p.11; quoted in Rebellato, 1999, p.92). While this attitude is certainly no longer the case, it could be argued that the residual effects of this historical hierarchy still linger in contemporary practice.

The recent 'scenographic turn' (Collins and Aronson, 2015) has occurred in part as a result of the recognition of the affective and dramaturgical potential of design and its impact on audiences, for example, as well as an effort by designers (set, costume, lighting, sound and video) to subvert the current hierarchies that not only constitute but are also constitutive of contemporary theatre working practices. An example of this can be seen in the ways in which lighting designers and the role of light (and thereby the teams responsible for its creation) are described in writing. The focus on the technical aspects of design is perhaps one reason for the apparent marginalization of lighting designers, whether that comes from inside or outside the industry. In *The Right Light*, Moran (2017) poses the question: 'If light on stage is so important, how come it is so rarely written about?' (p.22). One of the reasons for this, he posits, is that 'writers are intimidated by the apparent technical complexity of the *machine* that is needed to get the light onto stage' (Moran, 2017, p.22, emphasis in original). Related to this are 'the limitations of language', with Moran noting that 'a particular difficulty arises when we try to describe the ways in which light affects our experience' (Moran, 2017, p.25). Anecdotally, this can result in a dismissal of the lighting designer's creative contribution or the inability of outsiders to engage with it properly – and this lack of artistic and creative recognition or wider acknowledgement impacts the ways in which lighting designers and their work is sometimes seen within the industry.

The split between what is traditionally seen as art and technology, implied by Moran above, may be due to a historical belief that 'anything technical is out of the artist's realm' (Wrench, p.25), according to a 1954 article in *TABS* magazine entitled 'Who lights the set?', a title that is itself telling of the then-prevailing attitude towards lighting designers and demonstrates how light was widely seen at this time to be purely functional and facilitative. The title also shows the (ongoing) divide between art and craft (and the implicit hierarchies in British theatre practice). The role of the lighting designer and the dramaturgical role of light have advanced considerably since then, though it is interesting to note that the hierarchical distinctions between art and craft continue to prevail in some practices.

In the UK, where my research has taken place, the lighting designer will typically join the design team after the set designer and after the bulk of the production's visual aesthetic has been decided on. In what might be termed a 'traditional' hierarchy, the director and the designer work together to create the production's 'concept' and the visual elements that support this, including the set design (see both Constable and Breiner in this volume). This work tends to happen before the start of rehearsals (see Knowles, 2004, pp.28–9) and, crucially, for the purposes of this chapter, before the appointment of the lighting designer. These hiring practices point to a continued perception of lighting designers as secondary creative contributors, who often lack access and input to the initial design conversations and therefore miss a significant opportunity to contribute creatively to the process. This has implications for the nature of lighting design: while light obviously maintains its potential to be a dramaturgical force and to aid the visual narrative, it does so reactively, rather than proactively, with the lighting designer responding to 'the space that the designer has *given* me' (Fisher, quoted in Palmer, 2013, p.262, emphasis added). The lighting designer is typically responding to what is presented to them – usually drawings and a model of the set design – rather than being able to influence the design decisions from the very beginning. This has led some, including set designer Michael Pavelka (2015), to suggest that 'lighting designers can sometimes feel a bit marginalised [. . .], knowing that they often can't make a concrete contribution until the physical design starts to take shape' (p.61). That this opinion is still upheld and perpetuated by some practitioners only serves to reinforce existing production processes and the continued (perceived or actual) marginalization of the lighting designer (and video and sound designers, who often enter the process even later).

The integrative lighting designer

In *The Right Light* (2017), Moran introduces the 'integrative lighting designer' (p.16), who works against this 'traditional model of practice' and is 'more regularly part of the discussions about the production from the beginning' (p.17). These designers aim to 'reintegrate the creative use of light into the earliest creative discussions', though Moran admits that 'for many this remains an aspiration' (Moran, 2017, p.29). A closer look at Moran's interviews reveals the actuality of the working practices that lighting designers face. For instance, while lighting designer Natasha Chivers aims to be involved in discussions earlier than is typical – that is, at the initial 'white card' stage – her design decisions are still responses to the director's vision and the designer's model: 'looking at the designer's research material, learning why the choices have been made, and finding out what has been discarded' (quoted in Moran, 2017, p.35). Moran later notes that being involved 'right at the start of the process often well before even a white card model meeting [. . .] is quite unusual, and a lot of lighting designers say they would kill to have it' (Moran, 2017, p.39). Many of the lighting designers interviewed talk about their practice in reactive terms. Peter Mumford calls lighting design 'the last creative act in the process of making theatre' (quoted in Moran, 2017, p.49), and Johanna Town states that lighting designers are 'the third step' (quoted in Moran, 2017, p.32) in the creative hierarchy, noting that 'the director's vision for the play [. . .] may actually be different to what I feel' (quoted in Moran, 2017, p.32). Mark Henderson states that he is 'very driven by what I'm given as a set' (quoted in Moran, 2017, p.30), echoing Rick Fisher's comment earlier, while some lighting designers may 'see the model box for the first time with the actors, which is quite scary' (Ormerod, quoted in Moran, 2017, p.43). Ormerod continues: 'Sometimes you don't get booked until after the set's been designed, amazingly enough. Sometimes, you're actually not in the country when the set's being designed' (Ormerod, quoted in Moran, 2017, p.43). However, there are signs that these practices are beginning to change, as seen in the increased emphasis on process and working practices in industry-facing literature. Recent articles in theatre lighting magazine *Focus* have highlighted both how important early involvement in the process is becoming for lighting designers and the rarity with which this occurs. As lighting designer Elliot Griggs has observed in his own practice:

> As performances become increasingly technical, with tighter integration between lights, music, sound, video, movement and set, the need for collaboration between creative teams is becoming far more necessary than before. Early design meetings, which typically would've involved just the director and set designer, are becoming meetings with the entire creative team. (Griggs, 2018, p.36)

Lighting designer Lucy Carter notes that, ideally, lighting designers would be paid a more representative fee for time spent on each project, a point Griggs also touches on, which would allow them to

> commit more time to projects, which would in turn improve the collaborative experience. We could commit more time during the set design process so that we avoid the design being completed before we are involved and discover a difficult, if not almost impossible, set to light. We could have more time to develop our ideas with the designer and director so that everything is fully integrated and wholly of the concept. (Carter, 2018, p.4)

In concluding the second edition of *Performance Lighting Design*, Moran (2018) offers a series of provocations on the position of lighting designers. Among them, he states that 'If as LDs we are going to be useful collaborators with our fellow creative team members, rather than technical facilitators, we need to be steeped in the dramaturgy of the pieces we light' (p.262). This is inherently dependent upon having the opportunity and ability to speak for and about light creatively – with the director and other designers, in the rehearsal room, in production meetings and during technical rehearsals – with the ultimate goal to, according to Moran, 'make creating performance lighting more like making art' (2018, p.262). These distinctions are important because they govern the ways that lighting design is seen and lighting designers (and programmers) see themselves.

As we can see from these examples, a creative product must 'be the outcome of the right kind of process [. . .], one that non-trivially and essentially involves agency' (Gaut and Kieran, 2018, pp.13–14). Hunt (2013a), however, argues that agency is rarely applied to the 'technician or designer – roles that in many performance traditions are seen to have creative agency of a secondary order' (p.296). Fulfilling these roles is often said to be done in service of the text or the director's 'vision', and any agency is thus seen as secondary to the creative agency that is attributed to performers and the director. It is within this hierarchy (or, perhaps, within the shadow of this hierarchy) that most lighting designers work. When decisions 'trickle down' from the director to those lower in the hierarchy, this potentially diminishes those creative agents' contribution to the endeavour and can risk making them less likely to be intrinsically invested. Creative people tend to seek out work 'at the edge of their creative potentialities' as these 'have a certain baseline level of difficulty and interest for them' (Kieran, 2018, p.3). Furthermore, creative people will 'question or challenge conventional practice [. . .] and are self critically reflective' (Kieran, 2018, p.3) about their work and creative interests. This ideal is compromised in those hierarchical group arrangements in which 'the higher-up person determines the creative end, which is then farmed out to' other individuals in the group (Kieran, 2018, notes from seminar discussion).

There are, Richmond (2016) posits, at least three different types of agency at play during the performance-making process. The first is authorial agency, described by Isackes (2012) as an 'alternative way of making work' (p.2) in which the scenographer is not a 'reactive artist – one who responds to a playwright's text only through the mediation of the director's primary vision' (p.1) but rather a 'generative artist' who is not limited 'by a fixed position in a predetermined collaborative hierarchy' (p.6). Professional agency refers to how professionals 'influence, make choices and take stances on their work and professional identities' (Eteläpelto et al., 2013, p.61), which has had 'very positive connotations for creativity [. . .] connected to subjects' autonomy and self-fulfillment' (Eteläpelto et al., 2013, p.46). Finally, identity agency describes 'the habitual patterning of social behavior' (Hitlin and Elder, 2007, p.179), in which we 'select into situations that allow us to build and fulfill important identity commitments' (Hitlin and Elder, 2007, p.180). The following examples will show how these three types of agency are interconnected and enacted during technical rehearsals through a detailed analysis of naturally occurring language in the workplace.

Language and dynamics

In examining technical rehearsals, my focus was on the interpersonal and professional dynamics that characterize and constitute this particular working process. Analysing this particular creative process necessitated my presence in the environment at the time the work was taking place. This was a crucial consideration and led me, methodologically, to linguistic ethnography. As a subset of ethnography, linguistic ethnography is an emerging interdisciplinary field that, as the name suggests, uses analyses of naturally occurring dialogue to attempt to explain everyday interactions. Drawing on my own significant experience as a lighting designer, lighting programmer and production electrician, and using Melrose's concepts of 'expert spectating' (2007a, paragraph 1) and 'expert practitioner-specific modes of knowledge' (2007b, p.3), this approach has allowed me to articulate the 'expert-intuitive operations' (Melrose, 2007a, paragraph 8) that characterize the creative process during technical rehearsals. In doing so, this research positions the lived experience of lighting professionals during technical rehearsals as a valuable means of exploring the processes of theatre production and the production desk as a useful site of knowledge construction. Combined with field notes and thick description, this allowed me to explicate the nature of technical rehearsals as a fundamental element of the theatre production process, gaining valuable insights into the intricate and nuanced ways in which theatre professionals (lighting designers, especially) work together.

Lighting designers and lighting programmers have a variety of linguistic strategies to draw on to enable and facilitate dialogue at the production desk. Individually, these may seem insignificant, but taken together they form the basis for cooperative working practices, and for the creation and maintenance of an environment in which lighting designers and lighting programmers can enact authorial, professional and identity agency. The effects of agency and identity on process can clearly be seen in some examples. Both examples include what is known as 'relational talk', that is, talk that is primarily oriented to 'the construction, maintenance, reproduction and transformation of interpersonal relationships' (Locher and Watts, 2008, p.96). Being able to integrate the relational aspects of personal discourse with the transactional nature of professional discourse is crucial for assimilating effectively into changing workplaces, thus allowing lighting designers and programmers to exercise their authorial, professional and identity agency.

Example 1

The first example is taken during the technical rehearsal of a large West End musical. The lighting designer had never worked with the designer or director

PLATE 1 *The Litten Trees*, St Just, Cornwall, 2021. Installation on the same tree at different times. Lighting designer: Joshua Pharo. (Joshua Pharo).

PLATE 2 *The Litten Trees*, Alexander Palace Park, London, 2021. Lighting designer: Jackie Shemesh. (Hugo Glendinning).

PLATE 3 *The Litten Trees*, Leek, Staffordshire, 2021. Lighting designer: Daniella Beattie. (Tim Vickerstaff).

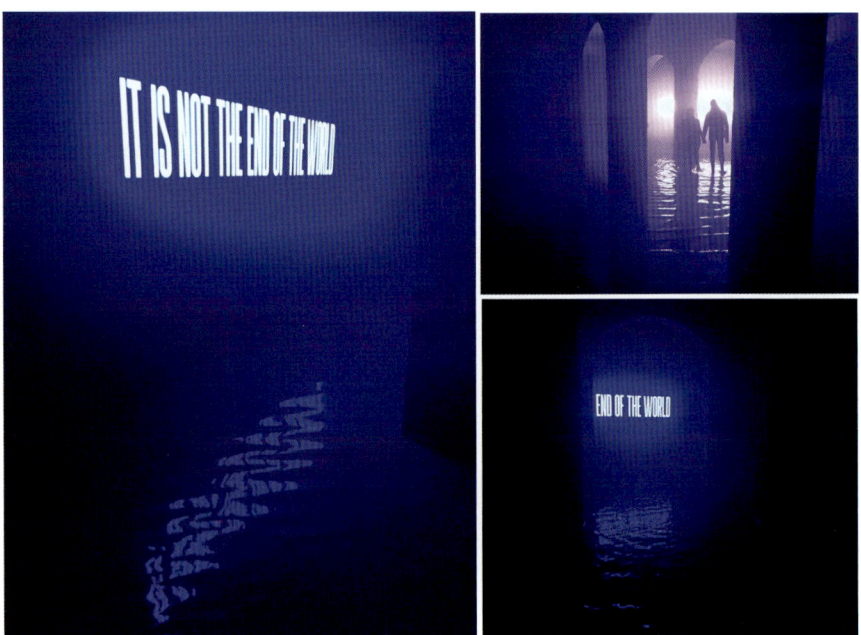

PLATE 4 *It Is Not the End of the World*. Superflex, 2019. (Scott Palmer).

PLATE 5 *Ungdom* (*Youth*). Fix and Foxy, 2015. Lighting designer: Michael Breiner. (Per Morten Abrahamsen).

PLATE 6 *Ungdom* (*Youth*). Fix and Foxy, 2015. Lighting designer: Michael Breiner. (Søren Knud).

PLATE 7 *The Drowned Man – A Hollywood Fable*. Punchdrunk, 2013. Lighting designer: Mike Gunning. (Alex Palmer).

PLATE 8 *and it all comes down to this…* David Shearing, 2012. Performance space without participants (David Shearing).

PLATE 9 *and it all comes down to this...* David Shearing, 2012. Spatialized screens layout, with double-sided projection (David Shearing).

PLATE 10 *and it all comes down to this...* David Shearing, 2012. Moments from the end sequence; paper birds with duo-tone light effect (David Shearing).

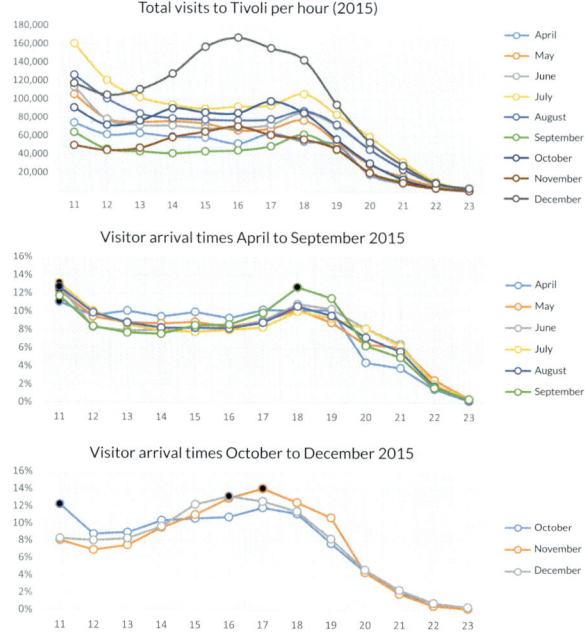

PLATE 11 Tivoli Gardens, Copenhagen. 2015 visitor data tracking.

PLATE 12 Tivoli Gardens, Copenhagen. Visitors experiencing the twilight. Lighting designer: Jesper Kongshaug. (Jesper Konshaug).

PLATE 13 The impact of light on the visitor experience of the Tivoli Gardens, Copenhagen. Lighting designer: Jesper Kongshaug. Clockwise from top left: 1. Daytime (Lasse Salling), 2. Nightime (Rasmus B. Hansen), 3. Chinese area with redesigned red lanterns (Lasse Salling), 4. Nimb Hotel decorated with historic coloured glass 'kuppels' (Jesper Kongshaug).

PLATE 14 *Woolf Works*, Wayne McGregor. ©Royal Opera House, London, 2015. Lighting designer: Lucy Carter. (Photograph by Tristram Kenton).

PLATE 15 *Woolf Works*, Wayne McGregor, Royal Opera House, London, 2015. Lighting designer: Lucy Carter. (Photograph by Tristram Kenton).

PLATE 16 *Hidden 3* (Light Store) from *No Body*, Sadler's Wells, 2016. Lighting designer: Lucy Carter. (Richard Davies).

PLATE 17 *F.LUX*, 2014. Lighting designer: Lucy Carter. (Richard Davies).

PLATE 18 *J3RR1: Programmed Torture*. None Collective, 2018 (None Collective).

PLATE 19 *Overcast*, Yaron Shyldkrot 2017. (Yaron Shyldkrot).

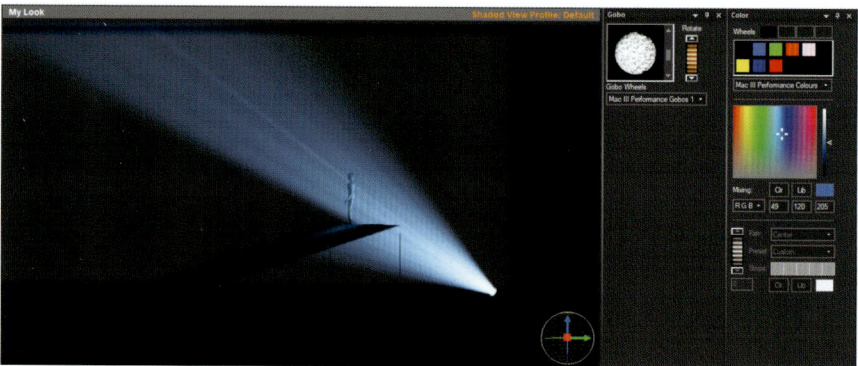

PLATE 20 Creating the Northern Lights effect for *The Valkyrie*. WYSIWYG previsualization by lighting designer: Michael Breiner.

PLATE 21 *The Valkyrie*. The New Opera (TNO) Esbjerg, 2017. Northern lights as realized on stage. Lighting designer: Michael Breiner. (Marie í Dali).

PLATE 22 *The Taming of the Shrew*, Hong Kong Academy for Performing Arts, 2014. Lighting designers: Psyche Chui and John A Williams. (Felix Chan).

PLATE 23 *The Taming of the Shrew*, Hong Kong Academy for Performing Arts, 2014. Lighting designers: Psyche Chui and John A Williams. (Felix Chan).

PLATE 24 *Two Man Show*, RashDash, 2016. Lighting designer: Katharine Williams. (The Other Richard).

PLATE 25 *The Darkest Corners*, RashDash, 2017. Lighting designer: Katharine Williams. (The Other Richard).

PLATE 26 *The Darkest Corners*, RashDash, 2017. Lighting designer: Katharine Williams. (The Other Richard).

PLATE 27 *Necessary Weather*, 1994. (Restaged at Baryshnikov Arts Center, 2011.) Lighting designer: Jennifer Tipton. (Photograph by Stephanie Berger).

PLATE 28 *War Horse*, National Theatre, London, 2007. Lighting designer: Paule Constable. (Brinkhoff and Moegenburg).

PLATE 29 *The Curious Incident of the Dog in the Night-Time*, National Theatre, London, 2013. Lighting designer: Paule Constable. (Brinkhoff and Moegenburg).

PLATE 30 *Angels in America*. National Theatre, London, 2017. Lighting designer: Paule Constable. (Helen Maybanks, courtesy of ArenaPAL).

PLATE 31 'The Trial of Queen Katharine, *Henry VIII*, Act II Scene 4' Covent Garden Theatre, 1831. Painted in 1866 by Henry Andrews (1794–1868), (Courtesy of RSC Theatre Collection).

PLATE 32 *We are Hull*. City Hall, Hull City of Culture, 5 January 2017. Installation by Zsolt Balogh. (David Graham/Alamy).

before, though their relationship with the lighting programmer was very well established, affording the programmer a large amount of creative and problem-solving input. The following exchange between the lighting designer and the lighting programmer demonstrates one strategy for realigning control and authority through the exercise of professional and identity agency. Despite potentially seeming to be a wilfully disruptive tactic, the strategy employed here is crucial in gaining time for the lighting designer to work productively at a critical time during the production process. Without this intervention, the significant limitations on time that are already present and the hierarchies at play during technical rehearsals actively work to negate the contribution of the lighting designer and lighting programmer, whose work would otherwise be forced to take place in the margins and achieved despite less-than-ideal working conditions.

1	LD: This is the new, slower tech style, isn't it?
2	Programmer: We are, absolutely. And I am more than happy to cop some of the flak for that. I will go slower if I need to go slower.
3	LD: It's just – it's a request from everybody.
4	Programmer: Good. I just – it's mad. [. . .]
5	LD: It's the conversation we had last night.
6	Programmer: But [the director] doesn't listen. Don't worry; I'll just be really shit at programming today. And then we'll just go back to the . . .
7	LD: Just let me know when you're being shit and when you're not being shit. [Laughter.]
8	Programmer: Thanks, [LD]. I would hope that you would notice. [Laughter.]

We can see in this excerpt a clear example of how the lighting programmer uses their professional agency to support the work of the lighting designer and wider production team. This transcript comes from the second day of technical rehearsals, after a particularly hurried first day. In speaking with the lighting team before the start of this session, I learned that the design and production team felt that the speed of the first day had not given them adequate time to focus on the design elements, specifically lighting or some of the more technical, logistical elements such as scene changes. This had been discussed informally after rehearsals had finished on the first day, without the director present, and there was a general feeling among the creative and production team that the director was more concerned about the dancers and the choreography than the design. The creative team, therefore, along with the deputy stage manager, decided to forcibly (but surreptitiously) slow down the technical rehearsal to ensure enough time was spent on the technical and design elements from day two.

The director of this production did not appear to be interested in meaningful collaboration with the design team. The lighting designer was provided with images from the production's previous incarnation and often seemed to be simply reproducing what had come before, reducing their role in many cases to that of a facilitator. Not only did this prove frustrating for the lighting designer (as well as the associate lighting designer and the lighting programmer), but it was also largely self-defeating for the director, who was in effect actively denying themselves access to the lighting designer's creativity and expertise. In instances when the lighting designer – or, indeed, the lighting programmer – did attempt to exercise some level of creative agency or input over and above mere facilitation, this was curtailed by the director. According to my field notes, this led to another instance in which creative decisions were mooted against the director's wishes. While this could have had a detrimental effect on both professional and personal relationships within the lighting team, this in fact served to strengthen group amity. The lighting designer's comment in turn 7 could potentially be taken as an insult in another context in which the interlocutors were not as friendly with each other. Here, however, 'it is as if they are saying "I know you so well I can be this rude to you"' (Daly et al., 2004, p.960). The insult is not taken seriously, and in fact the programmer makes a joke out of it.

During this exchange, the director was located at another production desk in the stalls, closer to the stage and was out of hearing range. As stated, the director had not been consulted about the proposed change of pace, and the creative team (led by the lighting programmer) was effectively subverting the director's authority in a subtle but highly coordinated way. The lighting programmer takes responsibility for the conditions in which the artistic and technical output of the wider team may be realized by taking control of the situation with the group goals in mind; they are exercising their professional agency in a way that both supports the lighting designer and their work and benefits the process as a whole.

It is notable that it is the lighting programmer who either has been designated or has volunteered to lead this shift in control. The programmer states, 'I will go slower if I need to go slower' (turn 2), and while this is clearly a deliberate choice on the part of the programmer, the blame for the lack of speed can easily be apportioned to the lighting console itself – the interface between the programmer and the actual lighting fixtures on stage and, crucially, an inanimate object. The level of sophistication of both the console and the lighting equipment provides the programmer with a 'buffer' for what could be seen by an outsider as the programmer's lack of skill or ability; the potential capacity for the technology to fail or be otherwise difficult to manipulate (independent of the programmer) provides a convenient and 'safe' way for the programmer to maintain their professional standing without fear of repercussions. The fact that this labour is both largely unseen and not understood by those without this specialist knowledge adds to this defence. The programmer is also clearly free to choose when to 'be really shit at programming' (turn 6), meaning they must constantly 'read' the situation and respond accordingly; they will only 'go slower *if I need to go slower*' (turn 2, my emphasis).

What is also particularly fascinating about this exchange is the way in which the programmer volunteers to 'cop some of the flak' for any potential challenge from the director, an act that is designed to save the lighting designer's professional face while simultaneously asserting the programmer's own identity agency. This is a clear example of how 'face is closely related to a person's sense of identity or self concept: self as an individual (individual identity), self as a group member (group or collective identity) and self in relationship with others (relational identity)' (Spencer-Oatey, 2008, p.14). The long-standing nature of the programmer's relationship with the lighting designer afforded them this ability to protect the lighting designer's authorial agency, using technology to disrupt the process as and when needed, but to the benefit of the lighting designer and wider creative team.

Example 2

Sometimes, establishing or preserving the dynamics of the team or the wider process requires an opposite approach, as in the excerpt that follows. The following example comes from a different production, with a different creative team, and therefore a different dynamic, both professionally and interpersonally. This can be seen throughout the linguistic interactions that occurred during my observations, one of which will be analysed in more detail.

Compliments and their responses help to create cohesion and to construct positive working relationships (Holmes and Marra, 2004); complimenting is 'a communicative act that impacts a person's identity' (Mirivel and Fuller, 2018, p.219). Compliments are part of a larger group of linguistic strategies called 'positive communication' (Mirivel and Fuller, 2018), which help to establish effective workplace interactions. Mirivel and Fuller suggest that such relational strategies can also 'strengthen professionals' competencies' (2018, p.224). When responding to compliments, English speakers are under two concurrent constraints that are not simultaneously satisfiable: compliments are assessments, and since assessments are usually followed by an agreement with the assessment as a preferred next turn (Pomerantz, 1984), a form of acceptance should follow after the compliment has been given. At the same time, it has been shown that when speakers praise themselves, such behaviour is routinely sanctioned (Pomerantz, 1978). (cited in Golato, 2003, pp.102–3)

Preference here (in conversation analysis terms) is a structural notion, not a psychological one; it refers to how we would expect someone to reply (things like question–answer pairs are a good example of this), rather than how speakers feel about each other or about what they're saying. One way of attempting to satisfy both of these response criteria is to provide 'the history of the object of the compliment (i.e. where or how one obtained it)' (Golato, 2003, p.118), which is precisely what the lighting designer does in turn 2. The use of 'just' minimizes the lighting designer's authorial agency and almost seems to separate their work and their creative agency from the effect of the light itself. The set designer praises the lighting designer's work in the previous scene without quite being able to articulate what they liked about it:

1	Designer: There was something you did at the end of that scene that just . . .
2	LD: I just added a bit of my backlight.
3	Designer: Yeah, it just made it . . .

The lighting designer offers a downgraded assessment of their involvement in the lighting state being referred to, as if the light were acting independently of the lighting designer's creative actions and intentions. The designer's language reflects this in their switch in pronouns: in turn 1, 'There was something you did', but in turn 3, 'it [the backlight] just made it . . . '. Following self-effacing or self-deprecating turns (such as in turn 2), the preferred response is disagreement, though 'a dispreferred can be couched as preferred' (Glenn, 2019, p.241) as it is in turn 3. The designer starts with an agreement marker ('Yeah'), then matches the lighting designer's mitigating 'just', perhaps sensing the potential for embarrassment or expecting another self-effacing remark from the lighting designer. To offer a 'preferred' response in either case would potentially be face-threatening (Sifianou, 2012, p.1560), which could serve to upset the dynamics of the team. The link between identity agency and face is noted by Layder (1997), who notes that 'much routine situated activity requires a great deal of creativity and ingenuity with respect to the notions of self, meaning, situational propriety and so on' (p.235). Throughout my observations of lighting teams at work, face-saving acts such as these occurred frequently, by all members of the creative and production teams. There were very few instances of overtly face-threatening acts; instead, there seemed to be an aversion to anything that threatened another person's face, even if these were not explicitly face-saving. Creative agency, therefore, seems to be strongly linked to the development and maintenance of a professional workplace environment that is founded on personal relationships, trust and a degree of autonomy and agency. Additionally, both of these examples show that the construction of personal and professional relationships is a process that is essential for creative collaboration and demonstrate ways in which this is enacted through language.

Conclusion

The examples I have shared here from my observations show just two ways in which creative relationships can shape scenographic processes. In the first example, we saw the lighting programmer subverting the hierarchical norms of the workplace, using their professional and identity agency in service of the wider production aesthetic. In the second, the lighting designer uses a linguistically face-saving strategy in order to preserve team dynamics, inadvertently downplaying their own authorial agency. Much like with Carter's *Hidden*, making these latent processes visible contributes to a fuller and wider understanding of how theatre is made and how creative individuals exercise agency throughout the process.

Using linguistic ethnography and discourse analysis to closely study the processes of the technical rehearsal opens up new ways of thinking about how theatre is made. These often hidden processes are integral to our understanding of theatre-making and how language can be used to either facilitate or disrupt these processes. Ontologically, research into the intricacies of the technical rehearsal also opens up potential theoretical and practical implications for theatre and production studies more widely through its focus on process over product: the processes of theatre-making in which lighting designers, programmers and directors engage (and, importantly, how they engage in them) have a direct impact on the final product, and thus on what theatre, at a fundamental level, is. The technical rehearsal should, therefore, be seen as an integral and essential part of theatre-making, part of a continual process of creative experimentation, personal and professional engagement, trial and error, and problem-solving, that serves to engender opportunities for collaboration in theatre production. Recognizing the centrality of this process marks a fundamental shift in the ontology of theatre-making and in the way the contribution of lighting designers and lighting programmers is understood.

The work of the lighting designer and lighting programmer is intrinsic to this process and deserves to be given more attention, in both the academy and the industry, as well as through public performance events such as *Hidden*. Demonstrating the creative contribution of the lighting designer and lighting programmer as integral to the creative process, as this research does, in turn opens up the possibility of light to act as an agential force in contemporary theatre practice.

Notes

1 Since the Covid-19 pandemic, some of this work has been happening remotely; however, the lighting designer and lighting programmer are still required to be present in the space, whether virtually or in person.
2 In opera, these are called 'stage and piano' rehearsals and, later, 'stage and orchestra' rehearsals.
3 See also Lucy Carter's chapter on pp. 72–81 in this volume.
4 There is evidence, however, that this practice is changing. In the United Kingdom, the Reset Better campaign (and others) has advocated for 'two-session' days during the technical rehearsal period, shortening the working day to eight or nine hours, and in the United States, data gathered by the group No More 10 out of 12s has shown the detrimental effect of long days on theatre workers' productivity, mental and physical health, and quality of life.

7

Northern Lights

Using natural light phenomena as stage lighting concept

Michael Breiner

This chapter explores the development of our lighting concept for Richard Wagner's opera *The Valkyrie*, staged at The New Opera (TNO) in Esbjerg, Denmark, 2017. The magnitude of the work, the time span of the project, and the particular nature of the collaborative working environment each impacted on how the lighting concept evolved and was ultimately realized in performance.

The director of TNO in Esbjerg, Lars Ole Mathiasen, set out in 2016 to form an artistic production team, which would work collaboratively on Wagner's *Nibelung Ring Cycle*, which includes four opera productions, *Das Rheingold*, *Die Walküre*, *Siegfried* and *Götterdämmerung*. This artistic team was to work closely to develop the concept together over the course of eight years (2016–24). This approach was intended to build a common design language throughout all four opera productions. When a new artistic team is formed for the first time, trust and confidence are essential, to create a common aesthetic viewpoint. Lars Ole arranged for several workshops, where director, conductor, set and light designer would meet, and slowly approach and explore *Die Walküre* together. In this environment it was clear that all questions were legitimate, and that any and all ideas could be discussed openly and without pre-judgement which also served the crucial purpose of allowing all of the members of the creative team to know each other better.

It was clear from the start of the process that all of the elements of music, direction, set, costume and light design would be treated with equal status and light would not be marginalized in the creative process, as can often be the case.

Many lighting designers have experienced working on productions where all of the key creative conceptual decisions have already been decided at an early stage before the lighting designer has been asked to contribute. This often leads to the lighting having to be reactive and therefore an illustration of the other artistic team members' ideas. In contrast, the creative process at TNO offered the potential for light to become a significant contributor to the way in which the productions in the cycle were staged and experienced.

In many ways this was the original intention of Richard Wagner when he developed the *Ring* cycle. Wagner was not only a composer but also wanted total control of all the elements of the staging of his operas or *Worttondrama*, as he described them, where all the theatrical elements would combine to create the *Gesamtkunstwerk* – a total art form, supporting a singular overall artistic vision.

Discovering the conceptual key

When I as a light designer first approach any theatrical production, I am actively seeking the conceptual key, which will in turn unlock the entire production concept. Once I find this key everything will hopefully start to make sense and all future questions will somehow be answerable by this conceptual framework. So, to find this key concept, many questions need to be asked: in which way do we intend to stage this production? What is the role of the light in this production? And what interests us as artists when we examine this particular artwork?

The natural occurring light phenomenon has, for some time, inspired me. Striking phenomena such as halos, lightning, rainbows, Northern Lights and solar eclipses of course create dramatic natural effects, but also more common light phenomena like the qualities of light at sunset and sunrise, misty weather, moonlight and the reflections of sunlight on a water surface have each arrested my attention, influenced my thinking and informed my professional practice in my approach to designing light. For example, in *Ungdom* (*Youth*) (2015), I created an environment in which the audience experienced a theatrical day as they were physically immersed in a festival landscape of tents, sand and a lake. Stage lighting was critical to allow the feelings of anxiety, joy, insecurity and ambition to emerge as the audience were gradually transported through the shifting light from daylight to night and through to dawn.

However, in working with *The Valkyrie*, the first opera in the Esbjerg *Ring* cycle, I wanted to draw upon other culturally embedded experiences of light in a very different way. Our cultural background, lived experience and physical geographical location all shape how we understand and relate to naturally occurring light phenomena. Throughout time, different cultures have tried to understand these phenomena, and the myths, stories and even religious practices that tell the tale of how humankind has tried to interpret these wonders of nature and found inspiration in them. It seemed to me that there were key opportunities in Wagner's mythical world to explore the potential for these wonders of natural light to drive the overall design concept.

What is the role of the light in this production?

This was the question I first set out to answer, in 2016, when starting to design the light for *The Valkyrie* opera in Esbjerg. This ambitious project seemed extremely daunting to me at the time. I had never worked with Wagner's music and never designed for opera on this scale before. Of course, I knew the *Ride of the Valkyries*. This classical music theme was forever burned into my memory, in the shape of a helicopter attack, in Francis Ford Coppola's legendary Vietnam War movie, *Apocalypse Now*. I also vaguely remembered seeing the opera in 1995. I attended a dress rehearsal with my classmates in primary school at the music house in Aarhus. At that time, as a young teenager, it did not leave a lasting impression.

During the years from 2003 to 2008 Lars Ole, the head of TNO in Esbjerg, produced all four instalments of Wagner's *Ring* cycle. However, each of the four productions were created by four different production teams and did not have an overriding artistic concept. Lars Ole felt that the dramatic material had a much bigger potential, and he had been thinking for some time about creating a true *Ring* cycle, with the intention of performing all four operas back-to-back in 2026.

Lars Ole wanted us all in the creative team to collaborate on equal terms; the idea was that anybody could have an idea for the set, lighting, directing or even the interpretation of the music. Of course, in the end somebody would have to make final decisions, in respect of each other's professions. An example of this collaborative workflow could be a lighting idea coming from the conductor, or a directing idea coming from the lighting designer. In practice this meant many meetings, where ideas were thrown on the table, only to be rejected, but some ideas stayed and were moved into new phases, models were built and actual technical tests were conducted. An example of this working method was the conductor, Lars Ole, coming up with the idea of a total blackout during a specific point in the opera. This posed the technical problem of light spilling from the orchestra pit onto the stage and so ruining the effect. So it was agreed to rehearse that passage of music to be played, without light in the orchestra pit, to allow us to create a true blackout on stage.

This kind of process is, of course, time-consuming and also filled with many dead ends, but in my experience, it is also much more rewarding as an artist. You really feel part of a whole, and nobody really owns any ideas; they all belong to the production.

It was on these conditions that I agreed to develop the lighting design for *The Valkyrie* in 2016. The rest of the production team all had previous experience with the dramatic material. Kasper Wilton, the director, had worked on the Nibelung *Ring* cycle before, directing *Siegfried* in the earlier Esbjerg *Ring*. The set and costume designer, Marie í Dali, was part of the Copenhagen *Ring* cycle from 2003 to 2006. Lars Ole had conducted all four previous operas in Esbjerg.

Early in the conceptual process, we had to decide on how to approach the Nibelung *Ring* cycle. We wanted to stay true to the story and at the same time create a version that would not alienate our audience. Lars Ole wanted to produce a *Ring* cycle for Wagner beginners: a version in which no prior knowledge of the libretto or overall plot was required from the audience, and a version that at the same time would stay true to Wagner's original intentions.

Many productions of the *Ring* cycle have been created in the past; the work will always and should always be reinterpreted. Keeping Wagner's mystical Nordic setting was important, as we believed that Wagner's complex plots and emotional motives would resonate with a contemporary audience, without adding an extra layer of interpretation, and at the same time providing the audience with a space for reflection.

We started to look at contemporary works of fiction with similar topics and soon realized that *The Lord of the Rings*, *Game of Thrones* and *The Vikings* television series were all good examples of fiction that employed magical realism, where gods, myths and magic played an equal part. And of course, they all borrowed heavily from Wagner and the Nordic myths.

In the Nibelung *Ring* cycle, gods and magic are part of the universe. I was still looking for a key to unlock this design problem, and at the same time, I wanted the light to have a symbolic function, much like Wagner's *leitmotif*, in which a character or central theme has its own musical motif, often foreshadowing an event in the future or referring to past events. Therefore, I was looking for a way to create light motifs that would function in the same way in the overall narrative.

Aurora Borealis and mystic light

As a lighting designer it is common practice to work on multiple productions at the same time. This has a tendency for the work to influence each other, a sort of creative spill-over effect.

The conceptual process for the *Ring* cycle started in the fall of 2016, and at the same time I was asked to teach a general lighting course at the National Theatre of Greenland. This suited me particularly well since I always wanted to visit Greenland, especially in the winter months, where the aurora borealis, the Northern Lights, is most visible. I had previously only experienced this light phenomenon in Iceland during a brief stay a couple of years earlier. This particular and mystical light had somehow occupied a special place in my creative subconsciousness.

During my stay in Nuuk, I was already working on *The Valkyrie*, and I was especially struggling with the *Ride of the Valkyries*. The whole scene takes place on a mountainside where the Valkyries gather before going to Valhalla, with the bodies of the fallen heroes. Wagner describes it in his libretto like this:

> On the summit of a rocky mountain. On the right the scene is bordered by a pine-wood. On the left is the entrance to a cave, above which the rock rises to its highest point. At the back of the view is quite open; rocks of various heights form the verge of a precipice, which apparently descends steeply to the background. Now and then clouds fly past the mountain peak, as if driven before a storm. Gerhilde, Ortlinde, Waltraute and Schwertleite are assembled on the rocky point above the cave: they are in full armour.
>
> A flash of lightning breaks through the clouds: a Valkyrie on horse-back becomes visible in it: across her saddle hangs a slain warrior. (Wagner, 1870, pp.201–3)

We had already decided that we were not going to actually fly any of the singers or to have horses on stage, but we still needed the Valkyries to enter the stage in some magical way. While I was pondering this problem, I had a conversation with my students in Nuuk about the Northern Lights and their meaning in Greenlandic myths. I was told not to whistle while seeing the lights, because this would attract their attention, and they might come to carry me off to the land of the dead. The lights were perceived as the souls of stillborn children, and they were now playing football with the skull of a walrus.

I had never heard this myth before. I knew of some beliefs of the Northern Lights having a connection with the souls of the dead trying to contact the living, but never before had I heard of the belief that the light actually had a purpose of bringing the souls to another realm. My creative curiosity was immediately tingling. Was this the conceptual key I had been looking for?

The same evening, instead of going straight home, I went for a walk in the bitter cold. I had seen glimpses of the Northern Lights on previous evenings, but not a full display, as the nights had been cloudy. This night the stars were out, so I walked to the old harbour district, where the city lights were less bright.

I saw only stars, but slowly, as the darkness descended, there appeared faint streaks of moving light traces on the night sky, like skating marks on ice, with slowly pulsating shifting hues of green. Watching the aurora borealis is like no other light phenomena: it is like seeing a living three-dimensional form. Unlike watching a rainbow that fades in and out but is a still, perfect, image, the Northern Lights constantly shift, change and produce an other-worldly presence.

Afterwards I went home to my apartment and found a time-lapse video of the Northern Lights. I watched the video and at the same time listened to the *Ride of the Valkyries*. Experiencing the magical, twirling Northern Lights alongside the music just felt completely right, and at that moment, I knew that this was the solution to my artistic conundrum.

A couple of years later I discovered a book in Trondheim, Norway, about the Northern Lights and their mythical interpretations. As I read the text, I realized that this light sign from ancient Norse mythology somehow had been with me subconsciously, and suddenly the light made sense to me in that moment:

> The Vikings believed that the Northern Lights were Bifrost, the magical bridge that leads from the human world, up to Valhalla, the home of the gods. Fallen Vikings were led over Bifrost by the Valkyries – women warriors chosen by Odin armed with shining armour, shields and spears. Bright spikes in the northern light were seen as light reflected from the Valkyries' shields. (Christensen, 2019, p.37)

The idea of the light functioning as a bridge between two worlds, a mystical force to transport the dead heroes to the eternal realm of Walhalla seemed just perfect.

So, this hunch, this gut feeling, maybe was part of my ancestral knowledge, somehow transported through time by stories and myths: the urge to understand a naturally occurring phenomenon and to translate it into something meaningful, for us to understand the unexplainable. This is where great tales of magic, wonders and poetry are born.

Creating the Northern Lights

In order to create the Northern Lights on stage I started to research the phenomenon in question. What science tells us about the Northern Lights is fascinating. A full understanding of the process that leads to the different types of auroras is still incomplete, but what we do know is that charged particles from the sun interact with the magnetic field of the Earth, and this causes a variety of different phenomena. The solar wind is constantly bombarding the Earth's magnetosphere with charged particles. The solar wind varies in strength, due to the activity on the surface and inside the sun. Eruptions on the surface of the sun, also referred to as solar flares, feed the solar wind.

The ancient Greeks observed the phenomenon of aurora borealis and the Roman philosopher Seneca describes it in his work *Naturales questions* circa AD 65. Galileo used the name 'aurora borealis' in 1619. Aurora was the name of the Roman goddess of dawn, and borealis was the Greek name for the north wind.

It was not until 1900 that the Norwegian scientist Kristian Birkeland laid the foundation for our current understanding of geomagnetism and polar auroras. He developed a theory in which energetic electrons were ejected from sunspots on the solar surface, directed to the Earth and guided to the polar regions by the geomagnetic field, which surrounds the Earth, where they produced the visible aurora. This is essentially the theory that is used to explain the aurora borealis phenomena today.

Although the experience of watching the Northern Lights can be very different, there is one frequently occurring feature: the lights are perceived as three-dimensional. It seems as if the light somehow stretches down in ribbons, slowly changing shape and colour, from ghostly green to cyan and sometimes flaring red.

I knew that I wanted the light to accompany the Valkyries to stretch into space and to appear as if it were a three-dimensional physical object, a bridge to another world.

Physics and mythology have always inspired me in my work, so I set out to conduct light experiments in the spring of 2017. I contacted the head electrician at the Esbjerg music house, Nicolai Thorsen, and we started to plan the experiments. I wanted to project light towards the audience to achieve a maximum visual effect, and I wanted the light to be visible in the air. Usually, light is not visible before it strikes an object, so in order to make the light visible in the auditorium we needed to fill the air with something.

Most of us have on some Sunday morning while lying in bed, witnessed the magical display of dust particles dancing in a beam of sunlight. This effect was for many years almost impossible to achieve in a controlled manner.

Many lighting designers had experimented with different smoke effects but not until the 1960s when the hazer was invented was this an artistic possibility.[1]

A haze machine produces a nearly undetectable cloud of very fine particles, and unlike conventional theatrical smoke machines, where the smoke evaporates within a few minutes, the haze cloud has a hang time of several hours depending on the level of ventilation and other atmospheric conditions.

Critically, I did not want to attempt the impossible task of replicating the aurora borealis on stage, and as this could easily become over-literal. Instead, I wanted to work with the atmosphere that this light phenomenon creates within the spectator, the feeling of an other-worldly presence.

The first experiments involved video projection. A video projector was placed upstage, at the far end of the stage, projecting directly towards the audience. At the same time, we filled the room with haze in order to project the video image directly onto the air. Doing so would create a three-dimensional image that traversed the entire stage and auditorium; however, we soon discovered that the video projector was not bright enough. The video content we were projecting was actual footage of the Northern Lights, but the contrast ratio and quality of the video material did not work as intended. Another problem was the visibility of the light source, in this case the front lens of the projector, which drew too much unwanted attention, and therefore detracted from the overall atmosphere and ruined the aesthetic.

I was rather disappointed with the tests. The idea was good, but we had to devise another technical setup to create the right light quality.

To recreate the atmosphere of the Northern Lights, we got rid of the video projector and instead installed an older moving light fixture that had some interesting features we wanted to test. We installed it on the floor, facing the audience, and built a mock-up of the set design in front of the fixture. The set for the third act was a cliff formation. The light source on the floor is hidden behind the set, in order not to destroy the composition and draw unwanted attention. This setup was also previsualized with computer-aided design (see Plate 20).

As soon as we turned on the fixture, we could see a major difference in the light quality. This light source was much brighter than the video projector, and by slowly rotating internal gobos we could create a sense of movement in the light. As we were testing the different colour options, someone accidentally opened the back door to the stage, and the light from outside poured in. This, of course, ruined the light effect but at the same time changed the depth of the room, and it made me wonder how we could create a bigger sense of three-dimensionality. We had previously been working with a black back wall, which created a sense of endless void, but when you look at the actual aurora in nature, the stars are always present in the background. I called the Royal

Theatre in Copenhagen, and they kindly lent us a fibre optic star curtain light system, which allowed us to create the illusion of spatial depth.

The value of testing and making mistakes can never be underestimated, light must be experienced in time and space, and other artistic and technical collaborators must respond to it, only then can real aesthetical decisions be made.

At this point, we had no more time to experiment, so we had to trust the knowledge we had gained in the process. It was not until the actual rehearsals on stage that we would see if the effect really would work as intended.

This is a typical situation for lighting designers. We have to trust our gut feelings and experience all the time. There is never enough time to experiment on stage and in the real setup. Artistic ideas must be neutered, bad ideas need to fail, and happy accidents happen. This can be nerve-racking, as decisions about renting expensive equipment must be decided. If the artistic idea fails, there will not always be enough time or money to change the lighting concept.

Reflections on light

As I think back on the whole process and this specific lighting design, one thing in particular comes to mind: natural light and all its fantastic possibilities and mysteries. In my experience, most audience members, and people in general, do not reflect on light in their everyday activities, even though everyone can recall a particular sunset or moonlight at a certain time, and we constantly navigate our everyday lives according to light and its changing conditions. This is a core principle in the understanding of light: it is constantly changing and, by doing so, it changes how we perceive the world around us. This hidden knowledge is embedded in all of us, and we subconsciously access it every second of our lives. As a lighting designer I work with this hidden knowledge, and the real magic happens when a particular lighting state on stage suddenly seems to click, and we can't really explain why; it's a gut feeling of a sense of truth in that moment. We work intentionally on producing a certain mood or atmosphere, but it really requires our attention to a particular moment in order to experience if this really is the right light.

Nick Moran sums it up beautifully in his book *The Right Light*:

> One key quality that we seem to be looking for, then, could be called purposefulness. The same quality the rose has; aesthetic beauty of form that also fulfils function – a beautiful rose is also very good at being a rose and a beautiful lighting look is also very good at doing the other things it needs to do for the production (support the text, reveal what needs to be revealed in the right way, etc.). An artistic lighting designer, working in an

artistic way, has to be able to plan for this, and has to be able to spot it if it happens by happy accident. It seems to me that what is important is to recognise when it is working, when the technical and aesthetic choices are appropriate in the moment and for the whole production. (Moran, 2017: 169)

I remember that moment in Esbjerg: the lights dimming in the auditorium, the orchestra starting to play the first eerie notes of *Ride of the Valkyries* as the curtain slowly rises, and the light fading to black. Out of the darkness, we see the stars, and slowly the Northern Lights appear, swirling and moving, ghostly greenish. In the light, two shadows appear, breaking the flow and slowly growing, two dark figures enter upstage, walking out of the light. Soon after, two more enter and are greeted by the first pair (See Plate 21).

I cannot explain why this particular series of light changes, in combination with the scenic action and music, works, but I can feel it. I sense how the audience let out an audible gasp, and how it set the atmosphere in that moment. I just want to stay in that moment and to prolong it. I do not need anything more to happen; it feels completely right.

Lighting design has always been driven by these moments for me, and the nerve-racking process of getting to that point in time where all the components are brought together: the moment of truth. Will our vision appear or fail miserably? This is the curse of the craft. Light is the last major component to appear on stage, and as everything else, always in need of more time.

Often the design process speeds up dramatically towards the deadline, the premiere. And often you do not entirely realize the full extent of your work until much later, an idea articulated as 'post-design rationalisation' by Rick Fisher (Palmer, 2013, pp.255–65). If you're lucky you get to revisit your work on a later date. I had the fortunate luck to restage *The Valkyrie* in Trondheim in March 2020. Seeing the production again and working with a new technical team was fascinating. Every production has its own problems and solutions, and sometimes these can be gifts in their own way. In Trondheim the stage was too small, and this forced me to come up with a new solution for the Northern Lights effect. And in the process, working closely with the lighting technicians, it became better than the original work. We changed the light source and moved the lighting position slightly upstage to hide the fixture from the balcony sightline. I knew exactly what I wanted to achieve, but I learned that other opinions and technical solutions can open the work and give it a new perspective.

The Northern Lights became a light motif, together with lightning, lava, sunrays, darkness and other naturally occurring phenomena, they became the conceptual key, the leitmotifs I was looking for and the magical glue that the production needed. Funnily enough, Wagner had already envisioned this in his music and staging ideas of the original production, but the technology and staging practices of the time were not ready and unable to compose this kind of aesthetics.

This design concept we developed together for *Die Walküre* was to stand the test of time two years later in 2019, when we staged *Das Rheingold*. Early in the first meetings, I had a sense of coming back home; the design process felt more relaxed and the whole creative team, much more confident and trustful. This is, for me, the core of stage arts, the collaboration over time and space where the work grows, and everybody somehow contributes to the making of a true *Gesamtkunstwerk*.

Now at the time of writing this chapter, we are working together on *Siegfried*, which will hopefully premiere in the summer of 2022. I am struck by the importance of the reflection time between the productions, and the collective knowledge we have developed together, but also by how writing this article brings new insights and a change in consciousness, a new active aesthetical realization into the work.

Notes

1 Svoboda's hazer was created for another visual effect in a Wagner opera. See Palmer, 2013, pp.113–114.

8

Light in contemporary Chinese opera

Psyche Chui

Traditional Chinese opera is a complex art based on multifaceted aesthetic elements. Many of these, such as gestures, movement, facial expressions, costumes and stage properties, are highly stylized:

> A traditional Chinese opera has a plot based on poetry, ingeniously combined with music, dance, as well as acrobatics and martial skills; using recitation style, through acting, mime, diction to perform on a small stage; a presentation of complex literature and art. (Zeng, 1991, p.2, translated by author)

Historically, light in this art form has functioned to support performance and has been bright, white and static while other stage elements have worked in an exaggerated way. This chapter will explore varying concepts of aesthetic values in theatrical representation between Chinese opera and Western theatre and how I integrate these approaches to lighting design in my own practice.

In the performance of Chinese opera, three artistic principles are adhered to: synthesis, stylization and convention. From these, several significant aesthetic elements are further derived: fluidity, plasticity, sculpturality and conventionality. The influences of Buddhism, Daoism and Confucianism heavily inspired artistic development in Chinese opera through the use of Hindu motifs, symbols, styles and forms. Chinese opera is not meant to convey reality but rather to offer something made to give pleasure, convey a mood or suggest an idea through perfect form. For lighting, therefore, there has been no need to be concerned with proper dimension and shadow. Chinese opera achieves the earlier objectives through the conventions of acting, space, properties, costumes, makeup and scenery. This chapter presents an argument about the potential of light in Chinese opera, drawing directly from my practice as a lighting designer working between traditions from the East and West. I will explore contemporary methods of lighting Chinese opera, which are sensitive to the artistic principles of the form but find space for colour and dynamic lighting changes alongside the traditional use of static bright white light.

The aesthetics of Chinese opera encompass all aspects of a production, from the set, costumes and lighting to performance-orientated experiences such as acting and musical accompaniment. Wichmann (1991) argues that Beijing opera 'exemplifies the concept' (p.1) of 'total theatre', defined by Kirby (1969, p.xiii) as 'the place of intersection of all the arts'; 'there must be an effective interplay among the various elements, or a significant synthesis of them'. Such synthesis is integral in Chinese opera where conventionality, as Martin (1999, p.78) notes, 'refers not only to form but also to xie yi, which has no exact equivalent in English but which can be understood as "essence"'. The significant synthesis of all components in an integrated whole can be considered a form of 'total theatre'.

The established 'total theatre' aesthetics of Chinese opera can be further enhanced by allowing light to have a more active role in the performance, in the way that had been previously advocated by Appia and Craig. These key lighting concepts also emerged out of a concern with the intersection of aesthetic elements.[1] Appia's concept of lighting distinguished between simple, diffused light and dramatically accentuated light by basing lighting designs on brightness and the direction of light (shadow value). Similarly, Craig's concept of theatre (Trainor, 2000, pp.160–1) looks for synergistic coordination of all the forces on the stage into a theatrical unity that captures not the illusion of reality but rather the essential spirit of the play. This harmonizes well with one of Craig's 'dreams' of 'a theatre where words and "visions", sounds and colours, dance and music would combine to make a feast for the eyes and ears' (Bablet, 1966, p.199). Craig stressed the need for organic inner rhythm and a sense of continuous and integrally connected movement to which all the various staging elements (acting, design, movement, costume, sound and light) had to be subordinated.

The fundamental aesthetics of Chinese opera apply to all aspects of the stage performance, including regional singing styles, costumes, movement and gestures. Even the performers' appearance and emotional expressions should be seen as beautiful and executed to perfection. The main aim of stylization in Chinese opera is to imitate, sublimate and beautify the real world into the essence of life. Aesthetically, such stylization aims to present constant streams of expression by each performer with the internal aspects of the character being made external.[2] In a similar way, Western lighting design elements can also encompass both expressionistic and symbolic responses to assist in the communication of key ideas. Compared to real three-dimensional objects or obvious actor-gestures, a symbolic response through light can be a less intrusive form of communicating with an audience. Indeed, the art of lighting is a non-material medium of conveying symbols that works freely and with fluidity in space and time.

The rhythm of Chinese opera is significant to both aural and visual elements. It includes the musical rhythm and tempo, singing and movement of the performers, and the flow of the whole performance. But it is as important to use lighting to create the visual rhythm on the stage. From an aesthetic point of view, a complete harmonious rhythm of the aural and visual components is required. The audience must hear the sound, see the shape and the colour and be touched by these audio–visual characteristics. In order to discover the organic merger of these rhythmic components, we have to focus on the colour and intensity of light in response to the music. Thus, the movement of light between states becomes as important as the stage picture in any given moment. The transition of lighting through the tempos of fast or slow movements is achieved by fast or slow fades that synchronize with the music and voices of the performers. Light should be in harmony with the performer and music.

An example of this is in *The Affection in Cold*, adapted from the Yueju opera *Jing Ke, the Loyal Assassin*, by the Zhejiang Xiaobaihua Yueju Opera Theatre and with lighting designed by Zhou Zhengping in 1996. Jing Ke was sent to kill the Qin king in order to rescue the state of Yan – a mission he knew he would never return from. In one scene, the crown prince and his courtiers appear in a mood of sadness and as they escort Jing Ke to the river, white colours dominate the costuming and indicate the colour of mourning. As Jing Ke faces them all and sings, 'Winds cry and the river waters are icy. A brave man goes but can never return', the stage is covered with pure white light to emulate sorrow, in stark contrast to the magnificence of the previous Yan farewell dance scene. Strong drum percussion, synchronized with a series of compelling directional light changes, reflects the bravery of sacrifice and the character's inner emotions. This moment was followed by a sudden loud army drum and a lighting change with twelve sharp beams of light focused on each character now poised in a frozen gesture, while two high-colour-temperature beams highlight Jing Ke to intensify the tension and pull focus to him.

As this brief example shows, because stage lighting is a non-material medium of conveying intentions symbolically, it perfectly fits in with the aesthetic sensibilities of contemporary Chinese opera. Light can be used both to freely interpret emotional feelings and can simultaneously create space and time through its fluidity and plasticity.

Synthesis, stylization and convention

It may be argued that Chinese opera has been most significantly influenced by Daoism:

> Daoism provided the Chinese with a sophisticated philosophical and religious outlook that permeated the dramatic theatre. Many Daoist principles guided Chinese society. Chance, change, spontaneity, non-purpose and reversion to origin serve as keys to understanding the Chinese drama's ideas about the relationship between individuals and society. Early Chinese theatre sought to give free rein to instinct, feelings, imagination, fantasy and idiosyncrasies. (Kuritz, 1988, p.84)

Many of these Daoist principles are reflected in Chinese opera through symbolism and stylization. To properly present such symbolism, performers are required to follow a basic set of aesthetic values: everything within the world of the Chinese opera must be beautiful (*mei*), internally and externally, in both appearance and emotional expression. The main objective of stylization is to make the world of Chinese opera performance look beautiful, in which the stage space stimulates the audience's imagination through the performers' improvisational skills and performance. This symbolic performance should not portray life as it is, but life as extracted, concentrated and typified. In other words, what appears on stage should be a reflection of real life: 'Traditional Chinese opera aims first to strike the audience with a resemblance of life – and then to convey the very essence of life' (Wichmann, 1991, pp.1–3). Therefore, stylization refers to the difference between the behaviour of daily life and its presentation on stage and non-realistic representations of behaviour. The communication of experience and the expression of inner life were qualities that the Chinese opera and the Daoist and Confucius schools of thought shared in common. In opera, these were often manifested in symbolic ways. In contrast,

> Zhan masters in the Dang Dynasty taught a more subjective technique to experience transcendental wisdom using many of the meditative practices of Daoism. Dramatic art became an important way to communicate the experience of nirvana, release from the self. The theatre in China expressed the inner life of things and helped facilitate nirvana. Theatrical art resembled both Daoism and the Sung Dynasty's (960–1279) Confucian idea of intuitive communion with nature through art. (Kuritz, 1988, p.85)

All conventional patterns of performance, which basically come from everyday life, play an important role in Chinese opera. The patterns are formed through artistic refinement in a symbolic way, rather than a realistic transfer of life to the stage. The actors rely upon these conventional patterns of performance to express the ideas and sentiments of their characters.

Acting gestures, costume, makeup, scenery and properties have been the trademarks of traditional Chinese opera.[3] I am questioning whether it is possible to make these aesthetic conventions more easily understood through enhancing the environment and atmosphere by referencing Western concepts of theatrical lighting. Generally, traditional Chinese opera lighting consists of bright white light with few cue changes and offers little aesthetic value to the production. Instead, it serves the primary function of visibility – to illuminate the stage to let the audience see the gestures, movements and facial expressions of the performers. Together with the performers' vivid costumes, makeup and painted faces, the bright lighting creates a high intensity of energy on stage.

I believe it is possible to retain the required functions of traditional Chinese opera lighting while enhancing the visual elements using Western styles of theatrical lighting, and I will further elaborate by briefly exploring some of the conventions used in sound, acting, settings, properties, costumes and makeup.

Elements of traditional Chinese opera

In 'the function of the introduction to a scene' (Hu, 1993, p.173), dramatist and critic Li Yu cites a convention of Chinese opera: '[T]here is always a "long introduction", followed by a couplet or a poem, the whole called "speech to set the scene", meaning that before the speech the audience does not know what the play is about, but after it they do and will settle down to listening' (Hu, 1993, p.173). In Chinese opera, 'the long introduction' and the 'speech that sets the scene' create the atmosphere, mood or emotional tone of the actors. It is critical at this point for the lighting designer to also establish conventions to secure the particular role and function of light in each performance.

Scenic decoration is usually limited to a carpet, a wooden table and two chairs placed before an elaborate satin embroidered curtain hanging between the two upstage doors (Duhalde, Tian and Wong, 2019). These objects can convey a multiplicity of meanings, and settings, depending on how they are arranged. A simple table and ordinary straight-back chairs could be arranged to suggest a throne, a bench, a tower, barriers or various obstacles for example. Chairs might become beds, walls, bridges or trees, and tables become hills or clouds.

Typical properties serve the same flexibility as scenic pieces. Placing an incense burner on the table can represent a palace, without the need for a literal or illustrative set or lighting changes. Performers show this flexibility in their interactions with props, and can, for example, show the traits of a character through the manipulation of different styles of a handheld fan through hand gestures with musical accompaniment.[4] A complex set of formal, symbolic gestures and objects fills the space with evocative images, suggesting the spirit of an object rather than its physical appearance.

One might ask what effect lighting might have in relation to the symbolic meanings of scenery and properties – especially where visible shadows can be seen as aesthetically problematic:

> Chinese art had no shadows or perspective because art was not an imitation of reality but something made to give pleasure, convey a mood and suggest an idea through perfect form. The Chinese artist sought a rhythm and an accurate line that suggested or symbolized the soul of a thing. Excellence in technique, rather than innovation in perception or power of feeling, seems Confucianism's contribution to the Chinese aesthetic. (Kuritz, 1988, p.86)

Contemporary settings which may be more intricate appear to require a new approach to stage lighting. Traditional Chinese opera lighting has centred on the bright and general illumination of setting, scenery and performers without creating strong shadows. Contemporary approaches to performance lighting (for instance, in Liu Xinling and Zhou Zhengping's designs for *The Peony Pavilion* at World Stage Design in 2017) offer potential not only for illumination of the setting and scenery but can also serve as new plasticity that gives shape and form to the look of a design and provides dimension and depth for the performers and the set on stage. In a Chinese opera production, the sustaining of an actor's high energy during a performance is essential, and therefore the requirement of bright light with tints of colour is of paramount importance. Even with these requirements, however, lighting can shape the perception of depth, texture, shape and pattern to create different kinds of atmosphere and environment in which the audience's imagination is free to interpret in new ways.

The use of aural conventions in Chinese opera was influenced by the contribution of Confucian thought to Chinese aesthetics. The Chinese artists sought a rhythm and an accurate line to suggest or symbolize the soul of a thing by using the individual elements of the music and their combinations to express specific emotions. However, aural conventions in Chinese opera require audience members to know their ascribed meanings beforehand. Very few aural conventions are immediately understandable without prior knowledge of their significance. Aural conventions can assist in presenting the internal and external conditions of characters and in creating the rhythm and tempo of the performance.

Using the theatrical conventions of song, speech and movement to express emotion, Chinese audiences appreciate correct pronunciation and strict adherence to rhythm. Speech and song are thus carefully timed to the players' movements. Singing is controlled by these conventions, for example, in the actors' codified gestures, such as the act of walking in a large circle, which connotes travelling a great distance. Other stylized gestures convey opening doors, climbing stairs and rowing boats. As an alternative approach to traditional Chinese opera lighting, light can enhance this virtual movement by visually transporting the audience through the mood and atmosphere in different scenes and becoming a unified part of the production. Frequently, in Western lighting designs, the lighting acts as a vehicle to transport the audience, not only through the time and space, but through the variation of mood and atmosphere.

Conventions used in Chinese opera can also indicate locations. The brushing down of a costume, for example, may signify an actor finishing a lengthy journey. Other movements might indicate travelling long, twisty roads. The bending or dodging of imaginary objects suggests walking through a wooded area or undergrowth. Up and down gestures in places can indicate the climbing of mountainous terrain. The audience can easily understand these actions even though they are conveyed through entirely symbolic forms of expression.[5] In order to create the best visual elements for use in a scene, characterization is an important consideration for the lighting designer in Chinese opera particularly the function of each character and the important relationships between them, and who should be the focus of attention at any given moment. A lighting designer must consider the audience's impression of the characters being portrayed by merging the emotional projections of the performer with the mood created by the lighting design.

In the conventional areas of costume and makeup, Chinese opera costumes were made to create impressive dramatic effects and to specify subtle nuances of characters. Symbolic colours and motifs, derived from traditional patterns, followed strict conventions for rank, status and character personality. For example, royalty is clothed in yellow, and the long silk *Shui Xiu* water sleeves resemble rippling water when extended. In this context, as an alternative to a traditional approach to Chinese opera lighting, selective lighting or using lighting to pull focus, can be used to highlight certain performers and areas of the stage that the audience is meant to see at a particular moment. This shift in focus is often imperceptible so that the audience is unaware that their focus of attention is being shifted.

Makeup is used to define a character in a conventional and symbolic manner and the essence of a character is often seen in the colours and patterns of their makeup.[6] As an alternative approach to traditional Chinese opera lighting, the psycho-physical qualities of colour, quality and intensity of light can be used to create the mood and feelings of the character in order to enhance expressions of beauty and nature.

The unique body movement accompanying Chinese music and costume design displayed in Chinese opera creates a special opportunity for the application of a lighting design that would serve to enhance these performance elements. Even to experienced Chinese opera audiences, these movements can be perplexing. For example, putting hands behind the back indicates anxiety or imminent danger, while rubbing hands together indicates that a character is worrying. In these situations, lighting can assist the audience in understanding the emotional tones of the moment. The task of creating a tangible atmosphere or mood – be it serious, comic, tragic or romantic – often relies on the skill of the lighting designer in Western theatre. For example, in a production of *The Zoo Story* by Edward Albee, lighting designers Streader and Williams note the 'two separate characters, and the unstable whole man they occasionally create, must be reflected in the approach to lighting' (1985, p.64). It is the expressive nature of light that allows the audience greater insight into the characters, and this potential of light is of critical importance when approaching a lighting design. Contemporary Chinese opera can additionally use the power and potential of contemporary stage lighting tools and techniques such as automated computerized lighting, video projection, effect projection, gobo and animation disc effects to create this kind of illusion (see Plate 22).[7]

Moods, especially those of passion, are often translated into songs in Chinese opera, rather than suggested through light. However, some moods, such as grief or commemoration, are often represented with less passionate energy and tend to lead to a more oppressive atmosphere. Conversational dialogue can also be accompanied by music when emotions of surprise, fright or even love are expressed. The music and singing in Chinese opera, which in contemporary Chinese opera also requires stage lighting to interpret the characters' moods, allows an audience to clearly understand the feelings and emotions of the actors.

It may seem obvious to a Western audience that lighting helps to establish the setting of the scene, the season, the time of day, as well as all interior and exterior atmospheric conditions. It is used for more than simply illuminating the stage. In Western theatre, firelight, candlelight, sunlight and moonlight are all made believable by lighting elements that back up and establish the nature of the emulated light source, but these elements are traditionally represented through gestures in Chinese opera. However, the artistic use of bright general lighting has its own functional and aesthetic value and can be artfully applied to many scenes. For example, for productions that incorporate a degree of acrobatics and martial art skills, which involve very fast action, good visibility must be provided to enable the audience to see all the movements and gestures clearly, such as in the 1999 production of *The Crossroads*. In this production when Song Jiang and Yan Xi Jiao awaken, although the light does not give any suggestion of dawn, the audience understands that night has passed. This is because of the stylized symbolism of traditional Chinese opera, in which time is indicated by diction and movement. In *The Crossroads*, the movement of the two men somersaulting under a brightly lit stage demonstrates to the audience that they are groping and fighting in the dark. Through the performers' acting, with musical accompaniment that was representative of their movements, a dark environment was portrayed on stage through the audience's influenced imagination.[8]

The Taming of the Shrew: A case study

To show how these traditional elements of Chinese opera might be enhanced by applying Western lighting techniques that offer more than mere illumination, I will discuss the Hong Kong Academy for Performing Arts' Chinese opera production of *The Taming of the Shrew* (2014). The lighting was co-designed by John A Williams and me, aiming to create a meeting of East and West. The production combined multidisciplinary theatrical styles of acting, singing and dance into a single production and special consideration was therefore given to the way lighting was used to 'illuminate' the diversity of styles: modern drama, contemporary dance, Chinese dance and Chinese opera. The play-within-a-play for *The Taming of the Shrew* was a Chinese opera interpretation of Shakespeare's work, performed in a traditional Chinese opera style against a backdrop of a contemporary set and lighting design.

It is perhaps important to note at this point that there was East/West diversity within the creative team. The producer/show director, Ceri Sherlock, was from the UK with a background in theatre, film and television, while the director of the Chinese opera piece, Hu Zhifeng, was Chinese, from Mainland China. John is also from the UK with a background in regional and commercial theatre both in the UK and internationally, while my background as a lighting designer is similar to John's except I am based in Hong Kong. John has lit Western opera and I Chinese opera. Between us, John and I have lit over 400 productions, including plays, contemporary dance, ballet and Chinese dance (all types of performance which were to be included in this production), so we were able to draw on those experiences, conceiving a lighting design and light rig that would serve the requirements of all of these art forms.

It was clear from the outset that Hu Zhifeng wanted her piece to be in the style of traditional Chinese opera. The staging area would be defined by a carpet with only a table and two chairs as set pieces, and costumes and makeup would be traditional. She was keen that lighting should not distract from or in any way change the makeup or performers' movements. Ceri was equally clear that the Chinese opera piece should not look bland and that the lighting needed to offer more than mere visibility, as might be found in more traditional productions of Chinese opera with the primary use of flat, white light. Of course, I shared the same ambition for the contribution of light and set about considering how we could still keep a traditional look for the opera while employing what might be considered to be Western lighting techniques.

As a student, I remember John (then my professor and dean at the Hong Kong Academy for Performing Arts) including in one of his lectures a trend developed by some UK lighting designers in the 1970s and early 1980s, influenced by Brecht's Berliner Ensemble, of using only white light in their lighting designs. As a pioneering lighting designer Rory Dempster, alongside Andy Phillips, established the Royal Court Theatre's white light principle that nothing was more important on stage than seeing the actors' faces.[9] Having met Rory Dempster and seen some of his productions, John explained how Dempster used white light while keeping shape, form and atmosphere. John was very influenced by this style, and he explained how he lit *Titus Andronicus*, *The Changeling* and *Timon of Athens* for the Bristol Old Vic (all directed by Adrian Noble), primarily with white light. I wanted to apply the same principle to the Chinese opera piece within *Shrew*, while surrounding the staged carpeted area with a highly contemporized look using the multimedia technologies we had at our disposal for the other components of the play, thereby satisfying the artistic aims of both directors.[10]

I discussed further with John about his and Dempster's work designing lighting using primarily white light and how it was championed by George Devine at London's Royal Court Theatre in the late 1950s and 1960s. Without moving light technology or the high colour temperatures that some light sources have today, the available colour palette was defined by the characteristics of conventional tungsten or tungsten–halogen fixtures. There was a critical choice of fixtures, either using a high lamp wattage that could be dimmed to warm a scene yet still provide visibility, or using lower wattage fixtures at full to give a contrasting whiter light. Careful consideration was given to the use of fixtures projecting either a hard or soft light; the extensive use of high side light to sculpt an actor's shape gave dimension, and backlight was used to add depth. This might seem obvious, but it was how the light levels were balanced using only white light that became the defining factor. As can be seen in Plate 23, we used only white light to illuminate the Chinese opera performers on the carpeted stage, while creating an atmosphere and spatial perspective with a contemporized, colourful look around the playing area.

Although I had moving lights at my disposal, I decided to only use conventional light fixtures to light the staged area of the Chinese opera piece. We had a sufficient number of fixtures to light the stage carpeted area from the front, a substantial number of fixtures for high side light, and a measured number of fixtures for backlight, all open white, without colour filters. I used the diversity of fixtures, their output and their position to balance the lighting states for each scene of the opera while at the same time employing moving light technologies and video/projection mapping around the outside of the staged area (as seen in Plate 22), to create a dynamic spatial perspective, transforming time and space according to the rhythm of the dialogue, movement and gestures of the performers with the accompaniment of music.

The distinctly contrasting methods worked well. Using white light to light the Chinese opera artists within their performing area, in juxtaposition with saturated colour elsewhere, contemporized the traditional opera elements while not detracting from the performers' gestures, makeup and costumes. This fascinated the audience as many had not seen such a combination of styles before.

New audiences

The cultural heritage of Chinese traditional theatre, which comprises more than 360 uniquely varied forms, must be preserved. At the same time, creative development of these traditional styles should be encouraged or they will be threatened with theatrical extinction. If well nurtured, this heritage could develop into a vital and thriving form of national expression.

A new generation of audience has emerged with a new interpretation of aesthetics and creative arts, often inspired by engagement with multimedia and visually orientated cultural work. Their interpretation of the aesthetics of creative arts is often considered a mixture of fast-paced multimedia, with trends changing and diversifying frequently. Therefore, I feel that if younger audiences are to be attracted to contemporary Chinese opera, there is a need to include some exciting and fascinating audio–visual theatrical elements to capture their imagination.

Lighting elements can assist in the preservation of some of the more complex features of Chinese opera by helping to decode the symbolic meanings attached to them. At the same time, lighting design can be useful in indicating time, location, character, atmosphere and mood of the characters or setting, rather than relying solely on their traditional form of expression in the performers' performance.

The contemporary Chinese opera lighting designer has the opportunity to influence the audience's visual perception. Lighting is not only to be used for general illumination; theatre lighting can be used effectively to express the actors' emotions, control the rhythm of the performance, create mood and atmosphere, form a visual perspective on stage and produce special effects. With the additions of new media technologies, such as multimedia projection, LED screens and automated lighting, Chinese opera can be brought into the twenty-first century.

In summarizing these thoughts, contemporary Chinese opera productions are grasping the same opportunity for the development of technical stage and lighting features as found in Western theatre productions. Present-day audiences have become accustomed to and have an expectation for a high level of technical sophistication in a production. A contemporary Chinese opera company production that employs such twenty-first-century techniques could see new faces in their audiences.

Conclusion

As I have shown in this chapter, it is possible to merge a Western style of lighting design with productions of contemporary Chinese opera, resulting in a new aesthetic experience and a synthesis of forms. Elements of Western lighting can be applied to Chinese opera and can therefore be used, in part, as a style to light contemporary Chinese opera. As in Western lighting, a three-dimensional style of lighting can better establish the physicality of the performer by the greater use of back, side and top light. This, in addition to the use of hard and soft light for key and fill, can sculpt the performer in relation to the scenery and backdrops and create a greater depth of field, further complementing the visual appearance of the stage. Furthermore, the selective use of complementary colours in lighting can enhance the vivid colours of the costumes and the sets typically used in Chinese operas. As in Western lighting, the employment of selective focus, rather than the general full-stage illumination that is currently in most traditional productions, can assist the dramaturgy by focusing the audience's attention to specific characters or parts of the stage that are of importance at any particular moment.

It can be considered that contemporary lighting concepts rather than established or traditional approaches can successfully enhance the aesthetic quality of contemporary Chinese theatre. The aesthetics of lighting design are based on the forms of plasticity, fluidity, sculpturality and conventionality, and in combination can create or enhance visibility, selective focus, modelling, psychological effects, time factors, mood and atmosphere in order to enrich the beauty of expressions. In applying these elements, contemporary Chinese opera can become more visually interesting to today's audiences and its aesthetic elements more easily interpreted. The increasing popularity of multimedia and other new technologies in the performing arts may be a factor in the decline in audience numbers attending contemporary Chinese opera productions,[11] and this decline may be mitigated by the increased visual appeal of the dynamic lighting I am proposing.

The development of worldwide communication and technological advancements in the field of performing arts has given rise to many famous contemporary Chinese opera productions, including Zhou Zhengping's lighting design for Yue Opera Ban Zhao at Hangzhou Yue Opera Theatre, which uses multimedia projections to transform the performance space. Zhou's lighting design work on this production was exhibited at World Stage Design 2013 in Cardiff, Wales. Since then, Zhou has also exhibited his work at World Stage Design in Taipei in 2017 and won Best Lighting Design at the Prague Quadrennial of Performance Design and Space in 2019, showing the potential of this approach to appeal to worldwide audiences.

From a historical viewpoint, we can see that the simple outdoor venues used by Chinese opera productions, lit under natural daylight, in many ways served to define the features of Chinese opera. Whatever changes are made or might be forthcoming in Chinese opera, one feature will remain constant: a high enough level of illumination for the performers and other elements to be seen and for the energy level to be maintained. There are three important considerations that must be taken into account:

First, for the pantomime and acrobatic scenes of a production (typically as used in the production of *The Crossroads*), high intensity levels are required in order to sustain the presentation of energy of the performers and to ensure the audience can see the symbolic values of the movements and gestures.

Second is a consideration of visibility. Traditional conventions such as posture and movement of the various parts of a character's body, both in isolation and of the entire body in or through the space of the performer, must be clearly seen. Lighting must help the audience to see a performer's characterization and to appreciate the aesthetic values of stylization in gesture and posture.

Third is mood and atmosphere. In Chinese opera, 'the long introduction' and 'speech' that sets the scene will create the atmosphere and set the mood or emotional feelings of the characters. Thus, traditionally, stage lighting in Chinese opera has played an insignificant role in providing mood and atmosphere or as a tool to draw an audience's attention to different locations.

In defining a new model of lighting that may work for Chinese opera, it may be of value to assimilate the following points of significance:

The conventions used in traditional Chinese opera are not always easily understood. The nature of Chinese opera, in its fluidity, plasticity, its sculptural qualities and its conventionality, can be applied to the concepts of lighting design. By using these visual elements through light, the audience can more easily understand the traditional conventions that are used to convey expressions, denote space, time and so forth.

Western lighting concepts of psychological responses associated with colour can also be applied to enhance the scenery and properties (examples can be seen in *The Taming of the Shrew* images), and to assist in properly interpreting the stylization of Chinese opera styles, such as commonly used movements and gestures; as a means of creating mood and atmosphere for varying scenes or moments; and to create visual climaxes and expressions.

To apply Western lighting concepts relating to the psychological aspects of space and form lighting design can enhance the visual dynamism of the performance and perspective of the stage space by pulling focus to localized areas of the stage and by texturing the stage with the use of gobo mottling or other special effects. Similarly, Western lighting concepts of rhythm and movement can be applied in order to harmonize with the music and synchronize with the dancer/actors. This can be achieved by analysing the opera in order to understand the total orchestration of the Chinese opera – its story/theory/structure/characterization and so on – and creating the flows, tensions and climaxes in the opera.

Transforming the current two-dimensional form of Chinese opera into a three-dimensional event can be achieved by applying the principles of fluidity/plasticity and the sculptural qualities of Western theatre lighting design. By considering all of the aforementioned possibilities, it is important to be aware that simply adopting a Western style of lighting design into a light plot for a Chinese opera will not work. There is a balance to be maintained if the fusion is to be successful. A lighting design that heavily relies upon dramatic directional or key lighting would create overly strong elements of light and shadow and would only result in the performer-orientated Chinese opera becoming more difficult for Chinese audiences to see and comprehend. Any use of overly saturated colours may reduce or even nullify the vivid colour ranges that are used in Chinese opera costuming, makeup and/or scenic elements. The director and lighting designer of a Chinese opera must be particularly astute when utilizing the Western method of 'selective focus'. Too much selective focusing may distract from the entirety of a stage performance where, unlike many Western operas that cast large choruses, all performers on stage in a Chinese opera have an essential relevance to a scene.

If lighting can re-define the representation of fluidity in the modern stage space in the Western theatre, then I believe lighting can also have an important role in the re-creation of the aesthetic values of traditional Chinese opera. This may be particularly true in the form of representation, expression and synthesis. In order to enhance the aesthetic of 'total theatre' and preserve the traditions of Chinese opera, as well as support the revitalization of Chinese opera for future generations, lighting must play a role. This can be achieved to a large extent by carefully adopting concepts of Western theatre lighting.

Notes

1 As exemplified in the work of Adolphe Appia and Edward Gordon Craig in the nineteenth century. (See Palmer, 1985, p.136; Trainor, 2000, pp.106–11; and Bablet, 1966, p.199.)
2 Watch *An Introduction to Peking Opera / Beijing Opera* at https://www.youtube.com/watch?v=SQSsL3I_Kac.
3 For more on the origins and conventions of Chinese opera, see Taiwan Review (1958) and Duhalde, Tian and Wong (2019).
4 See https://kknews.cc/photography/jrp5kby.html for an example of this.
5 Examples of this can be seen in Yandang Mountain for Beijing Opera (https://www.youtube.com/watch?v=HAo8Eyia420) and in the mime scene in *Autumn River* for Beijing Opera: (https://www.youtube.com/watch?v=9O6ZohS9M7E).
6 For example, the Jing can be very brave or very evil; his face is powdered and lustreless. The Chou character has white patches around the eyes and on the nose; the amount of white is determined by the extent of the clown's cunning.
7 Water flags (lighting ripple effect): https://www.youtube.com/watch?v=sVS6KIwJZUU (6:00–7:16) and wind flags (thunderstorm effect): https://www.youtube.com/watch?v=sVS6KIwJZUU (7:20–9:52).
8 See https://www.youtube.com/watch?v=IabMSb6LV7s.
9 In fact, Rory Dempster later co-founded a lighting company called White Light (https://www.whitelight.ltd.uk/).
10 Further images of this production can be seen at https://www.hkapa.edu/30th-anniversary/gallery/the-taming-of-the-shrew-photo.
11 https://factsanddetails.com/china/cat7/sub41/item2261.html.

9

RashDash

Fusing feminism and light

Katharine Williams

Introduction: A different kind of lighting

This chapter deconstructs the work that I have done with Abbi Greenland, Helen Goalen and Becky Wilkie of RashDash, and how our collaboration on their feminist dance theatre pieces, that also happen to be rock gigs, are an exploration of feminism in lighting design. The collaboration we have together, and the light art that those conversations become, is what happens when lighting becomes a feminist character in each project.

I'll start by including part of the card that writer Ellie Kendrick gave me on the press night of *Hole* at the Royal Court (another show that I made with Abbi and Helen). The card begins: 'Thank you for making the lighting in this show a living, breathing character that stuns me every night. You have found a beautiful language that speaks so eloquently. Well fucking done.'

So, what does that have to do with the process of fusing feminism and light?

A whole lot, it seems.

And so we begin.

~

A personal process

Lighting design for live performance is quite possibly the oddest art form to choose as an artist. It is ridiculously process heavy, in terms of the amount of work and absorption of the subject matter that you need to ingest in order to even start planning the art. And then there is the unwieldiness of the process itself, from the number of people-hours needed to assemble your lighting toolkit, through to the process of creating art during a technical rehearsal with so many pressures from inside and outside the process. So much of it is done at a time when you are not ready to make decisions because you've not seen enough of the show that you are collaborating on (because it isn't made yet) and still, you must make the decisions because it is the time in the process at which they have to be made.

It's daft, really: a massively complex art form that is unmanageable and nebulous and hugely stressful. But it is a huge part of the artist that I am. And the good bits, where you get to work in flow, connected to the technical process of the whole show, those moments are precious.

I'm an artist and a storyteller. In other parts of my practice, I tell stories with words.

In my lighting design practice, I tell stories with light.

Having light as your medium is hugely useful in terms of feminist theatre, because, as we'll get to in examining *Two Man Show*, almost every element of the English language exists in the context of patriarchy and has been shaped by patriarchy, so sometimes there literally aren't the words to tell a story outwith the patriarchal context. This is where light, choreography and music take over to tell a different story.

~

Two Man Show

Two Man Show is feminist to the core. It explores the relationship that we all have with Man, with men and with the patriarchy, but those explorations are by three women. Becky, Abbi and Helen make music, dance, act and sing. They shift shape regularly between inhabiting the masculine and inhabiting the feminine, most notably as they dance together.

There is something radical about this. We so rarely see women's bodies with the freedom to express themselves in the way that men's bodies do, and the freedom that Abbi and Helen channel as they move and dance is breathtaking. They've been dancing together for many years, and they know each other's bodies intimately, like they are extensions of each other. Again, powerful and radical and feminist and unforgettable all at once.

Much of the show is performed in various states of dress/undress, including nakedness, not because of some weird concept about sexiness and titillation (although the fact that I even have to qualify that demonstrates the need for feminist theatre even in this day and age) but because in exploring the physicality of how you channel these two energies of femininity and masculinity, it turns out that the one thing you need is freedom. And that somehow, clothes seem to get in the way of that.

Light in *Two Man Show* was absolutely set to become seemingly a living and breathing thing that would dance with the women on that stage – light to support, illuminate and dance with three fe(male) forms. The conversations I found myself having with the team considered what were the most feminist choices that light could make as a character. In addition, finding the flavour and the texture of what that light was, and how the quality of it worked with those three women, that was the game.

We are used to seeing naked female forms in a relatively limited number of ways in UK society. We see almost-nakedness far more often: we see almost-naked women in adverts, in the media and occasionally on our beaches or in our parks. If we start by stating that matter-of-fact nakedness (the kind you experience in naturism or in shared changing rooms) is fairly unusual, and then acknowledge that these women are on a stage, that means we can consider the more 'usual' (albeit unusual) ways of seeing naked women: in porn, or very occasionally in a love scene in a film, or perhaps in erotic photography.

Light in porn is generally overly bright, overly harsh and relatively cold. It appears to be designed to give the highest resolution for camera of the events being filmed, and there seems to be very little art or storytelling to the approach: it is all about serving the cishet male gaze with the maximum amount of stark imagery possible. What is missing from that light is humanity.

Lighting for love scenes, and erotic photography, seems to go to the other extreme: they romanticize the female form so much that it loses its power somehow. The warmth and generosity that is missing from those lighting states in porn becomes oversaturated and over-romantic in this context.

So what did we need for *Two Man Show*? Well, for starters a lighting tool kit and a language that goes against the clichés but absolutely supports the powerful vulnerability of the women on stage.

Light that is a character in its own right, that has opinions about the action and agency to illustrate those opinions by what it does.

Light that makes discernible choices that the audience can see and understand, as it shapes and illustrates the show.

Light that can dance with them as the drumbeats kick in.

Light that supports Helen as she stands centre stage on a pedestal like a classical statue, so we observe her form as a work of art.

Light that accesses the growling rage of centuries of being silenced.

Light, in haze, that becomes the cold, exposing, pointing finger of the patriarchy.

There were, as ever, practical constraints. The show was to be in traverse format, and a very intimate traverse at that: studio-theatre scale and opening at the Edinburgh Fringe, so with huge constraints in terms of the number of lanterns and dimmers we could use as well as a venue with a lighting grid not much higher than your living room ceiling. And this piece of dance theatre wildly needed sidelight to sculpt the bodies.

As always, collaboration was the answer. The main structures of Oliver Townsend's set were at the two ends of the long traverse stage, and Oli found a way that all the elements of the structures could have small halogen lights mounted on them to give us the dance lighting that we so urgently needed. Being a tungsten source was right on every level for this: the bodies needed a full-wavelength source that would kiss the skin of the performers and which would hold them in humanity.

There were two overhead battens with those same halogen lamps in them which joined the set structures at each end so that, coupled with the deep red dance floor, what you had was a space that completely surrounded the three performers from four sides and both held them in the light and gave them a full environment to perform in.

So the workhorse of the lighting tool kit were those halogen lights that Oli had embraced as part of his design. They looked beautiful in the set and then there was this amazing thing where the set and the lights and the music and the people all danced together (see Plate 24).

Light brought the audience into the stage picture even further (the audience are always in the stage picture in traverse) and made the audience and society beautifully complicit in all the stuff that was being explored.

It was right for *Two Man Show* to be a haze show. Seeing the beams hold the performers, and the beams in haze being more obvious in the wild dance sections, so that they were physically projecting their own pulses (banging their own drums) was an indescribably exhilarating part of the show. We used to dance up at the control position, because the whole space was alive with this animal energy.

The only time I ever used any colour aside from warm and cold white was later in the piece at a key moment where I could feel that we needed a deeper support for the performers, so I brought in a deep, deep red as they accessed an animalistic state in the dance and music. I didn't have a conversation with RashDash about that red, by the way. I could just feel that that was what was needed and so I added it. It looked right, but most importantly, it felt right, too. And when things feel right that impacts the performers and how they play and perform.

So, feminism in light? Well, I've talked about colour and intensity being part of the thing that holds the bodies and isn't too harsh. But what really is feminist about my lighting design for this show?

Okay, so.

Light is a character. What is this character? It is a mix of the political and personal. S/he is genderless, in that s/he chooses whatever form, texture and status s/he wants, as part of the show.

Play is important. The light plays and dances with the three performers.

Confidence is important. The light makes choices. Sometimes it is that aggressive pointing finger of the patriarchy. Sometimes it is a grainy, dark, almost tangible, wrap-around force. Sometimes it bounces and celebrates. Sometimes it is quiet and still, supporting the words and the breath to do the work.

Shapeshifting is important. That confident shapeshifting that I just outlined in the previous paragraph is important because it is part of the feminism of the piece. Why? Because a key aspect of the power in this piece is the fact that it allows all possible versions of being a woman playing a man or playing a woman or playing yourself, and the patriarchal model doesn't usually allow for three women to do that. It has a very specific set of rules for how three women should be, and shapeshifting just ignores that, without even noticing that it isn't toeing the party line. Confidence is feminist. And that's huge.

I mentioned early on in this chapter that RashDash makes feminist dance theatre that also happens to be a rock gig, and I don't think that you can really understate the power of the rock gig stuff. *Two Man Show* is Proper Loud. Powerful. Confident. Writing that makes it sound like something concocted by the 'nasty women' that the patriarchy so hates, and I suppose that is right. It is unashamed.

The publicity for this show says that RashDash is a feminist company 'making an unabashed show about gender and language, masculinity and patriarchy, but the words that exist aren't good enough, so there's music and dance too'.

The words not existing is in some ways what has driven the form of the whole show: the moment where the words stop working so we have to make music and dance instead. What do I mean by that? Well, almost all of the English language, despite its gloriously complex roots and evolution, consists of words hewn from a patriarchal context. Those few words that came into being from outside that have existed through years and years and countless years of the patriarchy and so what happens? What happens is that there are words to speak and write and sing within that context and when you start working outside of that context, the words fail you.

~

There is a reason it has taken me days and weeks and months of fighting with the words to write this section of the chapter. The words often don't exist. When I gave the talk that seeded this chapter into being several years ago, I was fresh from the process of making this show and the process of using words and ideas and the space of a university theatre and drawing with my hands in the air and leaving gaps so that our inner knowing could fill in the rest . . . that process worked. It flowed as easily as the dance in the show.

~

Articulating that process on paper, electronic paper, has been a different beast. The essay format is fundamentally different to the dance-theatre-rock-gig format and my free-flowing talk. And so, in the undeniably more patriarchal format of writing this chapter, I fought with the words, and also with the conviction. When I try to articulate why the lighting for *Two Man Show* was feminist, in this patriarchal context, I run out of words and wonder if it wasn't, really. If my work wasn't good enough. If there is any such thing as feminist lighting, really.

~

And there it is. In that rehearsal room, in that technical rehearsal and in those performances, the work meant that we were outside the patriarchy's grasp. RashDash had made it that way. And so: there was no need for me to articulate my decisions in the context of patriarchy/feminism. I just did what I do best: I worked from the heart. The process is natural, unarticulateable, based totally in freedom, and existing completely in flow. It engages in the intellectual when I do the nuts and bolts of the craft bit, but the art bit dances out of me like I am channelling it. Perhaps the term for this is matriarchal working. Maybe it is channelling the goddess and the divine. But it is what I do and it makes magic.

~

There was magic in that show, and my magic added to it.

~

When RashDash dance, they are the daughters of the witches you couldn't burn.

~

See the spell they cast. See us dance together.

~

The Darkest Corners

There are shows where you know at the development stage that you are working on something really special. *The Darkest Corners* was one such show. At the start of the year, RashDash was already working with the cast and the musicians, and the things that were happening in the rehearsal room, that special RashDash flavour of music/singing/dancing/rock gig were already extraordinary. There was power in this work.

To write about power in the context of *Two Man Show* and *The Darkest Corners* is interesting. That power of holding space, in an environment where you are expressly told that you can't hold space because you are vulnerable: that act of completely non-fragile vulnerability. That is truly powerful. It felt like there was electricity coming out of the rehearsal room. It felt like freedom. Angry freedom. But freedom nonetheless.

The subject matter for *The Darkest Corners* grew out of the Reclaim the Night movement. The show was part of Transform Festival in 2017, and it took place in an outdoor carpark on the border of Leeds' managed red-light zone. The contrast between the vulnerability of the mostly female bodies that performed within the unforgiving harshness of the city's concrete and brick was stark.

Headlights, lamp posts and confident shape shifting

The show was in a car park, it was about women traversing night spaces, and car parks have cars in them.

I think that it was Oli's idea to have cars in the car park, but I literally have no idea whose idea it was for us to use the car headlights as the main part of the lighting tool kit for the show. Maybe his, maybe mine. For the cars to be laid out in a kind of sidelight wash format . . . probably mine. To wire them up so they went through dimmers and we had full control of them . . . definitely mine. To make sure that was possible . . . the brilliant production electrician,

Alan. To keep fighting, in the cold, to get all the headlights working/reworking, that was Alan and Ariane, our lighting technician.

Using car headlights as sidelight was one of the best things I did for that show: it was the key element of the lighting toolkit, and it really paid off. It was a big gamble, though.

First of all, I wasn't sure that they would light far enough up people's bodies, as headlights are focused down to light the road and not blind other drivers. This turned out to be alright. The whole pointed-at-the-road thing wasn't really a problem. The performers were lit well enough, and the floor/landscape around them being lit, too, was good. It placed the human figures in this harsh, industrial landscape and made them more vulnerable. It was good.

I needed to demo the car headlights thing before we committed to using them properly, though. There was one idea that Abbi and Helen wanted to happen that I wasn't sure if it would work or not. It was the idea that a female performer would be lit in a single beam of light (in practice two, the headlights from one car) and that another person could be in darkness outside that beam, and then suddenly step forward into it and appear. It didn't really work. But the beams themselves were so theatrical (and yet utterly right for that place) that of course we were instantly wedded to using them, and the directors found another way to make that moment work.

Those car headlights did a magic thing: they allowed that woman (and the other women in the piece) to be so vulnerable in this industrial space: there was something about the implied violence of a car headlight catching their bodies, and yet that body being sculpted in such a beautiful way that it made her an object of desire or something to be looked at. The male gaze meeting the female form (see Plate 25).

There was one moment in *The Darkest Corners* where Maddie (who played the key female role) danced along a diagonal headlight beam so that she came to dance with her own shadow on the graffitied wall of the backdrop factory building. For some reason, this moment transformed the car headlights from being another of those accusatory pointing fingers that I wrote about before regarding *Two Man Show* into something kinder, more supportive. A holding space, made of light, where Maddie could be free and be herself.

The moving vehicles brought a different energy into the space: more aggressive, with a sense of foreboding travelling with them as they traversed the car park as part of the action of the show. The van headlights that caught Maddie in their beams before one of the male characters leered out of the window at her. The cold internal bus light that preceded the sexual assault that would happen on the bus.

Maddie lit only by a phone screen, tiny in that huge expanse of a space.

A couple lit only by a streetlamp, which they would then climb in a complicated choreography about consent.

And then there was the gig-like theatricality of the lighting battens on the static band trailer, recycled from the *Two Man Show* set and creating a much safer place, with music and song and safety and the atmosphere of a gig. In the dance numbers, that gig atmosphere spilt out into the centre of the car park stage. The headlights and the footlights danced together, as the cast led us into another dimension of the show.

We were certainly up against it with budget, so I made choices about lighting equipment that felt responsible in that context. As ever with these things, most of the money went on power, dimming and infrastructure. And so in the spirit of solidarity, you end up making minimalist choices for the art bit, to honour your commitment to the whole.

I specified a lot of Parcans on the show. They are cheap to hire, they focus (and refocus) fast, and they can deal with being rained on. We made a backdrop of them, in pink, to use in the only colour moment of the show because guess what, everything else was warm white or cold white again! When the Gulabi Gang of vigilante women from India, dressed in pink saris, made their entrance and we first turned them on it was a look and a moment and a feeling that we just hadn't had in the show before (see Plate 26). Sana, the assistant lighting designer, and I used to stand at the lighting desk and that pink blast of backlight would propel the silhouetted women onto the stage. I would feel myself smile and look across to see Sana smiling too.

~

Fusing feminism and light

A lighting designer is regularly the most experienced creative person in a technical rehearsal. Not because of their age or years of experience, but because we have to fit in so many shows back-to-back for economic reasons, and so our nomadic lives mean that we move from technical rehearsal to technical rehearsal. It makes sense to me that we are the ones whose eyes, in every different meaning of that word, have a wide perspective on the stories we tell and how we choose to tell them.

So when RashDash, or a lead artist, or a director bring you onto a project, what they are bringing is all of you. All your politics, all your art, all your ways of existing in the world and navigating it. As an artist, you create work through your own gaze. What else can you do? My gaze is one that has equality and feminism running right through it, so it stands to reason that feminism is a deeply infused part of any lighting design I create. My light makes political decisions as it illuminates, points out, reveals, supports and lets go of things.

I don't know if the light is an embodiment of me: if this is me personally performing through the light. I think it might be. But I never could have articulated it that way until somebody asked me if that is the case, during the writing of this. No wonder Ellie called it a 'living, breathing character' in that card she wrote for me.

My light dances, so the lighting and the words and the dance and the music all fuse together with that essence, and that is when the magic happens.

~

In a RashDash show, everything breathes. Everything dances.

~

Leading the way into the light.

~

10

Reflecting on light

Jennifer Tipton

Light is music for the eye. Music takes us to so many places; light can do the same. One of the ways that music takes us to these places is with its form – or sometimes with its lack of form. I feel that light works in exactly the same way. If you introduce pools of light in the beginning of a piece you have introduced a theme and should therefore use this theme more than once.

My light responds to actors' movement onstage much more than it does to the words spoken. The many themes for the light may be set by the words that are going to be spoken as I know them from reading the play, but then the focus of the composition comes to be on the movement of light using the themes as established. The light responds to the movement of the actors in the same way that it responds to the movement of dancers. The need for a change comes from a movement far more often than it comes from spoken words.

I grew up lighting the Paul Taylor Company on tour. I was the stage manager, as well as the lighting designer, and therefore I called the cues. I learned from my mentor, Tom Skelton, to call cues by counting them backwards. This way everyone knows where zero is and when to stop. By calling cues I could control the way that the change of light in a cue speeds up or slows down. Having been a dancer myself I knew that the counting could be different in each performance because a dancer's timing is a little different each time. Controlling the dynamics in this way taught me the full range of what light feels like and can do. It was good to have that level of control, allowing me to be able to respond to the performers and to have a dialogue with the dancers. Light became a partner to them. When a computer became the only way to control cueing the light I worried that the ability to control the tempo of the changing light was going to be eliminated. What I discovered, of course, is that

I loved the way that the computer made the timing always the same, always consistent. Cues that are longer than twenty or thirty seconds are difficult to do manually. Now, with a computer, one can have cues that are minutes long, that have parts of the cue that are programmed to begin later than when the cue is called, that have control over the timing of individual channels/lights within the cue, and so on. The ability to have different timings with computer control is wonderful. But, as in every circumstance, the tools are only as good as the person using them. It is always the eye that determines the composition of the lighting.

My evolving ideas about light have been greatly influenced by a dancer, Dana Reitz, who for the most part does not use music with her dance because the audience tends to respond to music more quickly than it responds to movement. In working with Dana, I learned that with her movement she can choose to reflect the light or not – she understands light and has learned that when she gives attention to it then the audience will as well. She feels very strongly that if she stands in a downlight, she wants to be in the middle of it. She can feel when it is a pure, straight, downlight. What is true for a downlight she feels is also true for all other lights. Sidelights are precisely from the side, backlights from the back and so on. We have spent much time doing some very precise focusing. Since that time and because of the careful focusing that I have done for her, I am very precise about any focus that I do. The audience may not be conscious of the light, but it is always aware of it in the air even if it is not entirely visible.

Dana also made me aware that between the reflecting of the light by the dancer and the receiving of the reflected light by the audience there is a membrane. There is a point where one flips into the other, shall we say. That point is often exactly where a person enters the beam of light, which then completely changes the perception of that light. It depends mostly on how the light hits the eye both inside and outside of the light. It is as if the person changes from the story listener/viewer to the storyteller by simply stepping into the light (see Plate 27).

Light does not really exist until it hits something. That characteristic is very mysterious and quite wonderful. That mystery is what allows the telling of the story of the dancers, the story of the actors, the story that is happening onstage. The story of the light can sometimes be separate from the other – the two existing parallel to each other. It is the performer who focuses the light onstage; the lighting designer both amplifies and supports that focus.

Necessary Weather is a piece made by Dana and me. It was devised – or perhaps the best word is imagined – by Dana. The light was very present – there in the now with everything else. The first thing Dana asked me was what light I felt was absolutely necessary for the piece. I chose sidelight. She chose the movements that she thought were necessary. We and another dancer put these together and spent a couple of weeks doing workshops and rehearsals. At the end of the two weeks, we invited people who we hoped would support it – financially – to see the piece. It was not finished. We knew how to make an end. We debated for a while about doing that and finally decided that we would not. We would explain that we had not finished and that we wanted to have the end grow out of our work rather than being hastily attached just for the viewing. We got the support. Finding the ending took time, and we allowed it to take that time. This process of taking time became very important to me and for my development. It is not often that one has time, but I learned so much by taking the time to find the stories that are in the depth of a piece rather than on its surface. I learned that to use how the light is reflected by the human body takes time to make mistakes, to realize that you're on the wrong path, that you need to go back and do it another way. A dancer like Dana chooses when to reflect and when not. Most dancers are not aware of the possibility of adding this dimension; it is the lighting designer who chooses when and how to use it.

I fear that I may make some directors feel that I'm being rude, but I like to keep my eyes on the stage even while I'm talking, changing the light so that they can see what I'm talking about. Talking in advance of setting cues is challenging and can be misunderstood and therefore dangerous. We lighting designers, choreographers and directors most often use words that were developed to describe painting when we are talking about light. We use the words, but they do not necessarily mean the same thing to everyone. You can say one thing and another thing pops up in the imagination of the person you are talking to. The light may turn out to be something entirely different when it is put onstage. It can be challenging to speak to directors in advance. Light is so ephemeral. It is easier to speak about light when it is onstage and you can look at it while speaking about the moment. In the end, what light is doing onstage is much more compelling than what it *might* do.

I try to look at each production that I do as an individual piece. I have a way of doing things, but I also like to experiment with other ways. The basic framework is there because I need it to feel confident. The stage or playing space must be lit from the front, the side and the back. This is the general light, and if this light covers the entire stage from each of these angles then there is a possibility to light a dancer or actor anywhere he or she may go. All too often the piece or the staging is not finished when the performers come to the stage. Or the first thing that happens is that the choreographer or director changes some of the staging. It is always wise to have light from various angles that cover the entire stage. But then comes the good part. Choosing the light that is specific to this production will allow the audience to remember it because it is special. This is the thing that challenges me to make the light in each production that I do different. It might be a different colour, it might be a different angle or intensity, but once I find the theme(s) that are appropriate to the piece then I have the key.

Having said that, I can't imagine lighting a dance successfully without sidelight. Of course, I end up using sidelight and frontlight and backlight and diagonal light and all kinds of light. But I begin with sidelight. Everybody says you should light dancers from the side and actors from the front. But what I have discovered is that the light that feels like a true source is the light lighting the face and faces rarely face the front; people are usually speaking to each other. Sidelight in theatre is just as important as sidelight in dance. Sidelight in theatre, as opposed to dance, must come from a higher place to get over the head of the speaking actor in order not to shadow the face of the other.

I think the language for a production has much to do with the way that the director, and the rest of the team, is thinking about the play, thinking about the production. That language might have to do with the range of colour. The distance from warm to cool may be very close in some productions or it may be quite far in other productions. Or there might be a lot of colour in one production and not so much in another.

One must build a vocabulary, the words, for each production. How you put these 'words' together to make sentences is how you make a cue – a change of light. And then you put the sentences together to make paragraphs. These paragraphs tell the story, the story of light, certainly – but also the story of the production, the story of the play. The light plot is a very important part of the process. It gives you that language, that vocabulary to begin. How is it that so often I sit down at the tech table to turn on the first light and realize that after all of the time I have spent preparing the plot I don't have that one light to begin the process (perhaps my ideas about the production have changed, or maybe the director has had other ideas since our discussions). If you don't have the proper tools, if you don't have the vocabulary, you can't speak the language.

I definitely consider myself an artist. What I do as a lighting designer is make three-dimensional compositions in time and space. I did hear somebody once say that a designer answers questions and an artist asks questions. I feel that it is the responsibility of the lighting designer to ask questions. A good playwright is asking questions, and it is not the job of the lighting designer to answer them.

I certainly am a terrible technician even though most people consider lighting designers to be technicians. I feel that it is sad that people do consider designers as technicians (like electricians). All my life I have wanted to make that different. I wanted to change the way that people looked at light and lighting designers. But I have failed. Light is compositional – composition is art – just like in painting and sculpture. It gives me such satisfaction to look at a production that I have lit, at the end of the process, just before the opening and to see the composition, to see how it moves, to see what the time of it is. That is art. Lighting on the stage is art.

I am reminded of being in Spoleto with the Paul Taylor Company early in my professional life. We had several days off so a group of us went to Florence for a break. We decided to go to the Galleria dell'Accademia to see Michelangelo's *David*. One of the (very beautiful) dancers in the group could speak a little Italian. She approached a guard and asked, 'Where is the David?' He took us to it and encouraged us to touch it. I was amazed; the marble felt like flesh – the shape of it in my hand, the texture of it made it feel like flesh. That memory for all of my life has made me remember that the art that I am making is human scale. That what we see is to remind us that it is flesh that we focus.

I teach at Yale in the School of Drama, and in the lighting classes we include the second-year directors. One of the things that I like for the directors to experience is setting a lighting state, looking at it, changing it and then looking at the light again from outside. Another thing that is helpful for any of us who make theatre is to set a lighting state, look at it and then go onstage and feel what it feels like to be in it. In the light feels very different. That is why it is such a skill to be able to find the light on stage. There are actors who are in the dark spot and there are actors who know exactly where the light is. Dancers also have a mixed ability in this department. Those who know where the light is know how to reflect it to the audience, to tell the story. Those who don't often wish that the light could erase them, an odd desire for a performer. Once there was a dancer in the Limón company who came to me one day and said, 'There's a bulb out. I know because it's the one that I put my face in after I do that step.' She knew how to use the light to her best advantage.

I went to Yale thinking that I was going to teach all ways of lighting. Of course, I quickly discovered that I could teach only one way. It's a three-year program, and in the first year I teach my way of lighting, but it's not really teaching. I guide the students through it so that they know it thoroughly, and then I spend the next two years encouraging them to find their own way of doing things. We only have two students a year because of the limited work that we actually do but the two students are totally different people. There is no 'right' way to light, only multiple ways. Instead, I say, 'This is not a good idea because . . . ' or 'There's a better idea than this because . . . '. I'm not a teacher but a provocateur.

As a teacher, you have to look at your own practice. I have always said that I would stop teaching before I stopped lighting, but because of the pandemic, I have stopped lighting before I have stopped teaching. It is much less satisfying to me because my work outside of school is not feeding into my teaching; I don't feel like I'm a teacher. I need that. I need the outside world to feed into the school world. When I started teaching, I heard myself saying things about light, and I said to myself, 'If I really believe this, I should change what I'm doing.' I had not been practising what I believed. I definitely became a better lighting designer after I started listening to myself and doing what I said I should do.

My eye does like incandescent light, particularly on skin. I recently lit *To Kill a Mockingbird* on Broadway, mostly with incandescent light. Because there's a tour coming up, I am being forced to redo it with intelligent lights, which all have non-incandescent sources of various kinds in them. It's been a steep learning curve for me.

I began as a lighting designer for dance, and the first big theatre production I did was with Andrei Serban as director, at the Lincoln Center Theater, of Chekhov's *The Cherry Orchard*. Santo Loquasto designed the costumes and scenery. It was a pretty remarkable set in a huge space. It was quite wonderful. We got to the second act, which takes place at dusk. Andre suggested that it might be actually dark. He meant DARK; he meant no light. Coming from dance, that was not an idea that I would have entertained at all, but I tried it. It was amazing; it made the voices sing out in the darkness in a way that I had never experienced in the theatre. Once I made the change I had to go back and adjust all the other cues; the range of intensity was different now. In this production we lit the third act, which is the party, completely with candles – a huge number of candles. Later, during a blackout in New York, we were the only theatre that could still have a performance. We did the whole performance in candlelight.

After that, I began using darkness in other design work. Dan Wagoner wanted to do a dance piece in the dark. We did not quite manage that because we were at Judson Church, and there was an uncovered window with the light from a streetlamp streaming in. It was not total darkness, but you had to listen to see this dance. I lit *Don Giovanni* directed by Sir David McVicar in Belgium; it was the first time I had worked with him. There was a wonderful, big, L-shaped wall in one scene. David asked me if I had ever considered having the space be totally dark causing what seemed to be the shadow of the wall. I had not considered that; we tried it. It was wonderful and appropriate; I loved it, but I never would have done it on my own. I needed to have a director to encourage me to work with darkness.

I worked a lot with Twyla Tharp, who talked about shadows as if they had substance. I wanted to fold up some shadows and put them in a box and give them to her for Christmas. It was very interesting to be able to work with shadow in that way. Twyla's shadows seemed to become people who had character separate from the bodies making the shadows. I have often wondered what was going on in her mind, but I never asked her.

I find that, in America, lighting designers are more often the initiators of their light. In Britain, I find that directors want to be in control of the light.

British lighting designers bring many suggestions and ideas to directors who then pick what they feel is best. It's a different approach. American designers must develop the entire design for the production, which leads to a necessity to change more than one part if the director asks for a change that affects another part.

Only by starting early enough to make the space with the set designer and the director can a lighting designer really be part of a true collaboration. That happens so rarely. The light is shaped by the space and, therefore, shaped by the set. It is nice to be included early enough to say, 'Oh, if you really want light like this, then you need to somehow change the set a bit to get a light in there.' That is hard to say when one is simply presented with the finished model. Early in my professional life, I looked at a model during a presentation and just knew that it would be a problem. But I didn't say anything. It became a problem for more than the lighting; the actual set had to be changed. I said to myself, 'From now on, I've got to say something.' But I do find it hard. The set design for *The Front Page* had a ceiling, and I felt that the ceiling kept the actors from being really well seen. I advocated for eliminating the ceiling from a lighting perspective rather than as an aesthetic choice for the design, and the director finally agreed with me. One has to do it, just gently. It is easier when you are there in person. Most collaborations happen over long distances; everybody is so busy. It is hard enough to get two people together, much less four or five. And let's face it: there are productions, rare productions, that pay a lighting designer a lot of money. Doing a large number of productions is about making a living. There is a balance between being able to spend more time on a production and being paid fairly for that invested time. Sometimes you can't always have both. There's just not much money in theatre.

My hope is that things will change here with the rupture, as I call it, of the pandemic. I don't think audiences are going to flood back to the theatre, and we depend on our audiences. Playing to half an audience does not pay for a production. A full audience doesn't pay for it so certainly half an audience does not. We shall see. A director friend of mine said, 'Wouldn't it be nice if instead of supporting institutions so much, people supported artists?' We'll see.

When I work with the Wooster Group, we rehearse with the light, the costumes, the makeup – and it takes years to develop the work. It is wonderful to have that kind of time; what happens is there are all these ideas, many of which do not make it into the final product. It becomes a soup. All the ideas come together; some drop to the bottom, but they are all part of the mixture. Working in these ongoing collaborations with the investment of time means that you don't need to talk with words. You talk with light. You have it there to look at. I feel very lucky to have had those times in my life to do that.

SECTION 3

Meaning

CHAPTER 5

Meaning

11

Aesthetics, materiality and meaning-making in scenographic light

Katherine Graham

The scope of light's scenographic action is vast and complex, and even somewhat weird. There is a fundamental strangeness to the light that ebbs and flows through a performance, to the constructed light that operates on an ever-shifting rhythm, that can transform objects in its path, and that creates instability around all that it envelops. In the creative and experiential encounter of performance, light sits between the material and the immaterial; we can sense its shifts kinaesthetically, we can trace its path through space and feel as though it could be apprehended haptically; light itself cannot actually be touched, and yet – if we are close enough to the sources – we can feel its heat on the skin, or, following Bachelard (1988), be drawn to reverie by its rhythms and glimmers. In addition to these bodily sensations of light, there is also, throughout the Western philosophical tradition, a metaphorical relationship between light and understanding. In an essay charting provocative and generative capacities of light, Joanne Zerdy and Marlis Schweitzer note that metaphorical resonances of light contribute to its material affectivity in performance, but also that such metaphors 'help us to read and interpret collective cultural and artistic performances in a fresh, new way' (2016, p.17). Elsewhere, Hans Blumenberg charts the history of light as a metaphor for truth, arguing that changing metaphors of light underpin wider shifts in world-understanding and self-understanding (1993, p.31). In this vein, common practices of theatrical lighting, such as 'selective visibility' (McCandless, 1958;

Pilbrow, 1997), directing the eye of the seer towards the 'most important' elements, are manifestations of a kind of thinking in practice. Accordingly, the traditionally established values of clarity in theatrical lighting are deeply tied to notions of representational seeing and to ideas of light as a means of providing understanding.

As a material of performance, then, light is both a substance that is encountered through the body, and a material that provides an offer to the imagination, indicating or presenting ideas in performance. This plurality, or this enfolding of the sensory and the cognitive, is an important, though under-explored, aspect of light's operation and its significance in performance. As Joslin McKinney (2013) has persuasively argued, the experiential encounter with scenography is a valuable site of understanding, and, moreover, the denigration of the bodily encounter with performance, or spectacle – tracing back in Western theatrical traditions to Aristotle – is productively troubled by scenographic practices which 'can stimulate aesthetic and intellectual engagement with the world rather than simply provide a diversion from it' (McKinney, 2013, p.64). In the same vein, there remains a great deal more to be explored about the nature of light in performance and about the generative and meaning-making potential of this immaterial material.

In tracing such generative and meaning-making potentiality of light in performance, this chapter uses the term 'scenographic light' to encapsulate the range and depth of light's operation in live performance. With the term 'scenographic light' I mean to do two things. First, quite simply, I intend to explicitly position light in relation to scenography. Light is widely acknowledged as a constituent of scenography, but there remains more to be uncovered about the particular ways in which light works to inscribe meaning in space and time as an interlocutor in performance. Through the expansion of its scholarship in recent years, scenography has come to be 'formally instated as a significant contributor to the production of knowledge' (Collins and Aronson, 2015, p.2), recognized as 'a distinct strategy for how theatre happens' (Hann, 2019, p.6) and a mode of 'doing, being and thinking' (McKinney and Palmer, 2017, p.16). While there may be a tension in claiming for a particular element a phenomenon that emerges through the confluence of materials in the event of performance, the term 'scenographic light' holds that the action and affectivity of light in performance must be considered in relation to broader contexts of dramaturgical and material operations of scenography, dramaturgy and performance, and indeed that close examination of light in performance enriches understandings of these.

The second, and perhaps more interesting, aim in the use of the term 'scenographic light' is to conceive of light as an explicitly active force in performance. By demonstrating light's unique mode of inscribing meaning in space and time as specifically scenographic, I hope to make clear that light is not only an important constituent of scenography but also a consequential and active component of performance. Contemporary thinking about scenography provides a useful foundation for this conception of light as an active performance element because it opens avenues of thinking about performance in which material, sensual and spatiotemporal experience become key factors in the reading of performance. Scenography encompasses multiple interactions – and, following Karen Barad (2007), intra-actions – between and among elements within space and the ways these interactions impact on the events unfolding. Significantly, expanded scenographic thinking foregrounds the experience of the spectator, and in so doing provides a lens with which to explore the 'spatial, multisensorial and material aspects of contemporary performance' (McKinney and Palmer, 2017, p.2). As a performance material that is at once affective, dramaturgical and ephemeral, light is an especially rich material to examine in this way. Much of the task of thinking scenographically, or thinking about what scenography does, involves attending to the relationships, and interrelationships, between bodies and space, between performers and audience and between space and stuff. Through its complex and multiple entanglements, scenographic light provides a provocative means of encountering shared materiality, where things are, to borrow Jane Bennett's phrasing, 'inextricably enmeshed in a dense network of relations' (2010, p.13).

Drawing on the framework provided in the term 'scenographic light' this chapter explores light's relationship with meaning-making in performance, arguing that this occurs through an affectivity that is principally aesthetic. This is not to say that light is principally a decorative or visual medium, but rather that it involves the complex modes of engagement that occur through aesthetic apprehension. As Timothy Morton argues, when 'you make or study art you are not exploring some kind of candy on the surface of a machine. You are making or studying causality. The aesthetic dimension is the causal dimension' (2013, pp.19–20). There are some productive connections between Morton's understanding of aesthetics as causality and Erika Fischer-Lichte's performance aesthetics that is centred on the possibility of a transformative exchange between performer and audience, where spectatorship is an activity in which the aesthetic experience of performance becomes 'an enabling factor' that allows for different and individual responses (2016, p.177). For Paul Crowther, the aesthetic operation of theatre is significant beyond 'mere entertainment' and is also an 'aesthetic education' for an audience (2019, p.104). Though he recognizes that the 'importance of the stage setting cannot be underestimated' (Crowther, 2019, p.104), Crowther's analysis of theatre aesthetics centres around the skill of actors, directors and playwrights. While it is significant that Crowther includes theatre within his wider argument that 'art's transformative effects involve *aesthetic self-becoming* –' wherein embodied subjects of all kinds can experience the world in a fuller way' (2019, p.1), his account leaves much scope for a deeper examination of the material conditions of performance and the enmeshed relations of scenographic practice. The performances discussed in this chapter are drawn from beyond the frame of dramatic theatre explored by Crowther, and yet by exploring the role of light in these examples it is possible to identify capacities of light that expand existing understandings of performance aesthetics.

Metaphor and material

Light is a polysemic phenomenon; designed light may serve to direct attention, to evoke a particular setting or mood, or may trigger a range of sensorial responses, including those beyond a designer's intention. Akin to the way McKinney writes about scenographic spectacle, there is an 'unruliness' to light in performance in that it 'makes a direct appeal to the body of the individual spectator and at the same time communicates images and ideas that spectators hold in common' (2013, p.74). The images and ideas that spectators hold in common in relation to light owe as much to cultural conceptions as to constructed similarities. 'Seeing light', Cathryn Vasseleu writes, 'is a metaphor for seeing the invisible in the visible' (1998, p.3) and the symbolism of this idea recurs in much dramatic theatre.[1] As Blumenberg writes,

> Light can be a directed beam, a guiding beacon in the dark, an advancing dethronement of darkness, but also a dazzling superabundance, as well as an indefinite, omnipresent brightness containing all: the 'letting-appear' that does not itself appear, the inaccessible accessibility of things. (1993, p.31)

Though this metaphorical link between light and understanding aligns with traditions of Western philosophy, the concept falters when considered with close reference to experiential conditions of light. The artist and researcher Barbara Bolt, for example, critiques this supposed connection between light and enlightenment, arguing – in virtue of the embodied experience of sunlight in her native Australia – that the idea of light revealing or uncovering what is there is one forged by a distinctly European experience of sun. For Bolt, the experience of living in the blazing light of the antipodean sun precludes absolutely the possibility of understanding (sun) light as a force of revelation. The glare of the Australian sun, for Bolt, conceals more than it reveals: 'Too much light on the matter sheds no light on the matter' (2004, p.124). The sunlight of her experience is one that necessitates a downward glance in order to see; raising one's eye line is to have one's vision bleached out by the sun.

Bolt's argument about lived experiences of the glare of the Australian sun shows that different experiential configurations of light can reformulate relationships with the conceptual. Performance, too, offers myriad ways of encountering light that depart from natural light and thus might offer new potential imaginaries. Bolt argues that the bodily encounter with the glare of the Australian sun 'takes apart the Enlightenment triangulation of light, knowledge and form' (2004, p.131) and thus demands a reconfiguration of the relationship between light and matter. This invitation to rethink the relationship between light and matter is, in the case of the Australian landscape, rooted in colonial history, of European colonizers imposing aesthetic and social constructs that were particular and not universal. Bolt argues that the bodily experience of the blinding glare of the Australian sun, in which light cannot be used to render form legible, does not only propel one towards 'a reaction against representation, but provides a different model of mapping the world altogether' (Bolt, 2004, p.137). This chapter argues that performance light may be a paradigmatic site for exploring these constructs, not only because differential experiences of light map on to a realm in which light is constructed and offered within what Hann calls the 'crafted ecology' (2019, p.20) of scenography but also because the particular materiality of light, its ephemerality, its challenges to tangibility and its imbrication with everything else offer a specific mode of aesthetic operation that enables ways of understanding intra-action.

Scenographic light in action: Three performance examples

In line with Bolt's insights about the situatedness of the encounter with light, and following Erin Manning and Brian Massumi's provocation that 'Every practice is a mode of thought, already in the act' (2014, vii), this chapter will now think *with* the light in three productions, as key points of orientation in exploring how the experience of light shapes the ecology of performance. The performances in question are *Plexus,* a piece of contemporary dance from Compagnie III (2015); Heiner Goebbels' *Everything that Happened and Would Happen* (2018); and Invisible Flock's installation performance, *Aurora* (2018). Each of these works features a distinct sensorial and dramaturgical configuration of light and considered in tandem they reveal much about the features and capacities of scenographic light in performance, elucidating the potential of light as both a material and medium in broader contexts.

Plexus features a single dancer, Kaori Ito, on an enormous floating structure, suspended by 5,000 cords through and around which she moved.

Aurélien Bory was both choreographer and scenographer for the production, a fact which may, in part, account for the foregrounding of the scenographic materials. A result of this foregrounding is that light, space and the body seem to coalesce within the aesthetic offer of the performance. Over the course of the performance, Ito moves throughout the space of the structure, sometimes pulling herself through the cords, sometimes suspended by them. The density of the tensioned cords makes traversing this space an act of negotiation for the dancer, but also creates a layering of textures as the light ripples through rows upon rows of dense black ropes. In much the same way that haze makes beams of light prominent in space, the cords here catch the light, making its every shift perceptible. Additionally, the movement in both the cords and the light creates a sense of light as a palpable, shimmering thing; every change in light is accentuated and every shaft of light is made distinct. To this end, the dominance of the light in *Plexus* seems to gain a material reality and can be read in terms of its physical presence. In the sheer materiality of its performance, then, *Plexus* focuses on the 'sensuous givenness' (Seel, 2005, p.22) of light as an aesthetic substance that is interwoven with the action of the dancer on stage.

By contrast, Heiner Goebbels' *Everything that Happened and Would Happen,* performed in an enormous, cavernous space in Manchester, centred around slippery relationships between bodies, space, materials and light. While *Plexus* hinges on the evolving interaction between a lone dancer and a single, if enormous, structure, *Everything that Happened and Would Happen* is driven by a large cast of actors hauling objects and materials through a vast space and forming them into new configurations and assemblages. Alongside these physical assemblies, light reaches across the space – as both light and as projection – and forms and reforms images which never fully resolve but are endlessly mutable. It creates geometric patterns in the space, at times creating kinetic optical illusions in which the architecture of the space seems to shift. Performers busy themselves with flight cases and set pieces (all of which were originally designed by Klaus Grünberg for a 2012 production of *John Cage: Europeras 1&2,* directed by Goebbels, and are repurposed here as part of the fabric of the emerging performance). These materials are continually manipulated and re-formed into fleeting structures, assemblages or impositions in space. Throughout the performance, light enfolds all it touches in a reciprocal relationship of instability.

The third performance discussed here, *Aurora,* unfolded between environment, materials and audience without the presence of (human) performers. Commissioned by Liverpool city council, and created by the Leeds-based interactive arts company Invisible Flock, *Aurora* brought its audience inside a cavernous Victorian reservoir, built in 1845 to house two million gallons of water. This performance installation, held by Ellie Barrett as an example of an art practice that tackles material 'head on' (2019, p.7), explores the interactions between tangible and intangible substances in ways that raise potent questions about scenographic encounters. On entering, the space was dark, filled with haze and appeared to be completely flooded with water. We were instructed to keep to the path around the space, and this was outlined with laser beams just hovering above the surface of the water. Across the seeming vastness of this space, blocks of ice would appear and disappear, seeming to glow from within as the light caught their slippery surfaces. The audience navigated a darkened space, flooded with water, with light pulsing between dozens of blocks of ice that slowly melted into a central pool. This was underlaid with a soundscape of music and field recordings taken of glaciers in Iceland. Water was both the principal subject and the core object of this piece, not only in the flooding of the floor but also in its transformed states of ice and steam. Furthermore, by pairing the mutability of water with the ephemerality of light and sound, the scenographic offering of *Aurora* exploited the fundamental properties of these materials as a means of examining its wider themes. The scale of the installation unfolded through continually shifting light that revealed clusters of sculptural ice as well as hidden recesses in the space. Thus, the focus on ephemeral materials in this piece – sound, light, melting ice – makes it an especially interesting proposition to consider in terms of its objects.

In discussing each of these, I offer my experience as a spectator as a means of accessing detail about how light worked in the encounter with each performance. McKinney and Palmer argue that the perspective of the spectator has proved productive in the development of scenographic scholarship, because it highlights the embodied nature of scenographic experience, and emphasizes performance as an event that is encountered rather than as something that might be analysed on the basis of 'static artefacts or on the intentions of the artist' (2017, p.8). By drawing close attention to what becomes possible through light in these particular examples, I hope to unpick some of the ways that light makes meaning in performance more generally. Building from attentiveness to the action of light in each performance, the analysis here aims to follow the experiential encounter with light as both medium and material of these performances, and in turn to connect these experiences with wider thinking on the nature of light. The three examples included here speak to light's potential as a meaning-making material of performance but they are not presented as a totalizing survey of modes of performance light. Rather, thinking with and through the particular materiality of light in these examples puts forward some of the ways in which light can operate as an agent of meaning-making in performance, and argues for its significance as a scenographic material.

Trick of the light

Plexus begins with a moment of deception. When the house lights fade, the audience is left in nearly complete darkness. Out of this darkness, three beams of light gradually fade up, appearing murky as though through dense haze or fog. These beams appear to float above the stage, reaching about halfway to the stage floor from the ceiling. These then fade out and are replaced by footlights, revealing the dancer, Kaori Ito, at the front of the stage. Behind her, there is a structure of some kind, covered entirely in a piece of black silk, and it was this that lent the sense of fog to the previous moment. Ito stands in front of the structure, with the silk at her back, and is lit by two visible lanterns at her feet. She uses a microphone, apparently to amplify the sound of her heartbeat and her breath, although it was unclear if this sound is being produced live or is recorded. Next, she starts to lean back against the silk, causing it to billow around her in the light, like waves. Finally, she begins to push back into the silk, wedging her body and the fabric through the cords. She continues to burrow backwards until the whole silk drops down around her and she pulls it back into the darkness behind her.

Light's opening gesture here – the appearance of the three strangely truncated beams – seems to announce the presence of light as something to be attended to in itself. The moment is fleeting; there was not enough time to clearly discern the silk, so the floating, hazy beams of light emerge as faint objects without immediate purpose or usefulness. Although the light is directed towards the silk, it does not illuminate the fabric such that it becomes clearly visible. In this moment my attention was held by the light beams appearing, and the uncertainty in the murky quality of the image. As a spectator, I was not at all sure of what I was seeing until the dancer appeared in front of the silk. This change, from hazily present beams of light, hanging high in the space, to footlights directed towards the dancer immediately sets up a kind of dialogue between the light and the dancer's body. The first act of light is not to make visible but to *be* visible; only afterwards does it reveal the presence of the dancer. First there is light, then there is a dancer in light. Both are given as aspects of the production to be experienced in themselves. Aronson observes that this degree of force is a prominent feature of light in modern dance, where:

> It is no longer tied to motivational sources but has taken on a physical force, making it a performer within the dance. Light is a force that draws dancers toward it; it is a force that pushes dancers across a stage; a wall of light may act as resistance against a dancer or create a sort of curtain through which the audience must struggle to see. (2005, p.35)

Aronson's discussion here of light's power in modern dance is tied to a conception of it as an active material agent within the unfolding dance. The language Aronson employs here is explicitly physical; light can push, resist and form walls, or block visibility. Such an understanding provides a productive frame for light as a *scenographic* power. Discussing light as a material with the power to compel a dancer to move, frames it as a material element and enables consideration of light as a bodily substance in performance. Thinking of light in bodily terms aligns with Reynolds' idea of kinaesthetic empathy in dance, in which it is not purely a dancer's body that triggers an affective response but the 'dance's body' (in Reynolds and Reason, 2011, p.123). Drawing from Vivian Sobchack's term 'the film's body', Reynolds uses the idea of the dance's body to convey the 'shared materiality and affective flow' of movement (Reynolds and Reason, 2011, p.123). Through this kind of kinaesthetic engagement with the emerging choreographed movement, the experience of watching dance blurs distinctions between individual bodies or movements such that, rather than seeing individual bodies move away from or towards each other on the stage, one instead sees the dance spread and gather. The dance's body in *Plexus*, then, encompasses Ito's body, the shimmering space of the cords, and the material shifting of the light, together with the affective responses and engagements of the spectator.

Light as aesthetic material

Perhaps inherent in the form of contemporary dance is an emphasis on more dispersed structures of meaning (Bleeker, 2015, p.67). Recent scholarship on dramaturgy in dance (as in, for example Hansen and Callison, 2015; Warner, 2016) speaks to the increasingly collaborative status of dance dramaturgy – both among collaborators in the rehearsal process and among multiple elements in the event of performance. There is a parallel here with Lehmann's discussion of 'parataxis' in postdramatic performance (2006, p.86). This is conceived as a kind of rebellion against the classical hierarchies of meaning in traditional theatre and as a means of liberating multiple elements in performance to contribute individually and collectively, without presenting immediate logical connections, and thus inviting the spectator to 'connections, correspondences and clues at completely unexpected moments' (Lehmann, 2006, p.87). Through this kind of attending, meaning is 'postponed', emerging over time rather than linearly or explicitly. Thus, the light here manifests as one element within a multifaceted aesthetic experience, and its role within that experience shifts and changes throughout. At times the light works to direct attention, or to pick Ito out against the large structure; at other times the light seems to modify the available space of the cord-strung structure; at other times it seems to present a kind of force in the space, with an apparently haptic relationship to the dancer and the structure. Through this kind of manifold operation, the light here asserts that it is doing something in this experience in excess of its formal properties of light and dark.

Comparably dispersed structures of meaning are also in evidence in the other two examples discussed here. In the case of Goebbels' *Everything that Happened and Would Happen* elements are continually drawn together, a roving sculpture that never reaches a fixed point. Set elements, already recycled beyond their intended purpose, are hauled across the stage, pulled into shapes and assemblages that defy their intended use. This action is layered over and around excerpts from Patrik Ouředník's *Europeana*, a postmodern text that resists the possibility of a single perspective and in which the history of the twentieth century is relayed as a series of accumulative facts, sweeping through events with a flattened ontology of detail and observations.[2] Sarah Lucie has already argued that this is a production in which a 'dramaturgy of connectivity and accumulation creates an atmosphere in which events – ways in which the atmosphere is built, affected and then active in the creation of the next atmosphere – are the basic ontological unit' (2020, p.17). This, as Lucie demonstrates, creates a performance in which the dramaturgical project, of connection, co-creation and entanglement between the human and the non-human, becomes a manifestation of Barad's intra-action. For Barad,

> The notion of *intra-action* (in contrast to the usual 'interaction,' which presumes the prior existence of independent entities or relata) represents a profound conceptual shift. It is through specific agential intra-actions that the boundaries and properties of the components of phenomena become determinate and that particular concepts (that is, particular material articulations of the world) become meaningful. (2007, p.139)

This conceptual shift has been influential in expanded scenographic thinking, drawing an increased attentiveness to the agency and vibrancy of materials (Bennett, 2010) and relationships between human and non-human that are significant to both 'how scenography works and how spectators experience it' (McKinney and Palmer, 2017, p.13). In this context, the entanglement of light, space, bodies and objects in *Everything that Happened and Would Happen* articulates the relationality of intra-action. Light and projection are used to transform both the performance environment and the ways in which it is perceived, with directional shafts of light cutting through the space, and shifting patterns of projected light moving across the stage. Here, light is an indivisible material component of an 'assemblage' (Bennett, 2010) of materials; rather than a medium through which a subject is seen, it is a thing among things co-constituting performance in the layered entanglement of bodies, space and stuff. In this cacophony of matter, light tracks across the vast space, shaping and reshaping the stage, but also joining with the flow of bodies and materials to create perilous sculptures, that seem to glow from within, or sometimes to draw light towards them. In the amalgam of light, materials and space it becomes impossible to think of light illuminating an already formed image; light is always already interfering, imbricating itself into the fabric of each shifting assemblage, and being remade in the meeting of light and matter. This is Barad's intra-action in action, the confluence of light, bodies and materials creating something new defined by the relationality between them. This disrupted causality exposes what is the case more generally; in their mutual transformation light and matter are each made anew. Bolt notes that we talk about 'shedding light on the matter' but not of any 'passage *from* matter *to* light' (2004, p.127). On a basic level, any lighting designer who has ever tried to look at a lighting state on an empty stage will know that light is made different by the presence of performers in it. But on a deeper level, this performance and its intense entanglement of shifting light and materials seems, to me as a spectator, to make their mutual and contingent transformation vivid.

Thinking through these examples, then, demonstrates something of the plasticity of scenographic light, but also its status as a kind of aesthetic material, distinct from other forms or appearances of light. There is, perhaps, a parallel between the aesthetic operation of light in these examples and Crowther's analysis of the structures of abstract art, in which he notes that abstract works of art engage 'virtual factors in excess of what they are as merely physical and/ or formal visual configurations' (2009, p.101). An aesthetic experience of light within the context of performance occasions a certain kind of excess, in which the light invokes a kind of consciousness or a particular kind of attentiveness to or engagement with the performance material, beyond what might be possible otherwise. An aesthetic experience of light, then, is a product of an affective encounter. This is not necessarily an explicit process; as Fischer-Lichte attests, light in performance is often received on the very 'threshold of consciousness' (2008, p.119). Yet many contemporary works of performance, including those discussed here, foreground light, enabling instances of what Crowther terms the 'wondrous apprehension of thinghood' (2006, p.41). The aesthetic experience of attending to light in performance is thus related to the specific characteristics of performance as an event of encounter. This is especially evident in work such as *Plexus* where the material seems to embrace its sheer theatricality; there is no sense of mimesis here, or of direct representation, instead the work unfolds within its own reality, like what Lehmann terms a 'scenic poem' (2006, p.111). Martin Seel argues that aesthetic experience 'has to *happen* and can happen only if subjects become involved with the sensuous making present of phenomena and situations that alter in an entirely unforeseen manner the subjects' sense of what is real and what is possible' (2008, p.100, emphasis added). The ways in which light works to shape understandings of what is real and what is possible underscores the extent to which the theatrical language of light relies on a symbiosis between form and content. In *Plexus,* we might recognize this symbiosis in the relationship(s) between movement, the body and light – or in the imbrication of body, space and light that is in evidence in different ways in both *Everything that Happened and Would Happen* and, as I will go on to show, *Aurora*. The content of the light involves what is in the light, but also the form of the light itself, as a visible beam. Furthermore, through this morass, and this parataxical coincidence of space, light and body, further kinds of content emerge, that of the affective or interpretational impressions experienced by the seer.

For Seel, the core facet of aesthetic understanding lies in the distinction between appearing and semblance. This distinction shifts emphasis away from appearance, or how things look per se, and towards appearing, or the dynamic play of appearances in a particular encounter. Further to this, Seel argues that when aesthetic perception becomes an event for the person perceiving this may be understood as aesthetic experience (2008, p.99). He also demonstrates that attentiveness to the presence of an aesthetic object calls attention, vividly, to our own presence. That, through the aesthetic encounter we 'allow ourselves to be abducted to presence. Aesthetic intuition is a radical form of residency in the here and now' (2005, p.33). I have argued elsewhere that the emphasis in Seel's work on emergence, temporality and event makes his concept especially relevant to an exploration of the nature of the aesthetic experience of performance (Graham, 2020a). This thinking is especially pertinent in relation to the ephemeral materiality of scenographic light as it is encountered in performance. Whereas an aesthetics of light based on appearance might seek to stress the image-making, or image-framing, capacity of light, attentiveness to the appearing of light speaks to its affectivity and its invitation to both embodied experience and imaginative encounter. This focus on temporality and encounter affirms understanding of scenography as something that happens (see, e.g. Svoboda in Burian 1974, p.15; Lotker and Gough, 2013; Hann, 2019, pp.67–77), and that the qualities and dynamism of this happening are integral to the ways in which scenographic process contribute to or construct meaning in performance. As Hann argues, 'Scenography is concerned not only with the material constructions of theatre, but how these constructions *relate* to one another; *relate* to the performers, *relate* to the spectators' (2019, p.72, emphasis in original). The aesthetic operation of scenographic light, then, is not concerned with the delivery of static images, or with a neutral revealing of what is already there, but in the contingent co-construction of a meaningful aesthetic event.

Haptic light

The emphasis on how light happens in these examples is in many ways emblematic of what Aronson describes as 'postmodern lighting' – in which light 'ebbs and flows, startles and surprises' reflecting a 'sense of instability' (2005, p.36). The happening or unfolding of light here is not only visual but also tangible. The foregrounding of physicality in *Plexus* seems to suggest that light is not only illuminating the cords but also *touching* them. This might be considered in terms of what Dempster describes as a 'haptic apprehension of space', noting that 'haptic perception fosters an intimate relationship with environment. The haptically attuned dancer is preoccupied with stage space; so too is the spectator' (2003, p.49). Dempster reasons that this sense of tangibility is acutely evident in dance spectatorship, where the kinaesthetic experience of watching entwines vision and touch (2003, p.46). In this framework, she draws on Gibson's ecological optics, noting how, in his work, processes of 'looking and seeing implicate us in the sensuous structure of the world' (Dempster, 2003, p.47). As Gibson argues, the overlap between looking and feeling is profound, as is the link between sensuous apprehension and action: 'the equipment for *feeling* is anatomically the same as the equipment for *doing*' (1968, p.99, emphasis in original). While Gibson's work, much like Merleau-Ponty's phenomenology, is primarily concerned with processes of perception, and the position of the perceiving subject, his approach, and the language he employs around light are useful reference points in approaching what light, in itself, is doing. He notes that, in addition to providing 'a stimulus for vision' and 'information for perception', light can also be conceived as 'a physical energy' (1979, p.47). The sense of light as a physical energy seems crucial in *Plexus,* where the interplay of body, space and light lies at the heart of the action. This bodily conception of light – or what Aronson terms its 'physical force' (2005, p.35) – is crucial in terms of understanding what light itself is doing in this performance. The physicality implied in these descriptions of light counters traditional assumptions in Western philosophical thought that light is 'an invisible medium that opens up a knowable world' (Vasseleu, 1998, p.1). As Vasseleu attests, 'in its texture light has a corporeality which constitutes the dawning of the field of vision' (1998, p.13). Or as Nigel Stewart puts it, 'the medium of light makes visible the medium of touch to reveal the body as tactile, and the medium of touch makes tactile the visible quality of light' (2016, p.61).

Light displays a similar kind of haptic presence in *Aurora*, where the tactility of the installation begins with the audience sloshing through puddles of water and encountering blocks of slowly melting ice. Light makes this ice shimmer and glow, and the textured shadows cast lend a heightened sense of materiality to the rivulets of water that run off the ice. As with the shimmering of the light on the cords in *Plexus,* the other-worldly glow of the light on the ice blocks in *Aurora* seems to suggest a kind of vitality to the light, or what Robert Edmond Jones calls the 'overwhelming sense of the livingness of the light' (Jones, 2004, p.36). The examples cited here certainly attest that in performance, there is a dynamism or an unpredictability to the light that emerges.

In this vein, attending to the relationships between light, bodies and spaces in the layered context of performance can reveal a great deal about the complexities of the material experience of live performance, in terms of both the ways performance is composed and, crucially, the meanings and associations it stimulates in its audience. Light is both a medium in which the performance happens and a material of that performance. As the pioneering lighting designer Jean Rosenthal evocatively put it: 'Dancers live in light as fish live in water. The stage space in which they move is their aquarium, their portion of the sea' (in Rosenthal and Wertenbaker, 1972, p.117; see also Carter in this volume, p.81) Rosenthal's metaphor is an apposite one, as it speaks to qualities of immersion in light, to the notion that light is something we are *in*, a medium. Crucially, this medium is a tactile one; just as limbs move and feel differently when held in a body of water, to be in light is a sensory as well as visual experience. More recently, Nick Moran has extended Rosenthal's metaphor to think about light in performance contexts beyond dance, stating that 'light is the water the production swims in' and that light 'on stage rarely works alone, and it is part of the thing that it supports – this *water* is inside the production as well as all around it' (Moran, 2017, p.169 and 170). This is the dual sense in which light is an element of performance: it is a component of a larger manifold, and it is also something elemental in the way that air or water might be.

Mercurial light

Invisible Flock's *Aurora* used the mutability of light as a substance in order to invite a reimagining of our relationship with water. For the artists, the piece was borne out of an understanding of the significance of water as a precious commodity, a life-giving substance revealing global inequalities as regards access and security and the installation was about trying to 'turn it into something precious, like a jewel, to create a beautiful hypnotic experience that brings us closer to water and allows us to interact with this substance that we take for granted with a newfound sense of wonder' (Eaton, 2018, p.1). The piece invited this 'hypnotic experience' by allowing its audience to move through the space that was once an active reservoir, the darkened space seeming to prompt a hushed kind of reverie. In this space, minimal light illuminated glowing blocks of ice, or reflected off the surface of the water, making the material all around us twinkle and glow in ever-changing ways. Using light and dark in this way to treat water as an object of contemplation is perhaps a very direct example of the 'making special' that Ellen Dissanayake identifies as at the core of aesthetic behaviour (1995). By casting the space of the Toxteth reservoir, melting ice, shimmering pools of water and shafts of light as its principal performers, *Aurora* explores the significance of water through aesthetic experience.

Here, the mutability of light partners with the shifting status of water, which we encounter in its various states of solid blocks of ice; as pools, drips, and streams of liquid water; and as haze or vapour in the air. Similarly, Azusa Ono's lighting design includes multiple textures and qualities of light. The laser beams that outline the path around the edges of the space are vividly coloured, and sharply defined by the haze in the air that makes them appear thick and solid. Later, more of these beams will pierce through the space, refracting through blocks of ice and multiplying in their reflections on the water. Blocks of ice illuminate from within, alternately appearing and disappearing as the lights within them fade in and out. We catch glimpses of the architecture of the reservoir as pillars are silhouetted by shafts of light across the space, or lit up in an other-worldly green. At one point a soft amber light highlights the textured surface of the brickwork in a recess beyond the pathway. It then begins to rain in this space, the cascading water caught by a pale light that makes it seem textural. The action of the sudden rain is arresting, an affective gesture that seems to work on me as a spectator in a way beyond associations of rainfall. This is what Hann describes as a 'scenographic scene' that is 'the felt experience of *being with* an affective atmosphere and its othering potential' (2019, p.27). The shifting qualities of the light in this installation afford a kind of openness to the atmospheres created, an attentiveness to the aesthetic events that operate as both a spectacle and as a means of triggering imaginative associations that link to arguments about the value of water central to the politics of the work.

The performance of the light here is one that operates through continual transformation. The mutability at play in *Aurora* unfolds materially at the juncture between the shifting states of water and the protean phenomenon of crafted light. This enfolding of light and what is lit recalls what Bolt describes as the conceptual shift from shedding light on the matter to shedding light for the matter. Shedding light for (the) matter, she argues, 'involves both an ecological and ethical challenge and presents a different conception of visual practice and visual aesthetics. Practice becomes imbricated in culture as an alternative mode of representation' (2004, p.147). This she links to methexis, or concurrent actual production, arguing that to 'think *methektically* is to think quite differently about the potential of visual practices. It involves thinking through matter' (2004, p.147). *Aurora* provides an invitation to think through the matter – and the mattering – of water, and this happens through the aesthetic transformation of water, ice and light.

Conclusion

This chapter has argued that scenographic light is not only a significant interlocutor in performance but also that it may be a paradigmatic mode of understanding what is at stake in the aesthetic offer of performance. As such, this chapter presented an expanded understanding of light in performance, that also enables a fuller view of the aesthetic operation of performance more generally. Light is a medium through which we come to see performance, and a constructive material that co-constitutes the appearing of what is seen. This is not a neutral facilitative process, but a transformative one in which light is imbricated into acts of seeing. Light, in performance, is not simply that which allows vision to take place but, through its construction and instability, is always already a form of mediation. Bleeker discusses the complexity of vision in the theatre, demonstrating that 'what seems to be just "there to be seen" is, in fact rerouted through memory and fantasy, caught up in threads of the unconscious and entangled with the passions' (2008, p.2). While Bleeker's argument does not take light explicitly into account, the examples drawn on here make it readily apparent that light adds a further layer of entanglement to the complex visuality of performance.

Through its scenographic framework, this chapter set out to explore what is at stake in how light performs, to tease out what light might offer to performance as a material, to think through the experience(s) it might invite and how we might trace the interactions between and the relationships that light has with everything else. As Kathleen Irwin argues, 'how performances materialize onstage and how they make sense are two inseparable aspects of thinking through matter' (Irwin, in McKinney and Palmer, 2017, p.126). Thinking through the matter of light reveals a productive complexity in scenographic practice and reception. Exploring how the light operates in the three performances discussed here, this chapter has attended to both the modes of embodied engagement occasioned by light and the ways that it trades on associations or expressive atmospheres. What emerges is an understanding of scenographic light as an ontologically complex phenomenon, an ephemeral material offering challenges to tangibility and perceptual stability. As such, examining the aesthetic operation of light in performance is to move beyond its decorative value and to engage with its multiple ways of constructing dramaturgical and experiential meaning. Light, I argue, is therefore especially valuable in exploring the nature of performance aesthetics, in unpicking the role of objects, materials and spaces, as critically embedded in the meaning-making processes of performance.

Notes

1 See Palmer, (2013, pp.118–24) for examples.
2 As an example, Ouředník's novel begins: 'The Americans who fell in Normandy in 1944 were tall men measuring 173 centimetres on average, and if they were laid head to foot they would measure 38 kilometres. The Germans were tall too, while the tallest of all were the Senegalese fusiliers in the First World War who measured 176 centimetres, and so they were sent into battle on the front lines in order to scare the Germans' (Ouředník, 2005, p.1).

12

Storytelling with light

Paule Constable

When I think about what I think light does and what it's for, I think it's about *releasing* things. I think it's about articulation and collaboration. I suppose there's quite a lot of different schools of lighting design; there are people who use light in quite a pictorial way – lighting that makes pictures that refer to themselves – that you see in things like rock and roll lighting or very overt TV lighting. This kind of lighting is often about an image, which may be visually striking or might be an intuitive response, but it's something that is added *on top*. For me, that's light that works from the outside in. I think my work is the opposite of that. I think my work starts from the inside and works out. I think I grew to work in this way because most of my early work was with more experimental and fringe theatre companies – people like Complicité – where we would all improvise and work together. And then in the end, I would respond with light. It was the understanding of the ideas and the story that we were trying to tell which was important to me. Light was the means with which I responded. So, I think I've been drawn more and more to light because of the things it releases rather than the stuff of it. I'm less interested in kit and technology than I am in what light smells like, really, how it tells the story. I like things that feel tangible. I often use the word 'smell' around what light is. I use loads of haze quite often because I like light that's thick. I don't use saturated colour very much, but if I do, I like it to be really thick. I like it to have some real kind of weight to it. It is edible at times, light. The way it kind of bounces off things and the way it meets other things, it's like it fizzes and it's alive. I love the word 'alchemical' because I think, when light comes into a space, it's transformative. I still feel really childishly excited by that. For example, the moment when the house lights go down at the beginning of a show is the moment you tell the audience that you are taking them by the hand and taking them on a journey. It shifts from being light to dark; from being open to being focused; from being an informal space to a formal one. I think that even that one moment alone is incredibly exciting.

Of course, in performance we have an emotional response to space, and I don't mean emotional in the sense of pictorial emotional, I mean the breath of space. This emotional response isn't about impressive images, but rather about lighting that makes you lean in, stop breathing, lighting that can shift the feeling in the room. A really simple way of thinking about that is that a person on their own in a space that you expose as very large can feel very, very solitary because you're aware of the emptiness around them. A person on their own in the dark can actually feel much more *held* because the darkness becomes the space where the audience imagines. The darkness becomes where the audience imagines the things that you're not showing them. You can make that feel safe or you can make it feel threatening, depending on what kind of angle of light you use on the person who is in the light as opposed to in the space of darkness beyond. I think light releases in that it allows a space to breathe and to be different things without it ever moving, because, essentially, light is about pressing darkness. You press it away or you allow it in. That's true of light and even of story, isn't it? In that, the amount of light you use takes an audience on a journey of revelation, or not. Or you can play with the idea of what can be seen in a space and what can't be. All of that is releasing information, releasing a relationship to an actor, and to a space because you're playing with scale a lot of the time. In a way, the rhythm of where light is going and what it's doing is releasing and closing down. Rhythmically, you're releasing space in terms of scale. You're also trying to capture and release the audience's imagination. And of course, none of it is definite. It's only what you imagine and hope.

Rigour in the lighting design process

My first meeting of the physical world of the piece tends to be at white card model stage. When I ask myself a very specific question, which is *what makes light walk into the room*? What is its function? Why is it there? If you're taking a kind of composite space like *War Horse*, where nothing was scenically delivered, every shift in time, space, place, time of day, season and size of space, everything was delivered by light, because it was a storytelling space (see Plate 28). The openness of the space offered and demanded a role for light in contrast to a stage restricted by a full ceiling piece, for example – which would prevent the story being told in a similar way. Or if you're doing a production of *Don Giovanni* or *Uncle Vanya* – one of those pieces, which is just a descent into darkness – and there's no naturalistic reason for light or dark to be in the room, then you need to really drill down into the question of what's the abstraction? Or, if there is a window in the room and the story of the light in the scene is that time is passing then you can potentially tell that story with a naturalistic sense of the light shifting behind that window. But if there is no window – how then do you make an abstract gesture that makes the space shift? Do you even need to? What game are we playing with the audience? How do we take them on the journey? One of the things about light is that you need to decide quite quickly what your rules are, to establish clearly the terms of engagement and the parameters of what you're doing.

Once you've created that set of rules, that kind of understanding – that light is heightened naturalism or it's abstract or it's delivering all of the different spaces – you just need to make sure that you can get light in the right way in each one of those. Once you've decided that, then you've got a framework that you can work within and you can then continue to ask the questions of what light is doing in the room. Can I achieve that with what I've got available to me with the way that the space is going to be? Is there a contradiction there? Is that contradiction interesting? That first moment of engagement is really critical; there are so many decisions you can make at that point. I often think, as lighting designers, we can spend a lot of time concentrating on the things we don't know because there's always a huge amount we don't know. But I've developed this process where I constantly bank the things that I *do* know; create rules for myself and have conversations. You also need to talk about what those rules are going to mean for a director and a designer really early on. If they've designed a one-room space with a ceiling and it's a ten-act play, and every act is different, and half of them are exteriors, there's a big question to ask about how you can deliver an exterior in a fixed room. That's a really extreme example. But if you don't have those conversations at this point, it will come and bite you later. That's your moment to create a mutual understanding and to key into the design language of what the interpretation of the piece is. As the lighting designer, this is where your creative engagement starts. It is not for you to be told what the piece needs, but to know the piece well enough to know the journey that it goes on and therefore come to these early meetings to discuss how to deliver that from the outset.

I create structure by understanding narrative and story. The more that I make clear decisions early on and plan based around that, the more I can respond intuitively, when I'm in the space. It's another one of those mad contradictions of lighting; that it's both technical and incredibly abstract and creative. I plan a huge amount and I make sure the deputy stage manager's (DSM) got all the cues. I have a rough idea of what the cues are going to be, and I create structures for them. All of that preparation is about allowing me to look. I work quickly because the sooner you've got something to look at, the sooner you can see what something might be, the possibility of something. Even if it's the possibility of seeing something that's rubbish, you've learned what it isn't then. All of that is useful learning, but the quicker you work, the more you can start learning about the piece. The more structure you've got, the less you've got to look down and the more you can look up. If you're trying to talk to a DSM (Deputy Stage Manager) about where to put a cue, and what number it is, that stops you from looking at the stage. Whereas if you've already given them a cue structure, you don't even have to think about it. You can get on with it, just light it. You can keep moving forward, then you've got more space to develop your language and heighten it to make it more sophisticated. I think sometimes people misunderstand what I mean by rigour, thinking that it's about narrowing it down. Actually, rigour is about creating a framework which gives you huge amounts of space to work within, but you've got a structure. And for me, structure is everything.

I think an obvious example, which is probably quite well-known, is *The Curious Incident of The Dog in the Night-Time,* which is an adaptation of the Mark Haddon novel that we originally did in what was the Cottesloe, is now the Dorfmann, at the National Theatre in London. When Bunny Christie and Marianne Elliott and I first met, Bunny's idea for the show was a piece of black graph paper with some light boxes just around the edge. The book talks about diagrams and maps and Christopher's love of space and of technology and things. So I introduced the idea of these pixels. Everywhere that the graph paper intersected there was a pixel so we could sort of draw diagrams and maps and respond to Christopher's sense of control (see Plate 29).

Then the way that Simon Stephens was developing the script, it was becoming Christopher's story. He was the narrative motor for the stories; it was his telling of his own story. And I thought he would probably love technical theatre. Essentially, the conceit for me became that I lit it in a way that I imagined somebody who's neurodiverse might enjoy or find stimulating. There's an incredibly restricted palette; we only used three or four different types of lights and they were sat in a grid above the stage and they responded to Christopher. It was almost like he was telling his story and he was using really supposedly simple (but actually complex) theatre elements to tell the story. There's very, very little colour in any of the light and it just directionally points you at the section of the show that you're in. Then we used diagrammatical elements to give that an edge and a shape, and perhaps an element of colour, so that the light boxes and the pixels might go blue, for example. He's Sherlock Holmes at one point and I transformed the whole space into a kind of *Mission Impossible* with red LEDs. So, you're imagining the sorts of things that we know Christopher likes from the book, but also the things that we imagine he would like, from understanding the sort of character he is and what he responds to and enjoys. It became an incredibly strict set of rules that made the show. Most of the time, colour came from people wearing a single coloured garment in this space, and because the palette was so restricted, that would really jump out to you, in the way that Christopher quite often experienced the world in the book. He notices very specific details about people. It was about playing with that level of perception and creating a sort of a box that's responding in the same way. It's infinite, what you can do through suggestion with light because you're also employing the audience's imagination to create new stories.

Releasing

I really like practical lights. I like real lights in the space, lights that *exist* rather than being secret. In my process there tends to be quite a lot of building and developing stuff, looking at things, and their possibilities. They have an evolution in the same way that through a rehearsal process you're honing your ideas down as you're mentally testing them, as you watch people develop their performances. Watching people rehearse can really help you to test out the strength and rigour of those ideas.

I think something that really helps me is to literally find the identity of light that might be in the space, and the landscape for what lights might be there. Sometimes it's not appropriate but I like trying to get some traction where you have lights that physically tell a story. We did a production of *Angels in America* at the National a few years ago and electricity in that play is really key. There's this sense of a kind of electrical charge of the world; the angel is essentially electricity. And she's charged. So, as she's coming nearer to the world, that all becomes quite unstable. In order for that to be the case, you need to establish electricity as a presence in the room. I felt it was important to make sure that we had electrical props for this multi-locational space. So quite often that might just be a physical light that indicates a change of space. But I also felt that it was important that there was a kind of lighting presence within the moving elements of the set – particularly in the three consecutive domestic room-sized revolves that made up the space for almost the whole of the first play. And also because of references to Jean-Jacques Beineix films, the idea of the 1980s, and the style of *Subway* and movies like that. The majority of the characters in the play are living on the periphery of society – in an impoverished world – where a small domestic light or a bit of old pink tat over a light or a neon tube might make their world feel and appear more glamorous. A small gesture that might push away the truth and where the landscape of night-time can hide both the realities of day-to-day life and be a safe space for them to exist within. This gave me a way to make the space have a kinetic quality as these different lights shifted as the space moved and also literally gave me an opportunity to feed lights and lights into the space (see Plate 30).

The pictorial lights in the space were already carrying huge amounts of narrative. In a way, with that play, it meant that I could create elements of fantasy as well, because so much of my work comes from a kind of heightened version of reality. I don't tend to think in saturated colour, so as soon as you put neon tubes all over a space and you can colour change them, then you can make a version of a 1980s kind of pop video or, as I say, the look of a Beineix movie or something like that. It becomes easier to add to those sorts of gestures but also it feels like the audience can see why they're there. They can see why it's gone neon blue in that *Diva* kind of way. Because you can see the tubes that are doing it. It's not like imposing from the outside; it's part of the world that you're looking into. I really like that, that light made its means visible. Having lights on stage also puts proximity between objects – between lights and people – which I think is brilliant because there's an amazing intensity. It's quite hard to achieve in theatre because so often lights are a long way away. I'm quite interested in the kind of physical reaction – and interaction – with light and how it makes us see and perceive people in different ways. Giving people lights that are *their* lights, as it were, be it a bedside light or a kind of little standard lamp or something, means that they're aware of their light and their dark and when they're there and when they're not. Rather than the light just being a perfunctory bit of set that sometimes is on and sometimes is off. You want a bit more traction around an object, a strong sense of it belonging to a character. If lights are in the space, then they share the space. They give light a visual sense of purpose and identity that is hugely useful.

I think as a lighting designer you're definitely thinking about a narrative. Even if I'm doing something that feels quite abstract, I create a narrative through-line for myself to follow. I don't draw, but I will tell myself the story of what light is doing in a show. What comes into the room, what it carries with it, what it is revealing, what it's hiding, when it's big and when it's small and when it's dynamic and when it's welcoming and when it's slow-moving and when it's fast, when it makes the audience just sit forward in their seat. I think all of those are absolutely story-driven. In a way, that's why I'm not naturally drawn to doing things like contemporary dance. Partly because it can so often avoid narrative, but you still have events. Choreographers, for example, will call little sections something and that section will have a scale and a quality that you can key into, that can fit into a larger picture of rhythm and dramaturgy.

It's like light is an actor in the play. So, you serve the play, but you might shape the moment relative to an actor. The relationship between light and the performers is something that you have to search for in the space when you're making. It's quite often to do with focus and making sure that, in simple terms, if somebody has a soliloquy, for instance, you can hear them. That might be about doing something like a ten-minute slow fade, just dropping the rest of the state and heightening where somebody is. Or you might make the space bigger and bigger and bigger. That's if you decide it is going to move at all. It might be you just let it be. That's obviously another decision: Does light need to move or not? Whatever it is, you're asking questions about how best that moment is shared relative to the rest of the text, but also relative to the choices that performer and director are making in terms of their interpretation. I think light has got a responsibility to the whole and then it's got the way it moves within the whole, which is like an actor – an actor who's on stage all the time and has to interact with every other character. It is definitely a character in every piece. It's got both a kind of collective responsibility and an individual responsibility. Obviously, there are things that I enjoy and that are part of the vocabulary of how I've refined my tendencies with light. But I think in terms of a structure and a response to a piece, I hope that that's a new thing each time. I always feel some sense of it being a puzzle that is there to be solved.

Collaboration

My initial response to a project is about a decision to take something on because it has to be something that I understand or have a relationship with or feel drawn to or feel interested in. That can sometimes be a juxtaposition; it can be that I think that I'm the least appropriate person in the world to do that. It's not any particular rule, but there has to be a reason for me to be there. There has to be a reason to engage.

Once I'm on board with the project, in a conventional structure, I would tend to leave a director and designer to wrestle their first thoughts together because I do think, as a lighting designer, my work is reactive. A set designer might say, 'I've only got one *Cosi fan tutti* in me' but I could do *Cosi fan tutti* twenty-five times, because every time, I'm responding to a different interpretative act. I don't think I'm an 'artist'. I'm a craftsperson, you know, I think I'm a creative, I'm a designer. I design and I have a craft, but I think the tyranny of a blank sheet of paper is something that terrifies me. I don't want to do anything on my own. I can extend boundaries and be quite extreme but it needs to come from a shared sort of sense of ideas. I let a director and designer do their thing, or a writer do their thing. I think they're much more creative, front end, and I'm interpretative. The interesting thing to me is when it feels like things add up to make the essence of a moment: gesture; the movement of a head; the amount of light that's catching it; the object next to it; the bit of costume you can see; what sound you hear.

Along with the decision about the piece, I think, the decision to take on a project also hangs on who you'll be working with and alongside. There are some directors and designers that I get on very, very well with and who challenge me, or we challenge each other and I think all of us aspire to make work that's greater than the sum of its parts. There are certainly specific colleagues of mine, friends of mine, who make me much better than I am, definitely. I think at the best of times, that's something mutual; you encourage – almost dare – each other to be better. Somebody throwing an idea into a room and not being received enthusiastically or being wrestled with and spat out as the same but more or different is the secret of collaboration – that it's alive. It's not about fixing something. It's about creating or finding yourself in a space where something can constantly evolve. And there is no right and wrong but it's exciting because it becomes this alchemical thing in front of you. I think that goes back to, also, releasing something. I think there are people who make work as a form of control and there are people who might work as a form of releasing. It's a bit like there being a way of working pictorially and as a way of working from the inside out.

I think there's certain sorts of people who are drawn to lighting design because it's never finished. It's never right. It's never one thing. It works on so many different layers and you're always working on so many different levels. I think it takes a certain sort of character to be drawn to something that is so infinite. I think that's also why people find it so frightening. And again, it goes back to that kind of control. It is quite a common thing for young directors to say, 'But I don't know how to tell somebody what I want.' The best bit of advice I can give is never talk about light, talk about everything else, but talk about things you're happy to talk about. Talk about the character of the scene. Talk about the time of day. Talk about the time of year. Talk about if it's shifting, if it's still. Talk about words that mean something rather than 'I think the light is *this*.' Because our job is to respond, which goes back to the idea that is light about releasing things in the story. In essence, to be a lighting designer is to be a storyteller, to shape the way a story is revealed. When light walks into a space it's transformational, it pushes and pulls darkness to change how a space appears and changes what a character looks like in that space. Light can have a relationship with actors and characters – a way of being that makes it feel like something muscular, something with its own smell. All of that allows a kind of storytelling where the air between actor and audience feels charged with possibility. Because our job is to be the creative in the room who's responding with light so responding to the same stuff that everybody else is responding to, but doing a different bit of it so that every element in a performance is doing something different and yet moving towards the same goal. That's gorgeous.

13

Tracing the light

A performance essay on space, light and the process of looking

Nick Hunt and Hansjörg Schmidt

A *blacked-out room. The floor is marked out with white tape: a rectangle, between 3 and 5 metres long, divided into four smaller rectangles. A further line extends out from the middle of one short side. From overhead, tightly shuttered lights pick out the tape lines without lighting the remainder of the floor. The light beams are invisible in the air, and the tape seems to glow of its own accord. To one side, a table, carrying several viewfinders, each comprising a piece of clear Perspex the size of an A4 sheet of paper, with a handle to hold it by.*

Traces is an interactive light installation by Nick Hunt and Hansjörg Schmidt, initially created for the *Performing Light* symposium at the University of Leeds in 2017. Since its initial appearance in Leeds, *Traces* has been recreated in a variety of forms, changing in scale and technical implementation, and in some instantiations including a performer/dancer as a surrogate participant. Arising from the *Library of Light* project at Rose Bruford College, *Traces* began as a response to the challenge of capturing and archiving light's role in the experience of seeing. As it has developed, *Traces* has become an artistic work in its own right, as well as an action-research investigation.

In the following interview, Nick Hunt and Hansjörg Schmidt of Rose Bruford College discuss *Traces* with their colleague Brian Lobel. They frame *Traces* as an apparatus for seeing, thinking and communicating experiences of light, which draws participants' attention to their own situated presence in a visual encounter with the physical world. Through the conversation, *Traces* is shown to prioritize experiential exploration and discovery over abstract, rationalized thought, embodying a research methodology particularly suited to the investigation of light and its often taken-for-granted role in everyday experience. *Traces* is also shown to be a vehicle to investigate the experience of seeing as situated, embodied and unstable. The kind of sensitivities and sensibilities an experience such as *Traces* can engender in its participants are foundational for those working creatively with light in performance, and indeed for audiences. Further, *Traces* proposes a methodology for future research into the experience of seeing, and the affective role of light in the performance encounter.

Brian Lobel: What is *Traces*? What is different every time you do *Traces*? And what stays the same?

Nick Hunt: The space is almost entirely dark, with just these slivers of light that pick up the lines on the floor. It's really all about the light in space; the floor is there so you can understand the architecture of the light in three-dimensional space. You are sharing that space with the light and finding out how the light lands on you, how it lands on other people, how you might see it through the viewfinder, how you might catch light on your own face and see that reflected in the viewfinder. And then, picking up the archival aspect of *Traces*, you might try and catch an image on a mobile phone and share that through social media. We've done it six times in different contexts now, and it's been different every time. The changes have been partly to do with our reflections on each time we do it; there are particular things that perhaps catch our curiosity or that we want to explore in different ways. The first time we did it was in a mid-sized black box studio theatre, with a high ceiling. The grid pattern of light on the floor was quite large, filling a big proportion of the floor area of the studio. We didn't have the performer at that point, so it was purely in lighting terms a static installation, and it was all about how people interacted with it. We had what we call the viewfinders – each a rectangle of Perspex about the size of an A4 sheet of paper, with a handle on it so you can hold it up in the light. With the Perspex, you can both see through it but also see reflections in it, and the idea is to try and catch some of the light with the viewfinder (Figure 5).

FIGURE 5 *Traces*. A participant's hand in the light, 2017 (Nick Hunt and Hansjörg Schmidt).

Hansjörg Schmidt: So the bodies in the space have always been there. What's quite beautiful about it is that, when people come into the space, not really knowing what to expect, they will see this grid on the floor. They will look at it and then as they step into it, they find out that there are light beams that come from the ceiling so that it is not just a 2D, but a 3D thing. That's magical, because of course they can only see the light when it hits something – so they see the light on the floor, but by the process of stepping into it they discover that this light comes from somewhere and there's light in the air. They've got these little Perspex screens to capture it, and it's quite balletic. You get people trying to twist their bodies to capture their own image in this piece of Perspex, and so it's a performance in itself. It's a performance that's not for an intended audience, but that exists in its own right. And then indeed, as Nick says, we invite them to take pictures of themselves or of each other. They can then post it to social media. That's the idea of archiving, as much as exploring and interacting with light as a material.

BL: Did you use a haze machine?

HS: No, for the reason I've just outlined haze would give the game away. When you go to a rock show or to a musical, they will often have haze – like smoke – in the air that will capture the light beam. That's exciting because it gives the light a solid form so you can see beams or cones of light appear; it can be very, very dynamic when the lights start to move. We've tried haze, but it wasn't right because it would make the audience into a more passive spectator. They would look at this sculpture and it looks beautiful, but we were worried they would be much shyer about stepping into it. The fact that they go into something that's incomplete – that they could step in and engage – is exciting.

NH: One of the things we learned from Leeds was that in the high space there it had quite a solemn, almost cathedral-like atmosphere to it. People tended to come into the room and stand around the edges and look at it as if it was a conceptual art installation, rather than something that's interactive and playful. We had to work quite hard to encourage people to engage with it in the way that we had envisaged they would, that was for us the purpose of it. In the later versions of *Traces*, it's been smaller in scale and that's been helpful – less formal, perhaps, so people find it less daunting to engage with. That has really cemented our thinking that haze would really push it as a 'thing' – an object that you look at rather than a space you enter and interact with.

BL: When it was just a piece that audiences were exploring on their own, was there any kind of introduction that was given to them, or context that was there? What did the audience enter with in terms of questions?

NH: Where *Traces* has been presented as part of an academic conference, we have done a presentation about it beforehand. There has always been a poster on the wall indicating how you might engage with it. I've always been a bit ambivalent about that, because it feels like the work ought to somehow explain itself, or people should just explore it. But the reality is that people are always slightly reluctant or slightly uncertain, asking 'how am I meant to do this?' – there isn't really a 'meant'. The smaller, less formal versions have worked better, but even then, people seem to need some encouragement and guidance (Figure 6).

BL: The fact that there isn't a poem or something on the outside shows us that you're not interested in this light being a metaphor for something else. You're looking at the material qualities of light.

HS: That's quite important. Mark Miodownik's materials library at UCL was always a model for the Library of Light – this idea of demystifying material culture and making it into something that's tactile and that you can explore – that's in front of you, rather than something that you look at on a screen or from the seat in a theatre. Quite early on, when I was still a freelance

FIGURE 6 *Traces*. Light viewed through the Perspex viewfinder, 2017 (Nick Hunt and Hansjörg Schmidt).

lighting designer, I got involved in this initiative about explaining light to theatre critics because in theatre reviews the light is very rarely mentioned or if it is mentioned it's because there is something wrong with it in really basic terms like 'I couldn't see'. That was quite a big source of frustration to lighting designers, so the Association of Lighting Designers[1] arranged a series of workshops where we invited theatre critics to come, and we would very simply show them how light works. That was a real eye-opener, I thought, because it turned out that critics don't mention light because they feel that they don't understand it. They don't have a vocabulary to talk about it. In a way, *Traces* is trying to do the same thing – it's trying to give people a vocabulary to talk a language of light. Light is a dark art; we feel we don't understand it because it's mysterious and we can't see it. Often people think it's very technical, and of course it's not. *Traces*, I think, very powerfully, empowers people and teaches them about light. People who might otherwise have not really thought about light at all will leave *Traces* maybe being much more aware of it, feeling empowered and feeling able to understand a little bit about how light works – within the performance context primarily, but beyond that also about the process of seeing and engaging with light.

NH: Something we discovered in the shift to the horizontal version of *Traces*, where we projected onto a wall rather than the floor, is that the grid is a coherent grid when it hits the wall, but as you move closer to the source it isn't because the sources aren't all in one place. The grid breaks up. It is a clean, neat, geometric shape at the wall end, and then as you work towards the light source it becomes little broken lines with gaps in and you lose the geometry.

HS: That's interesting, isn't it? It's worth explaining why that is. Each line has got its own light source. There are four lines for the frame, two for the cross in the middle and one for the handle, so we need seven lights. These are spots that you can focus, so you can have metal shutters that then make the shape of the thin line. They all sit in a cluster, and at the other end of the room is the image. The geometry of that is very interesting: as you go nearer to the lights the image breaks up and it becomes these component parts. In the horizontal versions of *Traces*, people tend to be more interested in that than in the actual image.

I think why we did it like that – with a light for each line – was there is something about replicating the process of drawing something. You draw lines and then out of those lines something appears. And I guess that's often what you do with light – it's very painterly. You have brushstrokes and then you apply those, and it's very similar to how you work as a lighting designer.

NH: Yes – building it up element by element. As lighting designers we're very used to thinking in three-dimensional space. We're thinking not just about the bit of light that's going to hit the stage; we're always lighting one-and-a-half to two metres above the stage, at head height. That's the volume that you're mostly interested in, at least with dramatic theatre, because you are primarily interested in actors' faces. But of course, that's not necessarily something that the layperson thinks about. We constantly visualize those volumes of space that the beam is marking out, rather than the flat bit when it hits something at the end. *Traces* reveals that.

HS: Yes, and that goes back to that workshop with the theatre critics. That was one of the things we had to explain to them – the way light behaves in a 3D space. And the fact that sometimes you might want the light to come from there, but you can't because there's a piece of scenery in the way, or there isn't somewhere you can put the light in the ceiling of the theatre. All of that was a complete revelation to the critics; they had no idea. But it's good because it empowered them – the next time they go to theatre, they'll look up and go, OK. They can connect thoughts and effect and impact and all of that. So that's an important aspect of *Traces*.

Something else worth talking about is the monochrome nature of it – it's black and white, and I think that's interesting. The lines on the floor that you can see are the white light coming from the source, but we also put white tape down to enhance that effect. What you see is the light lighting a piece of white tape, so it's got this very high contrast image, and it means that you can't really see the floor anymore. Nick was talking about the 'cathedral' effect, what the installation does for our perception of space. Maybe that has something to do with people being quite careful and nervous to enter it, because it takes quite a while for you to adjust to the space. You can't quite see where the walls or the floor is. When we are doing it in a non-theatre space, in a seminar room somewhere, where it's white rather than black walls, say, and there's an exit light that's annoyingly bright, then people tend to be much, much quicker with engaging with it because they feel that they understand the space.

NH: Yes, in a really good blackout, in a black box, you're right, it's quite a 'floaty' experience – your only point of reference is the glowing white grid. It's slightly disorienting in that way. I think the monochrome thing is interesting; it came up in a Q&A after one performance. One of the questions was about the light sources that we used, because that audience member was struck by the combination of the warmth – it's white, but it's a warm white, in contrast with some of the other light art exhibits which often use cool, crisp white LED light – together with the chromatic aberration. You get a little rainbow at the edges of the beam because of the relatively low-quality optics in theatre lights. The audience member noticed that, and I think he particularly noticed it on the skin of the performer, both the rainbow and the warmth. In theatre we love those tungsten light sources because they make people's skin look really good. The warmth is combined with some very subtle colour being introduced through this little rainbow fringing around the edges of the beams. This is something I've thought about a lot; occasionally as a lighting designer I worked on largely monochromatic shows where the sets were almost entirely neutral tones and then I was lighting with very little colour. Your eye's sensitivity to colour becomes so ramped up by being starved of colour for a time that the slightest colour you introduce suddenly looks really zingy and attractive, rich and interesting. So *Traces* is sort of black and white, but it sort of isn't, because your visual system is so starved of colour that it responds strongly to the little bit that's there (Figure 7).

BL: You've talked about what *Traces* can teach us about light – what does *Traces* tell us about seeing?

NH: For me that's a really important aspect of *Traces*, as a vehicle to explore the experience of seeing and particularly its instability. In a world where

FIGURE 7 *Traces*. A dancer interacts with the light, 2017 (Nick Hunt and Hansjörg Schmidt).

there's a huge amount of visual media that surrounds us all the time, and we are always looking at screens, through photography and video the world is constantly being framed, structured and organized. There's an assumption that when you look at a thing and I look at a thing, we're looking at the same thing. Of course, that, in a sense, is true of media, but it's not true of our everyday experience, because we are all always physically, spatially situated in a unique location. This is one of the things you find with *Traces* if you try to create an image using the reflective Perspex viewfinder. You think you're going to try to catch your own reflection, so you have to position yourself so a bit of light just skims across your face – a little sliver of light. Then you angle the viewfinder to see yourself in it and now you're going to do the thing you've been asked to do and take a photograph with your mobile phone, and you discover it's incredibly difficult because you have to get your phone exactly where your eye is and then you can't see what you're doing. The slightest turn of the viewfinder and you lose the image, and you realize how sensitive the conditions of seeing are. The slightest change means you don't see the same thing anymore, and I find that fascinating. *Traces* is a very simple, very embodied, experiential way of understanding that; it isn't a concept or theory or a description of that fact. It's an *experience* of the fact that we never see the same thing as somebody else, that it's almost impossible to capture what we actually see, that the act of capturing it changes it. The instability of vision comes through *Traces* really powerfully, I think, if you engage with it in that way.

HS: That's absolutely right, I think. *Traces* is a really interesting way to bring back the experience of seeing to oneself, rather than relying on the camera eye – to move it back to the human eye and to celebrate what the human eye can do as opposed to the camera.

BL: What did you learn the most by having a performer? What was the biggest change you saw in the performance, in the audience or about your own processes?

NH: I think the shift for an audience is that with a performer you are exploring the light field and the experience of the light through somebody else. Our performer was Lill Worden, who at the time was a student with us at Rose Bruford College on the European Theatre Arts BA. There were elements of what she was doing that felt like a performance – she was a dancer by background and training. But there was also a sense that she was a kind of surrogate audience person, who was just exploring through her curiosity what the light field was. She was an 'expert' curious person, who might explore *Traces* in a way that other people might not think to do. She was a kind of guide, pointing out ways in which you could be in the light, working with the light to create a play of light across her body and to reveal the architecture of the light in its three-dimensional form.

HS: In the process, the big thing for me was when we tried it out with her in the rehearsal room, I had a big urge for the light to become dynamic – to not be static anymore. Because suddenly we had this very dynamic body in the space. That might be because when I work with Clod Ensemble, light, movement and music are so intertwined. We did play a bit with the light changing, but it didn't feel right. That still feels like an open question to explore.

NH: Yes, absolutely. I think I've always been in two minds about that. I certainly enjoyed when we explored it with Lill. There was something about the music and her very dynamic movement that made it feel like a nightclub. She was moving through the narrow cuts of light very fast, so even though the lights weren't changing at all, it was very dynamic with lots of movement from the dancer.

HS: I think part of the reason why I'd chosen that music was to make up for the fact that the light didn't move. And actually, the stillness of the light was quite beautiful alongside the movement of the dancer and the music.

Traces has so far been presented six times, in various configurations and at various scales, to academic and public audiences, with and without a performer. As both an enquiry into the experience of seeing and a vehicle for experiential learning about light and seeing, it offers a powerful research methodology as well as being its own artistic outcome. *Traces* has the potential to engage with diverse audiences, and future iterations may be aimed at children, festival-goers or people in public spaces.

Notes

1 In 2021 it became the Association for Lighting Production and Design (ALPD) to recognise all practitioners working with light in live performance and events.

14

LX *ludens*

Mediations upon the play of light

Christopher Baugh

According to the Book of Genesis, the creation of light produced the first day, whereas the Sun, the moon, and the stars were added only on the third' (Arnheim, 1992, p. 303). Rudolf Arnheim locates light as being right at the heart of philosophy and metaphysics. Earlier in the century Edward Gordon Craig had posed the essential question for our research with a typically dogmatic answer: 'Can anyone on the stage tell us what is Light? Whence it comes from – what its power – NO!' (*Daybook* I (November 1908 to March 1910), p. 187). What mediates what we call the 'play' of light? Does that play have rules? If so, where do the rules come from – the dramatist? The lighting designer? Contemporary philosophy? The spectator? How does an audience see and experience light within their daily lives, and how does that affect what is seen on stage and in performance? Is there a contribution to an understanding of light in performance to be made by examining the nature of seeing and observation? Such questions imply important interactions between social appreciation and our understanding of the physics and neurology of vision. The great artist of stage light, Josef Svoboda, implied a methodology for analysis of such questions when he said: 'Contemporary art should present a ground plan of life, the life-style of its time.' (in Burian, 1971 p. 18). This chapter therefore asks in what ways might the 'ground-plan' of the observer, mediate the rules of the play of light?

In order to approach this, I will point to some of the cultural assumptions, conceptions and preconceptions of the nature of observation. In doing this, I hope to suggest that although new technologies of making light have been and are undoubtedly extremely important within theatrical change, the development and implementation of those technologies have always represented a complex reflection of, and interaction with, social change and development within the understanding of neurological perception and, especially, the contested balance between the objectivity of what is presented optically to the eye and its constructed meanings and significance. Just as the architecture of Shakespeare's Globe theatre is rightly considered as a social construct of theatrical space, so we should similarly consider the perception of light as socially and culturally constructed.

I will consider topics that illustrate significant historic changes and tensions, within the nature of observation and perception. Importantly, Jonathan Crary proposed the *camera obscura* (1990, p.6) as a model to represent the objective, monocular and hierarchical vision suggested by the dominance, until the close of the eighteenth century, of Renaissance single-point perspective. However, observation in the nineteenth century began to function within models of seeing that were understood as being subjective and located within the empirical immediacy of the observer's understanding. The increased understanding of the physiology of the human eye, the subjective temporality of the human body and especially the understanding of the neurological processes of human vision, effectively dissolved the Cartesian ideal of the impartial observer completely focused upon an objective reality. Movement, speed, disruption and change became characteristics of the ground plan of the first half of the uneasy, unstable twentieth century: electric lamps dimming, or brightening, the changing colours of a backcloth or cyclorama, the spectators' attention directed by the increasing materiality of the beam of light, increasingly set within powered moving scenery. The searchlights of the Second World War precipitated the subsequent technologies of scenic projection and the flood-lit attractions of the *son et lumière*.

Debates towards the close of the century concerning authorship and authenticity that questioned the superstructure of the modernist proposition of aiming for a universal understanding and appreciation, have precipitated the cultural destabilization that conditions our contemporary perceptions. Within this context, light becomes a dramaturgy: a medium that directs and defines attention and replaces language as the initiator of performance and may become the act of performance itself. As Arnheim suggested: 'light enters the scene of art as an active agent, and only our own time can be said to have generated artistic experiments dealing with nothing but the play of disembodied light' (1992, p.303).

Although on a number of occasions I have tried to account for changes of taste in dramatic literature, scenography and theatre space during the development of romanticism throughout Europe (e.g. Baugh 2004, 2007, 2013) what I want to consider in this chapter is its significance to an understanding of light, of transitions that took place towards the end of the eighteenth and throughout the nineteenth centuries in the understanding of the eye, perception and the philosophy of observation – and consequently of light. The technique and method of observing the *camera obscura* provide a useful and dominant paradigm through which may be described both the status and possibilities of the observer/audience. Crary (1990) has argued in his studies on vision and modernity that the *camera obscura* represented the relation of a perceiving and knowing subject to the world – for us, the perceiving subject becomes the spectator – the audience – and the 'world' becomes the theatre and the act of performance (Figure 8).

For over two hundred years – from the late 1500s to the end of the 1700s – the optical principles of the *camera obscura* existed as a model for articulating the physiology of the human eye within an understanding of optic neurology, and of course, it was a technical apparatus used in a large range of cultural activities. The *camera obscura* with its monocular aperture represents the incarnation of an objective single point of view: it serves as a metaphor for the rational possibilities of an enlightened perceiver within the mobile and dynamic disorder of the eighteenth-century world. The small 'pinhole' aperture within the camera projected an accurate image of the outside world onto a flat-surfaced viewing 'screen' within. The (frequently) solitary spectator observed and admired the presentation placed before them, while at

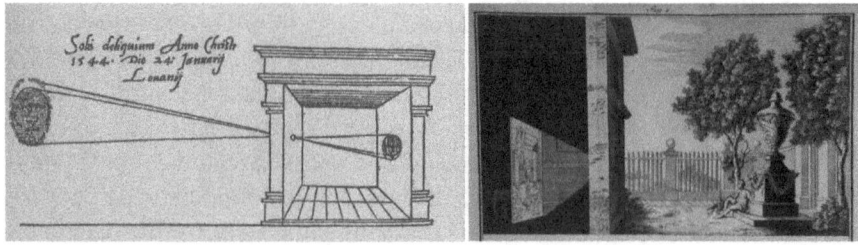

FIGURE 8 Camera obscura in Gemma Frisius' 1545 book *De Radio Astronomica et Geometrica* and an illustration of the principle of the camera obscura from James Ayscough, *A Short Account of the Eye and the Nature of Vision* (London 1755).

the same time, and significantly, retaining the independence of social self and cultural identity. This single dominating point of view, theatrically exemplified by Renaissance perspective scenography and its associated architecture, suggests a hierarchical and privileged relationship of the observer with performative representations of the world. The emotional distance inherent within that assumption of observation was reflected not only in the theatre architecture but also in the lighting of the stage in the late seventeenth and most of the eighteenth century. For most of that period, the auditorium shared its illumination with the stage. Within that context, an audience of the 1750s or 1760s, for example, would consider it unthinkable to *actively* connive at losing one's sense of identity in the theatre where a rigid social hierarchy was unquestioned. For *that* audience, the act of being engaged in performance involved balancing the socially identified sense of self, alongside an admiration of the skills of performance, painting, dancing and music. An enlightened spectator such as Dr Johnson may well have considered an immersive 'losing' of himself in art as an effective abandoning of his identity or indeed his soul – a form of heresy. One might be 'carried away' with anger, tears or laughter in witnessing the passions (or possibly be carried away drunk) but certainly not carried away or emotionally transported by observing and participating in an act of performance.

Daniel Dennett conceived of the 'Cartesian Theater' as a model to explain Descartes's late-seventeenth-century proposition that the function of the brain was to perform a sort of pre-processing on the sensory optical input in order to project it onto some kind of internal screen – just like the *camera obscura* – where it could be objectively viewed by the conscious self – its audience (Dennett, 1991, p.107). Such a fundamental binary of observation – between the presentation and the identity of the spectator – was effectively challenged by the emotional involvement of actor David Garrick, and the visual unification, harmony and spectator engagement sought by his scenographer Philip de Loutherbourg that aimed, through costume and careful attention to lighting, to locate the actors' characters holistically *within* their scenic environments. They both sought to actively 'transport' their audiences and significantly both were noted in their own day for radical developments in stage lighting: in removing the distraction of seeing the hanging lamps suspended over the forestage, and greatly shifting the balance of lighting between that *within* the audience and that upon and within the scenic stage. Their joint ambition clearly *anticipated* an attentive audience within a darkened auditorium, although the technology to achieve that was still a hundred years in the future. In his *Essai sur le peinture* appended to his report on the Paris Salon exhibition of 1765 (that included paintings by Loutherbourg), Denis Diderot provided the underlying thinking behind the decline of the *camera obscura* as paradigm and of Garrick and Loutherbourg's joint endeavour:

What is difficult is the correct distribution of light and shadow on each of these planes and on each infinitely small portion of the objects that occupy them; these are the echoes, the reflections of all these lights upon each other. When this effect is produced (but where and when is it?), the eye is halted, it comes to rest. Satisfied everywhere, it rests everywhere; it advances, plunges, is brought back on its track. Everything is linked, everything holds together. Art and artist are forgotten. It is no longer a canvas, it is nature, it is a portion of the universe that we have before us. (cited in Fried, 1980, p.87)

Michael Fried argues that 'The new emphasis on unity and instantaneousness was by its very nature an emphasis on the *tableau*, the portable and self-sufficient picture that could be taken in at a glance, as opposed to the "environmental," architecture-dependent, often episodic or allegorical project that could not' (1980, p.89). Garrick's seeming abandonment of reliance upon an 'episodic' performance of 'points' of acting, alongside Loutherbourg's harmoniously conceived scenic tableau, no longer reflected the architecture that focused upon the open, transformable liminality of the forestage. Fried goes on to cite Diderot urging the performer that 'Whether you compose or act, think no more of the beholder than if he did not exist. Imagine, at the edge of the stage, a high wall that separates you from the orchestra. Act as if the curtain never rose' (*Discours*, 231, in Fried, 1980, p.95). Diderot proposed the extinction of audience self-awareness brought about by the absolute engrossment or absorption of the performer within an environment of scenographic action. He recounts a recent dream that seems to prefigure the theatre of the late nineteenth century and indeed the beginnings of the cinema. Stimulated by reading Plato, his dream found him, along with many others, seated in a darkened cave, bound hand and foot and compelled to face the depths of the cave across which was stretched an immense canvas. From behind this captive audience, he explains, small transparent coloured figures were projected by a kind of magic lantern onto a canvas screen, thereby producing a remarkably convincing illusion of actuality. (The illusion was made virtually complete by assistants stationed behind the screen who provided voices for the images.) Finally, Diderot describes an especially memorable sequence of *tableaux* created in this manner (cited in Fried, 1980. pp.142–3). David Hume had echoed this in the *Treatise of Human Nature* (I, IV, VI) (1739–40) saying, 'The mind is a kind of theatre, where several perceptions successively make their appearance; pass, repass, glide away, and mingle in an infinite variety of postures and situations.' Sybil Rosenfeld in her introduction of Edward Burney's watercolour of de Loutherbourg's miniature theatre of spectacle, the *Eidophusikon* of 1781–2, accounts for the placement of the scenic representation high up and towards the back of the stage: 'The spectators looked up to it as to a cinema screen' (*Theatre Notebook*, Vol XVIII, No. 2, 1963/4, p.52). Significantly, she also cites W. H. Pyne's account of the model theatre that he visited in 1786 where he says that although Loutherbourg had displayed his graphic and painterly powers in Drury Lane Theatre he had not until now 'conceived the power of light that might be thrown upon a scenic display, until he made the experiment on his own circumscribed stage' (*Theatre Notebook*, Vol XVIII, No. 2, 1963/4, p.53).

By the middle of the nineteenth century, every possible aspect of architecture, scenography and its associated technologies – especially that of gas lighting – was used to pursue the complementary agendas of Diderot, Garrick and Loutherbourg: to absorb and to transport the imagination of the spectator into the representational space of the 'other worlds' which the theatre sought to (re)create (see Plate 31). The observer in the early nineteenth century *began* to function through models of vision that were increasingly understood as being subjective – located within the empirical immediacy of the observer's body. The guarantees of objective authenticity and enlightened identity that had been supplied by the *linear* optical system of the *camera obscura* with its fixed hierarchical viewpoint were too inflexible and immobile for rapidly changing cultural, political and eventually, scientific circumstances. By the 1820s, the observer is no longer conceived as a *passive* receiver of sensations. The objective hierarchy of the *camera obscura* made way for the unstable physiology and subjective, emotional temporality of the human body. The shifting qualities of subjective perception dissolved the Cartesian ideal of the impartial observer focusing upon an objective reality. The breakdown of this model of perception is well represented, for example, in the paintings of Turner. Based firmly upon an appreciation of the subjectivity of vision, his paintings of the 1830s and 1840s record the loss of a fixed source of light, the dissolution of a distinct, perspective cone of light rays and the collapse of the hierarchical distance separating the observer from the site of optical experience.

Early nineteenth-century scientific analysis analysis discovered that the eye does not have the objective neutrality of determining what we see: that in fact the subjective mind *constructs* a personal vision from data received through the optic mechanisms of the eye. Scientists and artists were especially interested in examining the seemingly irrational properties of the after-image; that is, the image that continues to appear in one's vision *after* exposure to the original image has ceased. This effect of this after-image accounts for the appearance of a complementary colour (the perception of the colour green after staring at the colour red) and the startling sense of three-dimensionality perceived when viewing through a stereoscope, offset photographs or later in the century, the appearance of the sensation of motion created by rapidly seeing closely aligned still images one after another. The cultural effects and performative opportunities afforded by these phenomena became a dominant concern throughout the century that began as early as Goethe's work on colour, *Zur Farbenlehre*, published in 1810, and became a leitmotif of the century's physiological studies of vision, as well as a predominant trope within photography. Additionally, the photograph introduced a concept of immediacy within perception (notwithstanding long exposures), of somehow 'taking, or catching life on the wing'. Lighting on the stage and especially in photography offered images 'on the wing' through the increasingly common experience of the flash of a magnesium flare for the photograph and the aiming of the beam of the limelight. In such ways light directed and organized the gaze upon pictures of life and 'moments' of performance.

Amy Holzapfel importantly considers that realist dramaturgy and performance practices were generated from the technologies and 'ways of seeing' of photography. The 'taking life on the wing' became illuminated stage images: 'moments of truth' being caught in the limelight of the stage and the light of the photographic electric lamp.

> For the spectators in Emile Zola's theatre [for example] the stage functioned as an optical apparatus revealing an unseen world [. . .] Zola used his stage to demonstrate that realism is not so much a descriptive attempt to mirror reality, as a penetrative process of exposing a hidden interior world – an examination performed by the emboldened eye of an experimenter. Zola relied upon consciousness of the corporeality of vision and positions his audiences as fellow seers of the unseen. (Holzapfel, 2014, p.19)

Light and the focus of photography provided the opportunity to expose realms of inner existence never before seen – as photographer Gaspard-Félix Tournachon (Nadar) used battery-powered electric arc lamps to photograph the sewers of Paris during the 1860s. In the context of developments in the philosophy of light and vision, the realist stage became, in Merleau-Ponty's words, 'a site of interaction between consciousness and the visible world' (cited in Macphee, 2002, p.32). Strindberg was a keen photographer with a passion for the exposing and revelatory power of light. In his essay in *Ny Nord* on 'Drama and Modern Theatre' in 1889, he said:

> This is photography, which includes everything, even the speck of dust on the camera lens. This is realism, a working method elevated to art, or diminutive art, which does not see the forest for the trees. This is the misconceived naturalism which believes that art simply consists in copying a piece of nature in a natural way, but not the greater naturalism which

seeks out those points where the big battles take place, which loves to see what one doesn't see every day. (cited in Holzapfel, 2014, p.141)

So the unmediated 'blind sight' of the *camera obscura*, or the neutral oil and gas-lit painted wing-flats and back-scenes of the eighteenth and earlier nineteenth centuries, gave way to the gas/oxygen limelight and, increasingly from the 1870s, to the electric carbon arc light. By the early twentieth century, the electric spotlight exposed and more precisely directed the gaze – lighting tells the spectator where to look and what to see. Lighting became the director of attention, a guiding Sherpa within the ground plan of observation. And if the electric spotlight beam focused attention, then its opposite – the depth and chiaroscuro of blackness – became especially significant. The ability of electricity to control and manage darkness, and furthermore to mediate the *quality* of that visibility became a radical new ingredient within the recipe of performance proposed by Adolphe Appia. Similarly, Gordon Craig's vision of the stage was one where blackness and the potential for the after-image was dominant, arguing that black was the most essential of all colours, and that it deserved special respect. The effect on the narrative method was significant since its dramaturgy effectively constituted a succession of carefully lit 'moments' of drama (like Craig's drawings of 'Scene'). The narrative method might be said to resemble a sheet of analogue photographic contact prints.

The nineteenth-century philosophical concern with subjectivity of vision may also be understood as underpinning the foundations of our contemporary notion of scenography. For example, in *The World as Will and Representation* (1844), Schopenhauer rejected the model of the observer as the passive receiver of sensations – the paradigm of the *camera obscura*. In its place he proposed a subject who was both the site *and* producer of sensation: 'The site of beautiful objects, a beautiful view for example is also a phenomenon of the brain. Its purity and perfection depend not merely on the object, but also on the quality and constitution of the brain' (Schopenhauer, 1958, p.24). For Schopenhauer and his disciple, Richard Wagner, the multifaceted and collaborative theatrical process – compounded by the seductive possibilities of the effects of light – could inspire an audience capable of losing itself through a process of *collaborative,* and interactive *perception*. In Wagner's *Artwork of the Future* (*Das Kunstwerk der Zukunft*) of 1849, he asserted that the work of art ultimately would be produced *within* the minds of the audience who encountered it, and the aesthetic unity – the harmonious scenic design – of this sensation would be central to its creative power. Both Schopenhauer and later Friedrich Nietzsche characterized the transition within observation, which I have described, by saying that it was the Dionysian that represented the intangible nature of the spectator's reaction and emotional response, as opposed to the pleasing, but distanced aesthetic beauty of a static image – symbolized by Apollo.

The nineteenth-century scenic artist, the painter who was also the lighting designer, wrote on the back of painted scenic canvases the type and quantity of lights to be used – the placement of gas battens, wing lights and portable units that would illuminate, blend with and make sense of the painting. And although embracing the detailed, costumed actor into the scenic environment of the painted scenes, the primary object was to illuminate the painting so that shadows and highlights were clearly seen. In essence, chiaroscuro was created by paint as much as it was by the absence of light. But Appia realized that this approach to light had little or nothing to do with the work of the actor: 'If we introduce the actor onto the stage, the importance of the painting is suddenly completely subordinated to the lighting and the spatial arrangement, because the living form of the actor can have no contact and consequently no direct rapport with what is represented on the canvas' (Appia, 1898 [1962], p.22). Appia perceived inseparable connections between dramatic action, the living actor and the scenic space that they inhabited. Movement of light was therefore inevitable within performance. Music provided Appia with language to express his concerns: 'Light is to production what music is to the score' (1898 [1962], p.72), and in consequence the lighting plot should be perceived as a score that expresses constantly evolving and changing states of light.

Georg Fuchs began working during the 1890s as an art critic in Munich. He was part of a group of artists who proposed a theory of spectatorship called *Einfühlung* or empathy. The theory articulated an 'urge to abstraction'; it sought a visceral, modernist response to art that it considered might be universal. *Einfühlung* described the viewer's aesthetic experience as a form of embodied vision – an emotional absorption within the work of art. Fuchs adopted the theoretical discourse of this movement to describe the spectator's experience of performance that he strove to achieve at the Munich Artists' Theatre where he directed and whose building he designed with Max Littman (a colleague of Gottfried Semper who had originally designed Wagner's *Festspielhaus* at Bayreuth) and which opened in 1908. The Parisian art critic Robert Brussel reported the opening of the Munich theatre on 18 August in *Le Figaro* No 233 (Figure 9):

> The rising of the curtain revealed an inner proscenium, a middle stage and an inner stage, sometimes on one level, and sometimes on different levels. At the sides and continually visible are two square towers of wood, each with a door and a window [. . .]. Light is the principal factor in the presentations of the Artists' Theatre. It is a light that liberates the imagination. Not the footlights, which are extremely reduced. [. . .] The actors are always illuminated from above and from the depths. They are always represented in relief.

FIGURE 9 Georg Fuchs, *Twelfth Night*, Munich Artists' Theatre, 1908, *Dekorative Kunst*, XIV, 3 (December 1910), p.140.

In the following year, 1909, Fuchs published an important book which is now almost totally forgotten: *Die Revolution des Theaters,* which has had one translation in 1959 as *Revolution in the Theatre: conclusions concerning the Munich Artists' Theatre.* In this, he echoed Schopenhauer's rejection of the passive spectator and pursued the subjectivity of perception to a logical extension in performance: 'For it is in the audience that the dramatic work of art is actually born – born at that time it is experienced' (Fuchs, 1959/1972, p.43). Importantly also he was among the first to appreciate the radical opportunities of the innovation of electric lighting, and in so doing he effectively constructed an agenda for the development of scenography and stage lighting throughout the twentieth century:

> Light has the power to dissolve a physical object, to dematerialise it, so that an intensively illuminated expanse of canvas changes for the eye of the spectator into an illusion of infinite space [. . .]. Light is, and will continue to be, the most important factor in the development of stage design. Modern electrical technique offers possibilities which it would be folly to disregard. To use them correctly, to distribute and regulate these immense and manifold masses of lights with artistic effect, requires the creative spirit of a sculptor. (Fuchs, 1959/1972, p.85)

In 1923, Craig, in response to the changing, restless societies post-First World War, extended Fuchs's understanding of light in performance practice. He was

FIGURE 10 Computer visualization of Edward Gordon Craig's concept of moving screens (ca.1911) Cat Fergusson and Gavin Carver, University of Kent, 1999.

precise in articulating the need for light to physically move *with* the scene as well as to change in colour and intensity working alongside the actors: 'This scene also has what I call a face. This face expresses. – Its shape receives the light, and inasmuch as the light changes its position and makes certain other changes, and inasmuch as the scene itself alters its position – the two acting in concert as in a duet, figuring it out together as in a dance . . . ' (Craig, 1923, p.20). Movement, he said, meets the requirements demanded by what he called 'the modern spirit – the spirit of incessant *change*' (Figure 10):

> Again, the relation of light to this scene is akin to that of the bow to the violin, or of the pen to the paper. For the light travels over the scene – it does not ever stay in one fixed place, travelling it produces the music. During the whole course of the Drama the light either caresses or cuts, – it floods or it trickles down, – it is never quite still though often enough its movement is not to be detected until an Act has come to an end, when [. . .] we find our light has changed entirely. Scene and light then move. (Craig, 1923, p.25)

Matthew Luckiesh, writing in 1917 for the architect and commercial lighting engineer in the United States, acknowledged the remarkable opportunities for movement and change offered by electric lighting:

Variety is a mobile painting in light, shade, and colour done by a master colorist, and it provides perpetual interest as it is altered to suit our mood or fancy. In thinking of variety in lighting the metaphorical phrase, 'painting with light' seems most appropriate. (Luckiesh, 1917, p.26)

In 1927, László Moholy-Nagy, a collaborator with Oskar Schlemmer at the Bauhaus, expressed a sense of modernist intoxication with transience and movement and the opportunities generated by new technologies:

Nothing stands in the way of making use of complex APPARATUS such as film, automobile, elevator, airplane and other machinery, as well as optical instruments, reflecting equipment, and so on. The current demand for dynamic construction will be satisfied in this way, even though it is still only in its first stages. (Schlemmer et al., 1961, p.67)

Increasingly through the 1920s, qualities of movement, speed, disruption, transience and change were keenly sought in the uneasy, unstable world and became defining characteristics of the ground plan life during the inter-war period: lamps dimming, or brightening, the changing colour of a backcloth or cyclorama, projected still and moving images, and attention increasingly directed by strong beams of light.

Benefiting from the mechanical and electronic technologies of the radio and talking picture industries of the 1930s, that, for example, enabled the remote control of lamps, stage light settled into its dominant twentieth-century role of guiding the spectators' gaze – the director of attention. The practice and theory of Stanley McCandless (1897–1967) epitomized this ambition for light on stage. In 1925, he and George Pierce Baker (1866–1935), who he had met at Harvard, created Yale University's School of Drama. Lighting at the time was primarily taught as an aspect of engineering and architecture, and accordingly in those departments. In 1926, McCandless offered the first academic programme of stage lighting and provided the first structured, formal 'method' for lighting the stage. The McCandless 'method' proposed a division of the stage into areas and the allocation of two to three spot lamps to each area that may, accordingly, be individually coloured and controlled. This approach reflected a summation of many of the ideas proposed by Fuchs, Craig and Appia earlier in the century, but it also reflected, during the 1930s, the predominant light-style of the domestic living space with its general cover coming from above, with individual 'table' lights providing points of focus – in fact very much still the form in our contemporary domestic living spaces. But implicit in McCandless's theory, of course, is the concept that lighting should begin upon a stage without any light. Furthermore, the lighting designer should 'lift' the darkness by employing precisely aimed spotlights whose focusing will be determined by the immediate dramatic action of the scene – light will follow the drama as it unfolds. In that manner light may be said to perform in partnership with the actors on stage.

The Second World War plunged Europe into a very intense darkness such that domestic 'general cover' became a forbidden luxury and the dim table lamp or the handheld, moving torch defined the experience of artificial light. But, at the same time, advanced wartime technologies began to significantly affect the experience of lighting. The necessary assumptions and social constraints of the blackout and conditions of domestic lighting probably found its most direct expression in what is now called *noir* cinema with its extreme 'Venetian blinds' lighting angles where light glimpses or fleetingly catches the human being – not too far in spirit from the searchlight trapping the aircraft in its beams. Such purposeful and intense beams of light became an important way for society to identify and control its environment – part of its ground plan of life. During the ensuing peace, the technologies of wartime searchlights transformed into high-power floodlighting of public buildings that proved to become a remarkable new phenomenon in the 1950s – and, for example, was a major innovation of the Festival of Britain in 1951 that consciously used light to herald the new technologies of modern living and, of course, to counter the rigour of wartime darkness. The popularity of those new technologies initiated a whole generation of *son et lumière* events that focused upon the spectacles of light and tape-recorded sound.

The projection of scenic environments had been explored in the craze for movement and change (and of course moving pictures) during the 1920s and 1930s, with the companies Schwabe and General Electric producing what were usually called 'horizon' projectors and were most successful in their ability to project meteorological effects such as cloud formations, storms and rippling sea scenes onto back-cloths and cycloramas. Erwin Piscator used projected film alongside dramatic action in the late 1920s, and in Prague, Frantisek Burian with his 1941 *Theatergraph* attempted to integrate projection alongside scene and live-action. But the huge size of high wattage incandescent lamps made focusing difficult and they generated considerable heat within their equally huge and unwieldy lantern casings. However, new technologies of the wartime searchlight added not only higher power tungsten lamps but also, and importantly, introduced more sophisticated lens grinding technologies that enabled projection to become more seriously effective within scenography during the 1950s and early 1960s. German projector manufacturers Reich & Vogel collaborated with lens grinders Ludwig Pani to make scene projectors that could dominate the stage with 'gobo' texture or fill the entire back-scene with powerful and increasingly clearly defined imagery.

Nevertheless, the great size of incandescent tungsten lamps and the equally considerable heat meant that projection equipment was extremely large, and the size of the light source filament continued to make precise focusing through a photographic diapositive very difficult. However, the combination of halogen gas and a tungsten filament within a quartz glass body produced a chemical reaction that deposited evaporated tungsten onto the filament. This greatly increased the life of the filament; it created a light with a very high colour temperature and also enabled a bulb that was very small. The General Electric Company patented the tungsten–halogen bulb in 1959, and its development during the 1960s enabled greatly increased light output to be focused into the very small area required to allow focused projection through a photographic diapositive. The use of tungsten–halogen lamps within ellipsoidal spotlights from the late 1960s gave the beam of light a new and significantly enhanced physical presence: 'I perceive light physically, not only visually. For me, light became a substance' (Svoboda in Burian, 1993, p.6). For Josef Svoboda light as atmosphere, and as the projected image with its possibilities for reflection and refraction using new plastic materials as screen surfaces, became the fundamental ingredients within his process of scenographic creation. They became qualities that well reflected and expressed the ground plan of the 1960s and 1970s: the abstract modernity of Prime Minister Harold Wilson's 1963 speech announcing the 'white heat' of technology and scientific revolution, robot mechanization and the automation of manufacture, and indeed President Kennedy's 1961 ambition to escape earthly reality into absolute space and to land a man on the moon. The absolute space of performance had been claimed by Svoboda describing his scenography for *Hamlet* at the National Theatre, Prague in 1959:

> It did not conventionally describe the place of action or even create it. It placed the action in absolute space, which can represent any place and any time. That is, the scene did not picture a concrete place. The movement of the abstract panels not only indicated spatial changes but was also a materialisation of rhythm, by means of which the action progressed. (Svoboda and Burian, 1993, p.57)

The rapid development of tungsten quartz-halogen lamps, and the invention of heat-resistant colour filters, also enabled the production of powerful moving followspot lights, which, unlike their lime and electric carbon arc-light predecessors, were much smaller, generated much less heat and most importantly could be effectively dimmed and coloured. By the early 1970s, subtly coloured and dimmable followspot lanterns could 'lock' onto actors and precisely follow their stage action while at the same time enabling the scenic areas of the stage to retain sufficient background darkness to enable extensive use of projected imagery. In addition, light beams of such considerable intensity could be created that their resulting form could present a solidity to match that of physical materials – with the ability to be transformed in intensity and translucency. From the point of view of stage lighting, Svoboda will undoubtedly be remembered by future generations for his experiments with a scenographic 'wall' of light consisting of battens of high-power parallel beam lanterns focusing upon the stage floor slightly downstage of their hanging position. In 1998 he was jokingly proud of the fact that in Italy this was called '*La contra-luce Svoboda*': 'contra' obviously referred to direction as in back-lighting, but also 'against', and he very much saw himself as working against or certainly contrary to the still-dominant McCandless theory of designer training and lighting the stage based on establishing a general cover of illumination, occasionally punctuated with spotlighting for emphasis.

But the 'ground plan of life' of the latter quarter of the century in many respects underwent a serious destabilization of understanding of manifestations of culture – whether visual, textual or performed. This effectively began within the theoretical debates of the 1970s and 1980s concerning the construction of meaning, authorship and authenticity, which collectively and inevitably questioned the viability of seeking the 'universal understanding' superstructure of the modernist proposition. The plurality and diversity of audience reflected in postmodern sensibilities affected responses to observation, and it underpinned the consideration by the middle of the 1990s of contemporary performance practices as being postdramatic, as moving beyond the realization and interpretation of a dramatic playscript as defining the fundamental operating mode of theatre.

In 1991 I accompanied a group of theatre students from London University, Goldsmiths' College to the Young Vic Theatre to see the RSC production of *Measure for Measure* designed by Maria Björnson, lit by Chris Parry and directed by Trevor Nunn. Its scenography was comprehensively located within a meticulously researched and realized context of late-nineteenth-century Vienna. A rather desultory post-production discussion with the students concluded with an outburst that went something like this: 'But it was so perfect; there was no place for me; they'd solved everything; they'd rehearsed it and decided what everything meant; there it was – fully interpreted and complete!' It seemed to me like a powerful and utterly instinctive rejection of the values of searching for a universal understanding and meaning. The students' responses confronted the concept of the rehearsal as the place where interpretation is undertaken, as the creator of theatrical 'truth', when scenic and lighting preparations are made, and where the ambition is to establish a perfected, completed, fully interpreted and authoritative performance.

However, in the same period other theatre-makers such as Théâtre de Complicité seemed to reject the autocracy of a modernist theatrical event as a finished, authentic, definitive, fully interpreted and completed work of art. For example, their *The Three Lives of Lucie Cabrol* (1995) was created by Simon McBurney in collaboration with, among others, lighting designer Paule Constable to construct this performance from the original John Berger story. Actors moving in and out of character, offering different possibilities and inflections offered a postmodern rejection of the authority of interpretation and presentation and was matched by the evanescence and apparent mutability of the audio and visual event. The full range of scenography (drawing *with* the stage) was explored in order to generate stories and *possible* meanings; the business of what was seen and heard upon the stage became the syntax of narrative method. Within a mutable telling of stories, the movement and changeability of light became a central ingredient within the dramaturgy of theatre-making, as Crisafulli has said: 'Light is therefore defined within the assembly of relationships, established when constructing the production, and coming to life through fairly dense exchanges with other actions and texts' (Crisafulli, 2013, p.199). McBurney and Complicité have continued to challenge and destabilize traditional relationships within performance and with their audiences. In *The Encounter* (2015) McBurney formally introduced and demonstrated binaural sound technologies that he would be using during his performance, and then consistently referenced and interacted with both technicians and audience as his narrative developed – in many instances, the technology *became* the narrative: theatre technology was active and became capable of dramatic action. 'I believe that light does not belong only to the technical or visual domain. Its fundamental functions are to shape time and space, to become a dramatic structure, and serve as a means of unfolding or producing "actions"' (Crisafulli, 2008, p.93).

Producing such 'actions', and central to the dramaturgy of Robert Wilson's work, his lighting collaborator, Beverley Emmons, describes how light and its tools became performative elements in his work during the 1980s, beginning with a firm dismissal of the theory of McCandless:

> What Bob does with a light which is extraordinary and difficult and unusual is to separate all the elements from each other and control them independently. [. . .] He wants the floor treated as a whole unit and separately painted with light. He wants the background treated as another whole, with maybe one colour shaded into another, but what's happening on that drop shouldn't affect anything going on the stage. Then he wants the human figure separately etched out with light, and very often he wants the head or even the nose of that figure separately lighted. (cited in Shyer, 1989, p.192)

The overturning of theatrical assumptions about interpretation and modality have served to invite the light and the scenographic to become an initiator of performance and to challenge the architecture of the theatre building as the principal location of performance. With its material abilities to articulate and define space, light has increasingly become the architect and constructor of places of performance. Dorita Hannah said: 'As a phantasmatic force, light plays a critical part in the spatiotemporal constructions, deconstructions and personifications emerging from the void. [. . .] The stage has left the theatre, seeking other sites with their own materialities, atmospheres, histories and phantoms, occupying the dislocated realms of immersive theatre and cyberspace' (in Crisafulli, 2013, p.14). If the stage has indeed left the theatre, then it is most frequently light that creates what Katherine Graham terms 'transient architecture [. . .] the ability of light to make definable, distinct spaces within given physical environments' (2016, p.76). But importantly, a significant quality of this constructive function is that the 'architecture' may be perceptibly, or imperceptibly, dissolved and remodelled. Graham argues that the liminality of such spaces created by light is a crucial quality within such performance and suggests that creating and moving the boundaries of such spaces represents a significant quality of control in performance.

The feeling and the embodied awareness of control (and its inevitable bestowal of degrees of interactivity upon the spectator) is an extremely significant quality in contemporary performance. The beam of a torch light shining into the darkened sky, through its materiality creates the space of vision, but its capacity for movement also enables a powerful feeling of control and power – for example, the searchlight sense of authority that excites the child when first holding a torch and shining it into the night sky. The great popularity of outdoor light shows and the projection of imagery onto computer-mapped buildings and environments offer a not dissimilar spine-tingling sense of power and control – enhancing an aura of presence and engagement and giving a distinctive sense of liveness. It is the action of generating the beams of light, the movement and the transience of the imagery that excites attention – a photograph may record individual moments of its achievement, but it is the ultimate transience of generating light that provides such strong feelings of authenticity.

Importantly also, such performance of light frequently acts as an immense and ungovernable iconoclastic graffiti artist (see colour Plate 32), echoing the daring, audacious and subversive wit of graffiti street artist Banksy. Consider our shared pleasure in participating in the bold appropriation and illumination of cathedrals, heritage buildings and respectable civic halls with bright, colourful and often bizarre imagery. The seemingly mysterious and 'coming out of nowhere' ability of powerful projected light to create 'alternative truths' by invading a well-known building facade with imagery that not infrequently shatters the dour respectability of public buildings: creatures crawling over the gothic tracery of cathedrals, converting Buckingham Palace into a downmarket terraced row of houses, tortured, nightmare figures taking over the respectability of Georgian architecture, while the pillars of the portico facade of a classical courthouse building crumble and shatter. In those instances, light has the aura of the superhero vandal whose power matches and stretches the capabilities that we all possess in our tablets and smartphones. Associations such as Banksy's with the 'underground scene', 'Massive Attack', using the Israeli West Bank dividing wall as a canvas for performance, creating a devolved parliament filled with chimpanzees as its members, 'what if the whole city were a theatre?' asks New Zealand artists of their capitol Wellington in 2021, and the responses of local councils spluttering with anger at the illegality of graffiti, or the New York police department using its NYPD Vandal Squad to track down and destroy. The stencilling technique of much graffiti 'writing' has similarities with computer mapping where light has the quality of being 'sprayed' through the computer map onto the building that serves as innocent and unaware projection screen. Within this context, it is the ability of computer-mediated light to 'play' subversively and dangerously – a renewed and restructured ludic 'feast of fools' quality – that marks its potency within contemporary performance. The stages for light have indeed left the theatre and have found and occupied other sites creating Dorita Hannah's 'new materialities, atmospheres, histories and phantoms' (quoted in Crisafulli, 2013, p.14), and occupying the dislocated and transient realms of immersive theatre and cyberspace.

Conclusion

This chapter has asserted that changes and developments in ways of seeing are more than a question of optics, that the way we see and respond to the visual is as much about the philosophical and social understanding of who and what we are, as it is about the retinal images at the back of our eyes. The *camera obscura* of the eighteenth century reflected a social appreciation of rational enlightenment that, while acknowledging the range and variety of human emotions, kept them in representation, at a coolly observed distance. The *camera obscura* offered pleasure to the eyes of the eighteenth-century enlightenment as Rachel Hewitt suggests in 'perceiving the order to which we belong' (Hewitt, 2017, p.366). Whereas the nineteenth century placed the spectator deep within the Platonic cave envisioned by Diderot with increasing attempts to engulf the observer ever more deeply within the emotional states of performance. In both instances, the use and operation of light have been closely reflective of these expressions of social philosophy. The advent of electricity allowed light to be owned and commanded in radically different ways. The twentieth century may be seen to have presented at different times sequences of oscillations of varying intensities between the allegedly objective exposure (e.g.) of a white-lit stage of Brecht or Complicité, to the intensely coloured and chiaroscuro stages of the finely detailed and interpreted productions of the dramas of Chekhov, Miller or, indeed, Shakespeare. But in both of these, for the most part, light has been a willing servant *within* performance operating in accord within a theory and practices codified by Stanley McCandless, although in later examples seen in the work of Svoboda, itching to break free and to take centre stage as a leading performer. But the narrative potential of light, enabled by the digital and its computer control, has significantly redefined the core ingredients of theatre and performance. The historic and classical relationship between an audience of spectators who assemble to attend to actors performing within an architecture dedicated to such a gathering is questioned, or perhaps rendered irrelevant. Light has discovered its agency to create and manipulate; it can define its spatial architecture; it can collaborate and empower its spectators as participants; and it can construct meaning (or not) and significance (or not) for the participants.

Of course, a wide range of performance practices continues to take place in theatres and studios alongside site-specific and found spaces. Artists and scholars such as Abulafia, Crisafulli, Hunt, Moran and Palmer (to put them in alphabetical order) have all undertaken impressive and ground-breaking engagements with the roles (and rules) of light in such contemporary work. But my remit in this chapter has been to point to some of the ways in which our ways of seeing and observation have and continue to reflect what Svoboda called the 'ground plan of life, the life-style of its time', and to have some forms of direct effect upon the practices of light in performance. This chapter began with the question 'how does an audience "see" within their lives and does that affect what is seen on stage and in performance?' To that extent the destabilization and disruption occasioned within the ground plan of our contemporary lifestyle with digital technologies, alongside their potential to instigate, manage and control narrative, has radically removed the sense of completion – a 'finished' work of art – that would be anticipated in traditional performance of plays within theatre architectures. If at creation it was light that produced the very first day, then its numerous contemporary manifestations, through a wide range of digital forms, provide the scale and the coordinates right at the heart of the ground plan of life in the twenty-first century.

References

Aardse, Hester and Astrid Alben (2016). *Findings on Light*. Zurich: Lars Müller Publishers.
Abulafia, Yaron (2016). *The Art of Light on Stage*. Oxon: Routledge.
Alston, Adam and Martin Welton (eds.) (2017). *Theatre in the Dark: Shadow, Gloom and Blackout in Contemporary Theatre*. London: Bloomsbury Methuen Drama.
Appia, Adolphe ([1898] 1962). *Music and the Art of the Theatre (La Musique à la Mise en Scène)*. Translated by Robert W. Corrigan and Mary Douglas Dirks. Coral Gables, FL: University of Miami Press.
Aragay, Mireia and Clara Escoda (2012). 'Postdramatism, Ethics, and the Role of Light in Martin Crimp's Fewer Emergencies (2005)'. *New Theatre Quarterly*, 28(2), pp. 133–42.
Armitstead, Claire (2022). *The Animal Kingdom Review – Thrilling Portrait of a Family in Collapse*. [Online] Available at https://www.theguardian.com/stage/2022/feb/25/the-animal-kingdom-review-hampstead-theatre (accessed 8 April 2022).
Arnheim, Rudolf (1992). *Art and Visual Perception. A Psychology of the Creative Eye. [The New Version.]*. Berkeley and Los Angeles: University of California Press. Reprint, 1992.
Aronson, Arnold (2005). *Looking Into the Abyss: Essays on Scenography*. Ann Arbor: University of Michigan Press.
Aronson, Arnold (2018). *The History and Theory of Environmental Scenography*, 2nd ed. London: Bloomsbury Methuen Drama.
Aurora (2018). Invisible Flock. [Live performance.] Available at https://invisibleflock.com/portfolio/aurora/.
Bablet, Denis (1966). *Edward Gordon Craig*, London: Heinemann.
Bachelard, Gaston (1988). *The Flame of a Candle*. Dallas: Dallas Institute Publications.
Bal, Mieke (2013). *Endless Andness: The Politics of Abstraction According to Ann Veronica Janssens*. London: Bloomsbury Academic.
Barad, Karen (2007). *Meeting the Universe Halfway: Quantum Physics and the Entanglement of Matter and Meaning*. London: Duke University Press.
Barrett, Ellie (2019). 'Material Sensitivity'. *IPPR Progressive Review*, 26(2), pp. 204–12.
Barrett, Felix (2014). 'Inspiring Innovators' interview with Isabel Lloyd, *The Economist: Intelligent Life Magazine*, September/October 2014.
Baugh, Christopher (2004). 'Stage Design from Loutherbourg to Poel'. In Joseph Donohue (ed.), *The Cambridge History of British Theatre Vol 2 1660–1895*. Cambridge: Cambridge University Press, pp. 309–30.

Baugh, Christopher (2005). *Theatre, Performance and Technology: The Development of Scenography in the Twentieth Century.* Basingstoke: Palgrave Macmillan.
Baugh, Christopher (2007). 'Scenography and Technology'. In Jane Moody and Daniel O'Quinn (eds.), *The Cambridge Companion to British Theatre 1730–1830.* Cambridge: Cambridge University Press.
Baugh, Christopher (2013). *Theatre, Performance and Technology: The Development and Transformation of Scenography*, 2nd ed. Basingstoke: Palgrave Macmillan.
Bellman, Willard F. (1974). *Lighting the Stage: Art and Practice*, 2nd ed. New York: Chandler Pub. Co.
Benjamin, Walter (1997). *One-way Street, and Other Writings.* Edited by Edmund Jephcott and K. Shorter. London: Verso.
Bennett, Jane (2010). *Vibrant Matter: A Political Ecology of Things.* Durham and London: Duke University Press.
Bergman, Gosta M. (1977). *Lighting in the Theatre.* New Jersey: Almqvist & Wiksell International.
Bentham, Frederick (1950). *Stage Lighting.* London: Pitman Publishing.
Bentham, Frederick (1968). *The Art of Stage Lighting.* London: Pitman Publishing.
Bille, Mikkel and Tim Flohr Sørensen (2007). 'An Anthropology of Luminosity: The Agency of Light'. *Journal of Material Culture*, 12(3), pp. 263–84.
Billington, Michael (2009). 'Michael Billington on Theatre's Technical Skills'. *The Guardian*, 21 October. Available at https://www.theguardian.com/culture/2009/oct/21/critics-notebook-michael-billington (accessed 31 July 2021).
Billington, Michael (2018). *Guardian Theatre Critic Michael Billington on the Power of Lighting Design.* Available at https://knight-of-illumination.com/michael-billington-talks-lighting-design/ (accessed 31 July 2022).
Bindu Shards (2010). James Turrell. Gagosian Gallery, London 13 October–10 December 2010.
Bishop, Claire (2005). *Installation Art.* New York: Routledge.
Bleeker, Maaike (2008). *Visuality in the Theatre: The Locus of Looking.* Basingstoke: Palgrave Macmillan.
Bleeker, Maaike (2015). 'Thinking No-One's Thought'. In Pil Hansen and Darcey Callison (eds.), *Dance Dramaturgy: Modes of Agency, Awareness and Engagement.* Basingstoke: Palgrave Macmillan, pp. 67–83.
Blesser, Barry and Linda-Ruth Salter (2007). *Spaces Speak, Are You Listening?: Experiencing Aural Architecture.* Cambridge, MA: MIT Press.
Blumenberg, Hans (1993). 'Light as a Metaphor for Truth: At the Preliminary Stage of Philosophical Concept Formation'. In David Michael Levin (ed.), *Modernity and the Hegemony of Vision.* Berkeley: University of California Press, pp. 30–62.
Bogart, Anne (2014). *What's the Story: Essays About Art, Theater and Storytelling.* London: Routledge.
Böhme, Gernot (1993). 'Atmosphere as the Fundamental Concept of a New Aesthetics'. *Thesis Eleven*, 36(1), pp. 113–26. https://doi.org/10.1177/072551369303600107.
Böhme, Gernot (2011). 'Un Paradigme Pour une Esthétique des Ambiances: l'art de la Scénographie'. In Jean-François Augoyard (ed.), *Faire une Ambiance/Creating an Atmosphere: Actes du Colloque International Grenoble 10–12 September 2008.* Grenoble: Editions la Croisée, pp. 221–8.

Böhme, Gernot (2013). 'The Art of the Stage Set as a Paradigm for an Aesthetics of Atmospheres' In *Ambiances*. [Online] Available at http://journals.openedition.org/ambiances/315; https://doi.org/10.4000/ambiances.315.
Böhme, Gernot (2014). 'Light and Space. On the Phenomenology of Light'. *Dialogue and Universalism*, 24(4), pp. 62–73.
Böhme, Gernot (2017). *The Aesthetics of Atmospheres*. Edited by Jean-Paul Thibaud. London: Routledge.
Bolt, Barbara (2004). *Art Beyond Representation: The Performative Power of the Image*. London: I.B. Tauris.
Breiner, Michael (2021). Personal correspondence via Zoom and e-mail with Scott Palmer.
Burian, Jarka (1971). *The Scenography of Josef Svoboda*, 1st ed. Middletown, CT: Wesleyan University Press.
Burian, Jarka (1974). *The Scenography of Josef Svoboda*, 2nd ed. Middletown, CT: Wesleyan University Press.
Bywater, Ingram (1967). *On the Art of Poetry by Aristotle*. Oxford: Clarendon Press.
Carney, Phil and Vincent Miller (2009). 'Vague Spaces'. In André Jansson and Amanda Lagerkvist (eds.), *Strange Spaces: Explorations Into Mediated Obscurity*. Farnham: Ashgate Publishing, Ltd, pp. 33–56.
Carter, Lucy (2018). 'The Ideal Collaboration?'. *Focus*, June/July, pp. 4–9.
Cavallo, Amelia and Maria Oshodi (2017). 'Staring at Blindness: Pitch Black Theatre and Disability-Led Performance'. In A. Alston and M. Welton (eds.), *Theatre in the Dark: Shadow, Gloom and Blackout in Contemporary Theatre*. London: Bloomsbury Methuen Drama, pp. 169–91.
Christensen, Dag (2019). *Nordlys Mystikk og Fakta*. Oslo: Bokstav og Bild.
Clapp, S. (2021). *The Week in Theatre: After Life; The Sun, the Moon, and the Stars – Review*. [Online] Available at https://www.theguardian.com/stage/2021/jun/13/the-week-in-theatre-after-life-the-sun-the-moon-and-the-stars-review (accessed 8 April 2022).
Collins, Jane and Arnold Aronson (2015). 'Editors' Introduction'. *Theatre and Performance Design*, 1(1–2), pp. 1–6.
Craig, Edward Gordon (1908–1910). *Daybook 1*. [Document] Harry Ransom Center, University of Texas at Austin.
Craig, Edward Gordon (1923). *Scene*. Oxford University Press.
Craig, Edward Gordon (1925). *Books and Theatres*. London: J.M. Dent & Sons.
Crary, Jonathan (1990). *Techniques of the Observer: On Vision and Modernity in the Nineteenth Century*. Cambridge, MA and London: MIT Press.
Crawley, Peter (2016). 'Pan Pan co-founder Aedín Cosgrove Gets Into the Mind of Samuel Beckett'. *Irish Times*, 21 April. [Online] Available at https://www.irishtimes.com/culture/stage/pan-pan-co-founder-aed%C3%ADn-cosgrove-gets-into-the-mind-of-samuel-beckett-1.2619535.
Crisafulli, Fabrizio (2008). 'Light as Action'. In Dorita Hannah and Olav Harslof (eds.), *Performance Design*. Copenhagen: Museum Tusculanum Press, pp. 93–104.
Crisafulli, Fabrizio (2013). *Active Light: Issues of Light in Contemporary Theatre*. Dublin: Artdigiland.
Crowther, Paul (2006). *Art and Embodiment: From Aesthetics to Self-Consciousness*. Oxford: Clarendon Press.

Crowther, Paul (2009). *Phenomenology of the Visual Arts (Even the Frame)*. Stanford: Stanford University Press.
Crowther, Paul (2019). *The Aesthetics of Self-Becoming: How Art Forms Empower*. London: Routledge.
Csikszentmihalyi, M (1990). *Flow: the psychology of optimal experience*. New York: Harper & Row.
Daly, Nicola, Janet Holmes, Jonathan Newton, and Maria Stubbe (2004). 'Expletives as Solidarity Signals in FTAs on the Factory Floor'. *Journal of Pragmatics*, 36(5), pp. 945–64.
Daw, Matt (2021). 'The Litten Trees'. *Focus*, April/May, pp. 11–15.
de Kort, Yvonne A.W. and Jennifer A. Veitch (2014). 'From Blind Spot Into the Spotlight: Introduction to the Special Issue "Light, Lighting, and Human Behaviour"' [Editorial]. *Journal of Environmental Psychology*, 39, pp. 1–4. https://doi.org/10.1016/j.jenvp.2014.06.005.
Deleuze, Gilles and Félix Guattari (1988). *A Thousand Plateaus: Capitalism and schizophrenia*. Translation and foreword by Brian Massumi. London: Athlone.
Delgado, Maria and Paul Heritage (1996). *In Contact With the Gods?: Directors Talk Theatre*. Manchester: Manchester University Press.
Dempster, Elizabeth (2003). 'Touching Light'. *Performance Research*, 8(4), pp. 46–51.
Dennett, Daniel C. (1991). *Consciousness Explained*, 1st ed. Boston: Little, Brown and Co.
Descartes, René (2002 [1637]). 'Optics'. In N. Mirzoeff (ed.), *The Visual Culture Reader*. London: Routledge, pp. 116–21.
Dewey, John (1958). *Art as Experience*. New York: Capricorn Books, G.P. Putnam's Sons.
Diamond, Elin (1996). *Performance and Cultural Politics*. London and New York: Routledge.
Di Benedetto, Stephen (2010). *The Provocation of the Senses in Contemporary Theatre*. London: Routledge.
Di Benedetto, Stephen (2013). 'Embodying Scenography'. *Performance Research*, 18(3), p. 190, doi:10.1080/13528165.2013.818333.
Di Benedetto, Stephen (2017). 'Cognitive Approaches to Performance Design, or How the Dead Materialize and Other Spectacular Design Solutions'. In Joslin McKinney and Scott Palmer (eds.), *Scenography Expanded: An Introduction to Contemporary Performance Design*. London: Bloomsbury Methuen Drama, pp. 155–68.
Dissanayake, Ellen (1995). *Homo Aestheticus: Where art Comes From and Why*. Seattle: University of Washington Press.
Donger, Simon (2012). *Gloom: Scenography as Praxis of Imperceptibility*. Unpublished PhD Thesis, Royal Central School of Speech & Drama. University of London.
Dorn, Dieter (1999). 'Making Light'. In Max Keller and Johannes Weiss (eds.), *Light Fantastic : The art and Design of Stage Lighting*. Munich, Prestel, pp. 9–10.
Dowd, Marion, R. Robert Hensey, and M. Dowd (eds.) (2016). *The Archaeology of Darkness*. Oxford: Oxbow Books.
Dreyer, Kevin (2020). *Dance and Light: The Partnership Between Choreography and Lighting Design*. London: Routledge.

Duhalde, Marcelo, Yan Jing, Tian and Dennis, Wong. (2019). *Cantonese Performing Art*. [Online] Available at https://multimedia.scmp.com/infographics/culture/article/3036661/cantonese-opera/index.html.
Dunham, Richard E. (2019). *Stage Lighting: Design Applications and More*. London. Routledge.
DV8 Physical Theatre (2008). *To Be Straight with You* [Live performance.]
Eaton, Ben (2018). 'What is Aurora?'. *Aurora Publication One*, Available at https://invisibleflock.com/portfolio/aurora-one-publication/ (accessed 22 July 2022).
Edensor, Tim (2015a). 'Light Art, Perception, and Sensation'. *The Senses and Society*, 10(2), pp. 138–57.
Edensor, Tim (2015b). 'The Gloomy City: Rethinking the Relationship Between Light and Dark'. *Urban Studies*, 52(3), pp. 422–38.
Edensor, Tim (2017). *From Light to Dark; Daylight, Illumination, and Gloom*. Minneapolis: University of Minnesota Press.
Erwine, Barbara (2017). *Creating Sensory Spaces: The Architecture of the Invisible*. London: Routledge.
Essig, Linda (2002). *The Speed of Light: Dialogues on Lighting Design and Technological Change*. Portsmouth, NH: Heinemann Educational Books.
Essig, Linda (2005). *Lighting and the Design Idea*, 2nd ed. London: Wadsworth and Thomson.
Essin, Christin (2015). 'Unseen Labour and Backstage Choreographies: A Materialist Production History of *A Chorus Line*'. *Theatre Journal*, 67(2), pp. 197–212.
Essin, Christin (2021). *Working Backstage: A Cultural History and Ethnography of Technical Theater Labor*. Ann Arbor: University of Michigan Press.
Eteläpelto, Anneli, Katja Vähäsantanen, Päivi Hökkä and Susanna Paloniemi (2013). 'What is Agency? Conceptualizing Professional Agency at Work'. *Educational Research Review*, 10(1), pp. 45–65.
Everything That Happened and Would Happen (2018). Heiner Goebbels. [Live performance.] Available at https://www.heinergoebbels.com/en/archive/works/complete/view/396/info.
Fenemore, Anna (2001). *The Pigeon Project: A Study of the Potential for Embodied Praxis in Performance Spectating*. Unpublished PhD thesis, Manchester Metropolitan University. Available online: https://ethos.bl.uk/OrderDetails.do?uin=uk.bl.ethos.392839
Fischer-Lichte, Erika (1992). *The Semiotics of Theatre*. Bloomington: Indiana University Press.
Fischer-Lichte, Erika (2008). *The Transformative Power of Performance: A New Aesthetics*. London: Routledge.
Fischer-Lichte, Erika (2016). 'The Art of Spectatorship'. *Journal of Contemporary Drama in English*, 4(1), pp. 164–79.
Fisher, Mark (2015). *How to Write About Theatre: A Manual for Critics, Students and Bloggers*. London: Bloomsbury Methuen Drama.
Fisher, Mark (2021). *Shadows and Spotlights: Conversations With Kai Fischer, Lizzie Powell and Simon Wilkinson*. Edinburgh: Envelope Room and Salamander Street.
Fix and Foxy. https://fixfoxy.com/en/ungdom/ (accessed 20 December 2021).
Fix and Foxy (2015). *Ungdom* [*Youth*], [Live performance.] Republique Theatre, Copenhagen.
Foster, Hal (ed.) (1988). *Vision and Visuality*. New York: The New Press.

Fraser, Neil (1999). *Stage Lighting Design: A Practical Guide*. Marlborough: Crowood.
Fraser, Neil (2002). *Stage Lighting Explained*. Wiltshire: Crowood Press.
Fraser, Neil (2003). *Stage Lighting Design: A Practical Guide*, 2nd ed. Wiltshire: Crowood Press.
Fried, Michael (1980). *Absorption and Theatricality: Painting and Beholder in the Age of Diderot*. Berkeley: California University Press.
Fuchs, George (1959 reissue 1972). *(Die Revolution des Theaters) Revolution in the Theatre: Conclusions Concerning the Munich Artists' Theatre*. Port Washington, NY: Kennikat Press.
Gardner, Lyn (2009). 'Bright Spark: The Rise of the Lighting Designer'. *Guardian*. [Online] Available at https://www.theguardian.com/stage/theatreblog/2009/feb/16/stage-lighting-design (Accessed 29 April 2017).
Gaut, Berys and Matthew Kieran (2018). 'Philosophising About Creativity'. In Berys Gaut and Matthew Kieran (eds.), *Creativity and Philosophy*. Abingdon: Routledge, pp. 1–21.
Gibson, James J. (1966). *The Senses Considered as Perceptual Systems*. Boston: Houghton Mifflin.
Gibson, James J. (1979). *The Ecological Approach to Visual Perception*. Boston: Houghton Mifflin.
Gibson, James J. and Dickens Waddell (1952). 'Homogeneous Retinal Stimulation and Visual Perception'. *The American Journal of Psychology*, 65(2), pp. 263–70.
Gillette, J. Michael (1989). *Designing With Light: An Introduction to Stage Lighting*, 2nd ed. Mountain View, CA: Mayfield Pub. Co.
Glenn, Phillip (2019). 'Conflict Interaction: Insights from Conversation Analysis'. In Matthew Evans, Lesley Jeffries and Jim O'Driscoll (eds.), *The Routledge Handbook of Language in Conflict*. London: Routledge, pp. 215–45.
Golato, Andrea (2003). 'Studying Compliment Responses: A Comparison of DCTs and Recordings of Natural Occurring Talk'. *Applied Linguistics*, 24(1), pp. 90–121.
Gong, W.D. (1991). 龔和德，《梅蘭芳藝術評論》梅蘭芳與舞台美術，千華出版社.
Graham, Katherine (2016). 'Active Roles of Light in Performance Design'. *Theatre and Performance Design*, 2(1–2), pp. 73–81.
Graham, Katherine (2018a). *Scenographic Light: Towards an Understanding of Expressive Light in Performance*. Unpublished PhD Thesis, University of Leeds.
Graham, Katherine (2018b). 'In the Shadow of a Dancer: Light as Dramaturgy in Contemporary Performance'. *Contemporary Theatre Review*, 28(2), pp. 196–209.
Graham, Katherine (2020a). 'Between Material and Perception: Towards an Aesthetics of Scenography'. *Theatre and Performance Design*, 6(1–2), pp. 9–25.
Graham, Katherine (2020b). 'The Play of Light: Rethinking Mood Lighting in Performance'. *Studies in Theatre and Performance*, doi:10.1080/14682761.2020.1785194.
Griggs, Elliot (2018). 'The Importance of Collaboration'. *Focus*, December 2018/January 2019, pp. 36–38.
Grondahl, Laura (2014). 'From Candle Light to Contemporary Lighting Systems: How Lighting Technology Shapes Scenographic Practices'. *Nordic Theatre Studies*, 26(2), pp. 20–32.

Hamed, Uzma (2015). Programme notes for premier of *Woolf Works*. The Royal Ballet, The Royal Opera House.
Handke, Peter (2002). 'Offending the Audience'. Translated by Michael Roloff. In *Contemporary German Plays II*, edited by Margaret-Herzfeld Sander. New York: Continuum.
Hann, Rachel (2019). *Beyond Scenography*. London: Routledge
Hansen, Pil and Darcey Callison (2015). *Dance Dramaturgy: Modes of Agency, Awareness and Engagement*. Basingstoke: Palgrave Macmillan.
Harman, Graham (2011). *Tool-Being: Heidegger and the Metaphysics of Objects*. Open Court.
Hazel, Spencer (2018). 'Discovering Interactional Authenticity: Tracking Theatre Practitioners Across Rehearsals'. In Simona Pekarek Doehler, Johannes Wagner, and Esther González-Martínez (eds.), *Longitudinal Studies on the Organization of Social Interaction*. Basingstoke: Palgrave Macmillan, pp. 255–283.
Henry VI Trilogy (2002). [Live performance.] Stratford, Shakespeare Festival Theatre.
Hewitt, Rachel (2017). *A Revolution of Feeling: The Decade That Forged the Modern Mind*. London: Granta.
Hitlin, Steven and Glen H. Elder (2007). 'Time, Self and the Curiously Abstract Concept of Agency'. *Sociological Theory*, 25(2), pp. 170–91.
Holmberg, Arthur (1996). *The Theatre of Robert Wilson*. Cambridge and New York: Cambridge University Press.
Holmes, Janet and Meredith Marra (2004). 'Relational Practice in the Workplace: Women's Talk or Gendered Discourse?'. *Language in Society*, 33, pp. 377–398.
Holzapfel, Amy (2014). *Art, Vision, and Nineteenth-Century Realist Drama: Acts of Seeing*. New York: Routledge.
Hopper, Edward (1960). *People in the Sun*, Painting – oil on canvas, Smithsonian American Art Museum, Gift of S.C. Johnson & Son, Inc., 1969.47.61.
Howard, Pamela (2002). *What is Scenography?* London: Routledge.
Hu, T. Ch. (1993). *Li Yu Xi Ju Yi Shu Lun*（李漁戲曲藝術論）. Zhong Qing: Xi Nan Shi Fan Da Xue Chu Ban She.
Humalisto, Tomi, Kimmo Karjunen and Raisa Kilpeläinen (eds.) (2019). *360 Degrees: Focus on Lighting Design*. Helsinki: University of the Arts Helsinki.
Hunt, Nick (2013a). 'Exosomatic (Light) Organ: Creating and Using an "Expressive Instrument" for Theatre Lighting Control'. *International Journal of Performance Arts and Digital Media*, 9(2), pp. 295–313.
Hunt, Nick (2013b). 'The Virtuosity of the Lighting Artist: Designer or Performer?'. In S. Palmer, *Light: Readings in Theatre Practice*. New York: Palgrave Macmillan, pp. 232–240.
Hunt, Nick (2015). *A Commanding View: The Scenography of the Production Desk and the Technical Rehearsal*. International Federation for Theatre Research, 6–10 July, Hyderabad, India.
Hunt, Nick and Susan Melrose (2005). 'Techne, Technology, Technician – The Creative Practices of the Mastercraftsperson'. *Performance Research*, 10(4), pp. 70–82.
Hurley, Erin (2004). 'Blackout: Utopian Technologies in Adrienne Kennedy's Funnyhouse of a Negro'. *Modern Drama*, 47(2), pp. 200–18.

Ingold, Tim (2005). 'The Eye of the Storm: Visual Perception and the Weather'. *Visual Studies*, 20(2), pp. 97–104.
Ingold, Tim (2011). *Being Alive: Essays on Movement, Knowledge and Description*. London: Routledge.
Ingold, Tim (2022). *Imagining for Real: Essays on Creation, Attention, and Correspondence*. Abingdon, Oxon: Routledge.
Isackes, Richard M. (2012). *Rethinking the Pedagogy of Performance Collaboration: Two Case Studies That Assert Authorial Agency in Scenographic Education*. Performance: Visual Aspects of Performance Practice, 13–15 November, Salzburg, Austria.
Isenstadt, Sandy, et al. (eds.) (2015). *Cities of Light: Two Centuries of Urban Illumination*. London: Routledge.
It Felt Like A Kiss (2009). [Live performance.] Punchdrunk co-production with Adam Curtis, BBC and Manchester International Festival, Manchester, July 2–19.
It Is Not The End Of The World (2019). Superflex. Installation at Cisternerne, Frederiksberg Museum, Copenhagen, 16 March–30 November 2019. Available at https://frederiksbergmuseerne.dk/en/udstillinger/superflex-it-is-not-the-end-of-the-world/.
Janssens, Ann Veronica (2020). *Hot Pink Turquoise*. Louisiana Museum of Modern Art. Available at https://www.louisiana.dk/en/exhibition/hot-pink-turquoise (Accessed 17 August 2020).
Johnson, Dominic (2012). *Theatre and The Visual*. Basingstoke: Palgrave Macmillan.
Johnson, Nicholas E. and Jonathan Heron (2020). *Experimental Beckett: Contemporary Performance Practices*. Cambridge: Cambridge University Press.
Jones, Jonathan (2010). 'Warning: Art That Will Blow Your Mind'. *The Guardian*, 17 November 2010. Available at https://www.theguardian.com/artanddesign/jonathanjonesblog/2010/nov/17/bindu-shards-james-turrell-gagosian?CMP=twt_gu (Accessed 20 December 2021).
Jones, Robert Edmond (1941). *The Dramatic Imagination*. New York: Theatre Arts Books.
Jones, Robert Edmond (2004). *The Dramatic Imagination: Reflections and Speculations on the Art of the Theatre*. London: Routledge.
Keller, Max (1999). *Light Fantastic: The Art and Design of Stage Lighting*. Munich: Prestel.
Kendrick, Lynne (2017). 'Aural Visions: Sonic Spectatorship in the Dark'. In A. Alston and M. Welton (eds.), *Theatre in the Dark: Shadow, Gloom and Blackout in Contemporary Theatre*. London: Bloomsbury Methuen Drama, pp. 113–30.
Kieran, Matthew (2018). *Creativity, Conformity and Individuality*. [Seminar notes.] 24 January, University of Leeds, UK.
King Lear – Contemporary Legend Theatre (李爾王) (2003). Live Performance. Hong Kong: City Hall Theatre.
Kirby, E.T. (1969). 'Introduction'. In E.T. Kirby (ed.), *Total Theatre: A Critical Anthology*. New York: EP Dutton, pp. xiii–xxxi.
Kitching, John (2015). 'Tracking UK Freelance Workforce Trends 1992–2015'. In Andrew Burke (ed.), *The Handbook of Research on Freelancing and Self-employment*. Dublin: Senate Hall Academic Publishing, pp. 15–28.
Knowles, Ric (2004). *Reading the Material Theatre*. Cambridge: Cambridge University Press.

Kries, Mateo and Jolanthe Kugler (eds.) (2013). *Lightopia*. Weil am Rhein: Vitra Design Museum.
Kuritz, Paul (1988). *The Making of Theatre History*. New Jersey: Prentice Hall.
Laganier, Vincent and Jasmine van der Pol (2011). *Light and Emotions: Exploring Lighting Cultures. Conversations with Lighting Designers*. Basel: Birkhauser.
Lai, Kin (2003). Information obtained from the interview with Mr. Lai Kin on April 4, 2003 regarding his opinions of traditional Chinese opera aesthetic.
Layder, Derek (1997). *Modern Social Theory: Key Debates and New Directions*. London: UCL Press.
Leder, Drew (1990). *The Absent Body*. Chicago, IL: University of Chicago Press.
Lehmann, Hans-Thies (2006). *Postdramatic Theatre*. Translated by Karen Jürs-Munby. London: Routledge.
Levinas, Emmanuel (1978). *Existence and Existents*. Translated by Alphonso Lingis. Dordrecht, Boston and London: Kluwer Academic Publishers.
Locher, Miriam A. and Richard J. Watts (2008). 'Relational Work and Impoliteness: Negotiating Norms of Linguistic Behaviour'. In Derek Bousfield and Miriam A. Locher (eds.), *Impoliteness in Language: Studies on its Interplay with Power in Theory and Practice*. Berlin: Mouton de Gruyter, pp. 77–99.
Lotker, Sodja and Richard Gough (2013). 'On Scenography: Editorial'. *Performance Research*, 18(3), pp. 3–6.
Lucie, Sarah (2020). 'Atmosphere and Intra-action: Feeling Entangled Agencies in Theatre Spaces'. *Performance Research*, 25(5), pp. 17–23.
Luckiesh, Matthew (1917). *The Lighting Art: Its Practice and Possibilities*. New York: McGraw-Hill.
Macauley, David (2005). 'The Flowering of Environmental Roots and the Four Elements In Presocratic Philosophy: From Empedocles To Deleuze And Guattari'. *Worldviews*, 9(3), pp. 281–314.
Machon, Josephine (2013). *Immersive Theatres: Intimacy and Immediacy in Contemporary Performance*. Basingstoke: Palgrave Macmillan.
Mackerras, Colin, et al. (1983). *Chinese Theatre From its Origins to the Present Day*. Honolulu: University of Hawaii Press.
Mackrell, Judith (2014). 'How Lighting Design and Technology are Transforming Dance on Stage'. *Guardian Online*. Available at https://www.theguardian.com/stage/2014/feb/04/lighting-design-technology-transforming-dance (Accessed 11 October 2020).
Macphee, Graham (2002). *The Architecture of the Visible*. New York: Continuum.
Manning, Erin and Brian Massumi (2014). *Thought in the Act: Passages in the Ecology of Experience*. Minneapolis: University of Minnesota Press.
Martin, Carol (1999). 'Brecht, Feminism, and Chinese Theatre'. *Art. TDR/The Drama Review*, 43(4). Available at https://direct.mit.edu/dram/article/43/4%20(164)/77/9220/Brecht-Feminism-and-Chinese-Theatre.
Massumi, Brian (2002). *Parables for the Virtual: Movement, Affect, Sensation*. Durham: Duke University Press.
McCandless, Stanley Russell (1941). *A Syllabus of Stage Lighting*. New Haven, CT: Drama Book Specialists.
McCandless, Stanley (1958). *A Method of Lighting the Stage*, 4th ed. New York: Theatre Arts Books.
McEntee-Atalianis, Lisa (2019). *Identity in Applied Linguistics Research*. London and New York: Bloomsbury.

McKinney, Joslin (2013). 'Scenography, Spectacle and the Body of the Spectator'. *Performance Research - A Journal of Performing Arts*, 18(3), pp. 63–74.
McKinney, Joslin (2015). 'Vibrant Materials: The Agency of Things in the Context of scenography'. In Maaike Bleeker, Jon Foley Sherman and Eirini Nedelkopoulou (eds.), *Performance and Phenomenology: Traditions and Transformations. Routledge Advances in Theatre & Performance Studies.* London: Routledge, pp. 121–39.
McKinney, Joslin (2018). 'Seeing Scenography: Scopic Regimes and the Body of the Spectator'. In Arnold Aronson (ed.), *The Routledge Companion to Scenography.* Routledge Companions. Abingdon, Oxon: Routledge, pp. 102–18.
McKinney, Joslin and Phillip Butterworth (2009). *The Cambridge Introduction to Scenography.* Cambridge: Cambridge University Press.
McKinney, Joslin and Scott Palmer (eds.) (2017). *Scenography Expanded: An Introduction to Contemporary Performance Design.* London: Bloomsbury Methuen Drama.
Mei, Lanfang (1961). *Wutai Shenghuo Sishi Nian (Forty Years on Stage)*, Vol. II. Beijing: China Theatre Press.
Mei, Lanfang (1962). *Mei Lan Fang Wen Ji (Selected Works of Mei Lanfang).* Beijing: China Theatre Press.
Melrose, Susan (2007a). *Introduction.* [Online] Available at https://www.sfmelrose.org.uk/ (accessed 20 March 2020).
Melrose, Susan (2007b). *Still Harping on (About Expert Practitioner-Centred Modes of Knowledge and Models of Intelligibility).* AHDS Summer School: Digital Representations of the Performing Arts, Edinburgh, Scotland.
Merleau-Ponty, Maurice (1968). *The Visible and the Invisible*, Translated by A. Lingis. Evanston, IL: Northwestern University Press.
Merleau-Ponty, Maurice (2002). *Phenomenology of Perception.* London: Routledge.
Mirivel, Julien C. and Ryan Fuller (2018). 'Relational Talk at Work'. In Bernadette Vine (ed.), *The Routledge Handbook of Language in the Workplace.* New York and London: Routledge, pp. 216–27.
Miss Saigon (1997). [Live performance.] London, Theatre Royal Drury Lane.
Monkey and the Cave of Spiders, Pan Si Dong （盤絲洞） (n.d.) Video. Directed by Hong Tu SHI. Hong Kong: Overseas Video Recording.
Monkey Business in Heaven, Nao Tian Gong（鬧天宮） (n.d.) Video. Directed by Li Ping FANG & Fu Yuan Xu. China: CCTV.
Moran, Nick (2007). *Performance Lighting Design: How to Light for the Stage, Concerts and Live Events*, 1st ed. London: Methuen Drama.
Moran, Nick (2017). *The Right Light: Interviews With Contemporary Lighting Designers.* Basingstoke: Palgrave.
Moran, Nick (2018). *Performance Lighting Design: How to Light for the Stage, Concerts and Live Events*, 2nd ed. London: Bloomsbury.
Morton, Timothy (2013). *Realist Magic: Objects, Ontology, Causality.* Ann Arbor: Open Humanities Press.
National Theatre (2013). Programme. *The Drowned Man: A Hollywood Fable.*
Nibbelink, Liesbeth Groot (2019). 'How Does Scenography Think?' in Maaike Bleeker, Adrian Kear, Joe Kelleher and Heike Roms (eds.), *Thinking Through Theatre and Performance.* London: Bloomsbury Methuen, pp.100–14.

NONE Collective (n.d.) *'J3RR1'*. [Installation] Available at https://nonecollective.it/artworks/j3rr1/. (Accessed 28 August 2020).

O: A Cirque Du Soleil Production (2002). [Live performance.] Las Vegas, Bellagio Hotel.

Ouředník, Patrik (2005). *Europeana: A Brief History of the Twentieth Century*. London: Dalkey Archive Press.

Öztürk, Maya Nanitchkova (2010). 'An Uncanny Site/Side: On Exposure, Dark Space, and Structures of Fear in the Context of Performance'. *Contemporary Theatre Review*, 20(3), pp. 296–315.

Pallasmaa, Juhani (1996). *The Eyes of the Skin: Architecture and the Senses*. London: Academy Editions.

Pallasmaa, Juhani (2005). *The Eyes of the Skin: Architecture and the Senses*, 2nd ed. London: John Wiley & Sons.

Pallasmaa, Juhani (2019). 'The Atmospheric Sense: Peripheral Perception and the Experience of Space'. In Griffero Tonino and Marco Tedeschini (eds.), *Atmosphere and Aesthetics*. Basingstoke: Palgrave Macmillan, pp. 121–31.

Palmer, Richard H. (1985). *The Lighting Art: The Aesthetics of Stage Lighting Design*. 1st ed. Englewood Cliffs: Prentice Hall.

Palmer, Richard H. (1994). *The Lighting Art: The Aesthetics of Stage Lighting Design*, 2nd ed. Englewood Cliffs, NJ: Prentice-Hall.

Palmer, Scott (2013). *Light: Readings in Theatre Practice*. Basingstoke: Palgrave Macmillan.

Palmer, Scott (2015). 'A "Choréographie" of Light and Space: Adolphe Appia and the First Scenographic Turn'. *Theatre and Performance Design*, 1(1–2), pp. 31–47.

Palmer, Scott (2017). 'Harnessing Shadows: A Historical Perspective on the Role of Darkness in the Theatre'. In A. Alston and M. Welton (eds.), *Theatre in the Dark: Shadow, Gloom and Blackout in Contemporary Theatre*. London: Bloomsbury Methuen Drama. pp. 37–63.

Palmer, Scott (2018). 'Light and Projection'. In A. Aronson (ed.), *The Routledge Companion to Scenography*. Abingdon: Routledge, pp. 48–62.

Palmer, Scott and Sita Popat (2007). 'Dancing in the Streets: The Sensuous Manifold as a Concept for Designing Experience'. *International Journal of Performance Arts and Digital Media*, 2(3), pp. 297–314.

Pan Pan Theatre (n.d.). *All That Fall*. [Online] Available at https://www.panpantheatre.com/shows/all-that-fall (Accessed 8 April 2022).

Parker, W. Oren and Harvey K. Smith (1963). *Scene Design and Stage Lighting*. New York: Holt, Rinehart and Winston.

Pavelka, Michael (2015). *So You Want to Be a Theatre Designer?* London: Nick Hern Books.

Pilbrow, Richard (1970). *Stage Lighting* London: Cassell & Co.

Pilbrow, Richard (1979). *Stage Lighting*, Rev ed. London: Studio Vista.

Pilbrow, Richard (1997). *Stage Lighting Design: The Art, the Craft, the Life*. London: Hern.

Pilbrow, Richard (2010). *Stage Lighting Design: The Art, The Craft, The Life*, 3rd edn. London: Nick Hern Books.

Pine, B. Joseph and James H. Gilmore (1998). 'Welcome to the Experience Economy'. *Harvard Business Review*, 76(4), pp. 97–105.

Plexus (2012). Aurélien Bory and Compagnie 111. [Live performance.] Available at https://www.cie111.com/en/spectacles/plexus/.

Pomerantz, Anita (1978). 'Compliment Responses. Notes on the Co-Operation of Multiple Constraints'. In Jim Schenkein (ed.), *Studies in the Organization of Conversational Interaction*. New York: Academic Press, pp. 79–112.

Pomerantz, Anita (1984). 'Pursuing a Response'. In J. Maxwell Atkinson and John Heritage (eds.), *Structures of Social Action: Studies in Conversation Analysis*. Cambridge: Cambridge University Press, pp. 152–163.

Popat, Sita and Scott Palmer (2008). 'Embodied Interfaces: Dancing with Digital Sprites'. *Digital Creativity*, 19(2), pp. 125–137.

Pringle, Trish (2002). 'The Space of Stage Magic: A Study of the Application of Optical, Mechanical, and Psychological Principles in Classic Stage Illusions and Their Possible Relation to 20th-/21st-Century Experiences of Interior Architectural Space'. *Space and Culture*, 5(4), pp. 333–45. doi:10.1177/120633102237476.

Punchdrunk *It Felt Like a Kiss* (2009). [Live performance.] co-production with Adam Curtis, BBC and Manchester International Festival, Manchester, July 2–19.

Punchdrunk. *The Drowned Man: A Hollywood Fable* (2013). [Live performance.] Punchdrunk and National Theatre Co-production, Paddington, London 17 July 2013–6 July 2014.

Ratcliffe, Matthew (2013). 'Why Mood Matters'. In Mark Wrathall (ed.), *The Cambridge Companion to Heidegger's Being and Time*. Cambridge: Cambridge University Press, pp. 157–76. doi:10.1017/CCO9781139047289.008.

Rebellato, Dan (1999). *1956 and All That*. London: Routledge.

Reid, Francis (1996). *Designing for the Theatre*. London: A&C Black.

Reid, Francis (2001). *The Stage Lighting Handbook*, 6th ed. London: A&C Black.

Renmin, Xiju (1979). 'The Possibility of Major National Forms Assimilating Characteristics of Regional Forms is a Real One, However. For Discussion of the Relationship of Regional Traditional Forms to Major National Ones'. *Renmin Xiju*, 11: pp. 23–27, 37 and (1980)10, pp. 22–24.

Reynolds, Dee and Matthew Reason (2011). *Kinesthetic Empathy in Creative and Cultural Practices*. Bristol: Intellect.

Richmond, Harriet (2016). *Relationships Between Power and Agency: The Role of the 'Theatre Designer' in Performance-making Processes*. European Group for Organizational Studies colloquium, 7–9 July, Naples, Italy.

Robertson, Nan (1984). 'Jennifer Tipton, The Theater's Magician of Light'. *The New York Times*. Available at https://www.nytimes.com/1984/02/11/arts/jennifer-tipton-the-theater-s-magician-of-light.html [Accessed 9 November 2021].

Romance of the West Chamber （西廂記） (1990). [Live performance.] Zhijiang Xiaobaihng Yueju Opera Theatre.

Rosenthal, Jean and Lael T. Wertenbaker (1972). *The Magic of Light: The Craft and Career of Jean Rosenthal, Pioneer in Lighting for the Modern Stage*. Boston: Little, Brown.

Sadler's Wells Theatre (2016). *No Body – Hidden – Lucy Carter*. YouTube. [Online]. Available at youtube.com/watch?v=pQB2XJIlqfI.

Saraceno, Tomas (2007). *Cosmos of the Breath*. Installation.

Schechner, Richard (1994). *Environmental Theater*. New York: Applause.

Schivelbusch, Wolfgang (1988). *Disenchanted Night: The Industrialisation of Light in the Nineteenth Century*, London: University of California Press.

Schlemmer, Oskar, Farkas Molnar, Walter Gropius, Arthur S. Wensinger and László Moholy-Nagy (1961). *The Theater of the Bauhaus*. Baltimore and London: Johns Hopkins University Press.
Schön, Donald A. (1991). *The Reflective Practitioner: How Professionals Think in Action*. Aldershot: Ashgate.
Schopenhauer, Arthur (1958). *The World as Will and Representation*, Vol. 2. Edited by E.F.J. Payne. New York: Dover.
Seel, Martin (2005). *Aesthetics of Appearing*. Stanford: Stanford University Press.
Seel, Martin (2008). 'On the Scope of Aesthetic Experience'. In R. Schusterman and A. Tomlin (eds.), *Aesthetic Experience*. Oxon: Routledge, pp. 98–105.
Sha Xi（殺惜）(1998). Video. Performed by Yong, Zhi ji（童芷苓）and Li, Dou Sheng（李 多盛）. Shanghai: Shanghai Audio Visual Recording.
Shearing, David (2012). *and it all comes down to this . . .* [Live performance].
Shearing, David (2015). *Audience Immersion and the Experience of Scenography*. Unpublished PhD thesis, University of Leeds. Available online: https://etheses.whiterose.ac.uk/9467/.
Shearing, David (2017). 'Audience Immersion, Mindfulness and the Experience of Scenography'. In Joslin McKinney and Scott Palmer (eds.), *Scenography Expanded: An Introduction to Contemporary Performance Design*. London: Bloomsbury, pp. 139–54.
Shyer, Laurence (1989). *Robert Wilson and his Collaborators*. New York: Theatre Communications Group.
Shyldkrot, Yaron (2019). 'Mist Opportunities: Haze and the Composition of Atmosphere'. *Studies in Theatre and Performance*, 39(2), pp. 147–64. ISSN 1468-2761. https://doi.org/10.1080/14682761.2018.1505808.
Sifianou, Maria (2012). 'Disagreements, Face and Politeness'. *Journal of Pragmatics*, 44, pp. 1554–1564.
Solnit, Rebecca (2006). *A Field Guide to Getting Lost*. Edinburgh: Canongate.
Sørensen, Tim Flohr (2016). 'In Praise of Vagueness: Uncertainty, Ambiguity and Archaeological Methodology'. *Journal of Archaeological Method and Theory*, 23(2), pp. 741–63.
Spencer-Oatey, Helen (2008). 'Face, (Im)politeness and Rapport'. In Helen Spencer-Oatey (ed.), *Culturally Speaking: Culture, Communication and Politeness Theory*, 2nd ed. London: Continuum, pp. 11–47.
Stewart, Nigel (2016). 'Flickering Photology: Turning Bodies and Textures of Light'. In T.F. DeFrantz and P. Rothfield (eds.), *Choreography and Corporeality*. Springer, pp. 51–66.
Streader, Tim and John A., Williams (1985). 'Create Your Own Stage Lighting'. Englewood Cliffs, NJ: Prentice-Hall.
Superflex (2019). *It Is Not The End of The World*. [Installation] Available at https://superflex.net/exhibitions/it_is_not_the_end_of_the_world.
Svoboda, Josef and Jarka Burian (1993). *The Secret of Theatrical Space: The Memoirs of Josef Svoboda*. New York and Tonbridge: Applause Theatre Books.
Taiwan Today (1958). *Special Section on Chinese Opera: CONVENTIONS OF CHINESE OPERA*. [Online] Available at https://taiwantoday.tw/news.php?unit=20,20,29,35,35,45&post=25988.
The Crossroads（三岔口）(1999). [Live performance.] Peking Opera Troupe of Beijing.

The Crossroads（三岔口）(n.d.). [Video.] Hong Kong: Tai Ping Yong Jing Yin.
The Dream of Red Chamber (紅樓夢) (1993). [Live performance.] Auhui Provincial Huangmei Opera Theatre.
The Drowned Man: A Hollywood Fable (2013). [Live performance.] Punchdrunk and National Theatre Co-production, Paddington, London 17 July 2013–6 July 2014.
The Far Side of the Moon (2003). [Live performance.] Robert Lepage. Hong Kong Academy for Performing Arts, Lyric Theatre.
The Litten Trees (2021). Fuel Theatre. Available at https://fueltheatre.com/projects/the-litten-trees/.
The Phantom of the Opera (1997). [Live performance.] Her Majesty's Theatre, London, UK.
The Red Detachment of Women (1972). Hongse Hiangzjium 紅色娘子軍 [Live performance.] VCD. Jiangsu Province School of Xiqu.
Thoreau, Henry David (1886). *Walden*. London: Walter Scott.
Thorne, Gary (1999). *Stage Design: A Practical Guide*. New York: Crowood.
Tian, Han (1958). 'Zhongguo Huaju Yishu Fazhan De Jinglu He Zhanwang'. In Tian Han et al. (eds.), *Zhongguo Huaju Yundong Wushi Nian Shiliao Ji, Diyi Ji*. Beijing: Zhongguo Xiju Chubanshe.
Trainor, Patrick W. (2000). *The Aesthetic Principles of E. Gordon Craig Placed in the Imaginative Context*. Thesis (PhD). University of Maryland.
Trueman, Matt (2016). *Lighting Designers are the Unseen Heroes of the Theatre*. [Online] Available at http://www.whatsonstage.com/london-theatre/news/matt-trueman-blog-lighting-designer-awards-knights_41809.html (Accessed 22 July 2022).
UNESCO (2002). 'From Diversity to Pluralism'. *UNESCO Universal Declaration on Cultural Diversity*. [Online] Available at http://www.unesco.org/culture/pluralism/diversity/html_eng/index_en.shtml [Accessed 22 July 2002].
Vasseleu, Cathryn (1998). *Textures of Light: Vision and Touch in Irigaray, Levinas, and Merleau-Ponty*. London and New York: Routledge.
Volbach, Walther R. (1968). *Adolphe Appia. Prophet of the Modern Theatre: A Profile*. Middletown, CT: Wesleyan University Press.
Wagner, Richard (1870). *Die Walküre WWV 86B*. Wiesbaden: Breitkopf & HärtelPage.
Warner, Vessela S. (2016). 'Borderless Dramaturgy in Dance Theatre'. In M. Romanska (ed.), *The Routledge Companion to Dramaturgy*. Oxon: Routledge, pp. 348–53.
Welton, Martin (2012). *Feeling Theatre*. New York and Basingstoke: Palgrave Macmillan.
Welton, Martin (2013). 'The Possibility of Darkness: Blackout and Shadow in Chris Goode's Who You Are'. *Theatre Research International*, 38(1), pp. 4–19. https://doi.org/10.1017/S0307883312000958.
Welton, Martin (2017). 'In Praise of Gloom: The Theatre Defaced'. In A. Alston and M. Welton (eds.), *Theatre in the Dark: Shadow, Gloom and Blackout in Contemporary Theatre*. London: Bloomsbury Methuen Drama, pp. 244–64.
Westling, Carina E.I. (2020). *Immersion and Participation in Punchdrunk's Theatrical Worlds*. London: Bloomsbury Methuen.

Wichmann, Elizabeth (1983). 'Traditional Theater in Contemporary China'. In C. Mackerras (ed.), *Chinese Theatre: From its Origins to the Present Day*. Honolulu: University of Hawaii Press.

Wichmann, Elizabeth (1991). *Listening to Theatre: The Aural Dimension of Beijing Opera*. Honolulu: University of Hawaii Press.

Zeng, Y.Y. (1991). *Chung Kuo Gu Dian Xi Ju Di Ren Shi Yu Xin Shang* (中國古典戲劇的認識與欣賞). Taipei: Zheng Zhong shu ju.

Zerdy, Joanne and Marlis Schweitzer (2016). 'Provocative Atmospheres, Refracted Nations, and the Performance of Light'. *Performance Matters*, 2(2), pp. 4–22.

Zezulka, Kelli L. (2019). *The Language of Light: How Lighting Designers Use Language and Exercise Agency in Creative Collaboration*. Unpublished PhD Thesis, University of Leeds. Available online: https://etheses.whiterose.ac.uk/26799/.

Index

Note: Productions are listed under the performer, director or theatre company. An italicised lowercase 'n' in a reference denotes a footnote, e.g. 144 *n*.1 refers to footnote 1 on page 144. Similarly, '*f*' refers to a figure in the text, while '*p*' refers to a colour plate.

Abulafia, Yaron   4, 7, 9, 11, 18–20, 218
Actor. *See* performers
aesthetics   19–20, 36, 38, 58, 68, 167, 173, 175–6, 179
affect   5–6, 12, 14, 179
agency   105, 107–8, 111, 113, 116
Alston, Adam   13, 45 *n*.8, 83–4
Appia, Adolphe   5, 6, 21, 34, 44, 45, 50, 131, 144 *n*.1, 207, 208, 211
architecture   2, 204, 216
Arnheim, Rudolf   200–2
Aronson, Arnold   5, 34, 36, 37, 172–3, 177
Association for Lighting Production and Design (ALPD)   24 *n*.7, 24 *n*.9, 199 *n*.1
atmosphere
   created   126–8, 139, 153, 174
   embodiment   59, 179–80, 213
   emotion   77, 79
   experience   47–9
   immersion   36–41, 75, 216, 217
   as invitation   15, 43–4, 193
   mood   6, 58, 134–7, 142
   and weather   51
   in writing   10
audience
   behaviour   37–8, 193
   engagement   15, 140–1, 194
   experience   2, 13, 30–6, 208, 216
   mindfulness   61
   relationship to light   30–3, 171, 172, 191, 200
   visitor behaviour   64–71, *p*12, *p*13

auditorium   28–9, 34, 37–8, 74, 76, 128, 203. *See also* architecture
aurora borealis (Northern Lights)   120, 123–7, *p*21

Bal, Mieke   87, 88, 92–3, 97
Banksy   216, 217
Barad, Karen   33, 167, 174–5
Barrett, Felix   41, 42, 44. *See also* Punchdrunk
Baugh, Christopher   9, 11, 23 *n*.1, 61, 202
Beckett, Samuel   13. *See also* Pan Pan Theatre
Bennett, Jane   167, 174
Bentham, Frederick   8, 24*f*8
Bishop, Claire   91–2
Bleeker, Maaike   83, 86, 87, 97, 173, 180
blindness/blinded by light   35, 82–4, 89, 152, 169
Böhme, Gernot   7, 30, 37, 38, 48, 51, 59, 89
Bolt, Barbara   168, 169, 175, 179
Bory, Aurélien   170
Brecht, Bertolt   139, 218
Breiner, Michael   39–40, *p*5, *p*6, *p*20, *p*21
Burian, Frantisek   212

camera obscura   202–3, 202*f*8, 205, 207, 217
candles/candlelight   3, 137, 160

Carter, Lucy 72–81, 88, 104–6, 110, 117, p14, p15, p16, p17
  The Dream of Gerontius 80
  FLUX 79–80, p17
  Hidden 77–9, 88, 104–6, 117, p16
Cavallo, Amelia 84
choreographer 72–5, 104, 157, 170, 187
choreography 15, 68, 72–81, 114, 146, 152, 173
Chui, Psyche 8, 23, p22, p23
city. *See* urban environment
collaboration 18, 109–10, 114, 121–2, 151–2, 161, 182, 188–9
colour 67–8, 182, 185–7, 196
Compagnie III
  Plexus 169–70, 172–3, 175–8
Complicité (also Théâtre de Complicité) 182, 215, 218
Constable, Paule 182–9, 215, p28, p29, p30
contemporary dance 15, 16, 72, 138, 169, 173, 187. *See also* choreographer; choreography
control of light 207, 211, 215–16
Cosgrove, Aedín 18, 24f12, 86, front cover image
costume 41, 73, 78, 130, 134, 136, 203
Craig, Edward Gordon 5, 21, 41, 44, 50, 56, 131, 144 n.1, 200, 207, 209–10, 210f10, 211
Crary, Jonathan 201, 202
creative process 105–6, 111
Crisafulli, Fabrizio 4, 9, 11, 21, 23 n.1, 215–18
Crowther, Paul 167–8, 175

dance 17, 173. *See also* contemporary dance
dancer 73–6, 81, 104, 114, 143, 155, 156–9, 169–70, 172–4, 177, 178, 190, 197f7, 197–8, p14, p15
Daoism 133–4
darkness
  affect 13, 29, 51, 65, 66, 96
  beyond the theatre 3, 5–6, 71, 212
  as canvas 74, 183
  complete 160, 172

  as descent 34, 55, 95, 128, 184
  disorientation 40–4, 82–99
  dramaturgy 6, 13, 38, 41–2, 50
  experience 14, 15, 27–30, 34, 39–41, 53, 91, 92, 171
  obfuscation 82–8, 94
  perception 93, 97, 98, 204
  relationship to light 13–14, 50, 56, 67f3, 78, 88–90, 99, 168, 189
  as symbol 3, 6, 35, 44
  theatrical 37, 39, 207, 211, 213–14
  urban 5, 66–7
  vulnerability 35, 42–3, 75, 152
De Loutherbourg, Philip 204–5
  Eidophusikon 204–5
Dempster, Rory 139, 144 n.9
Dennett, Daniel 203
Descartes, René 83, 203
design process 6, 108, 120–1, 126–9, 183–4
Dewey, John 60–1
Di Benedetto, Stephen 4, 32, 34, 45 n.3, 62
Diderot, Denis 203–5, 217
director
  attention 207, 211
  collaboration 18, 74, 106–19
  role in lighting design process 17, 121–2, 143, 153, 157–61, 184, 188–9
Donger, Simon 82, 83, 86, 90
Dorn, Dieter 5, 6, 35
dramaturgy
  and agency 16, 108, 201
  and darkness 38, 41–2, 55
  and feeling 14, 46–7, 55–6, 59
  and light 4–7, 9–11, 19, 21–2, 56–63, 76, 77, 103, 109, 141, 166–7, 201
  and meaning 19, 39, 46, 47, 110, 166, 181, 215 (*see also* leitmotif)
  and space 11, 52, 54–5, 59, 61–3, 135, 151, 173–4
DV8 Physical Theatre
  To Be Straight with You 8

Edensor, Tim 3, 5, 12
Edinburgh Fringe 148

INDEX

electric carbon arc   31–2, 206–7, 209–10
electricity   16, 76, 86, 186, 201, 206–7, 209, 212–14, 218
Eliasson, Olafur   14–15, 86
   The Weather Project   14–15
embodiment   47, 168, 180
emotion   10, 46, 56, 60, 63, 75, 76, 78–81, 122, 132, 137, 141, 183, 203, 205, 208, 217
English National Opera
   The Dream of Gerontius   80
environment   203, 204. *See also* tuned space
equipment. *See* theatre production process
Essig, Linda   24*f*8
experience. *See* audience, experience

feminism   146–7, 149–50, 153–4
festival   2–4, 8, 35, 38–40, 79, 80, 120, 199, 212
fireworks   3, 33
Fischer-Lichte, Erika   18, 36–7, 167, 175
Fix & Foxy
   Ungdom (*Youth*)   38–40, 120, *p*5, *p*6
fog   15, 49, 61, 91–3, 95, 96, 172. *See also* haze
Foster, Hal   86, 93
Fraser, Neil   24*f*8
Fried, Michael   204
Fuchs, Georg   208–9, 209*f*9, 211
Fuel Theatre
   The Litten Trees   3–4, *p*1, *p*2, *p*3
Fuller, Loïe   8, 16–17

Garrick, David   203–5
gas lighting   205, 207, 208
Gibson, James Jerome   49–50, 56, 90–1, 177
Goebbels, Heiner   40–1
   Everything that Happened and Would Happen   169–70, 174–5
Goethe, Wolfgang Johann von   206
Graham, Katherine   9, 11, 16, 38, 83, 85, 98, 176, 216
Gunning, Mike   *p*7

Handke, Peter   6
Hann, Rachel   11, 16, 19, 166, 169, 176, 179
Hannah, Dorita   216, 217
haze   15, 39, 51, 53, 55, 58, 59, 61–3, 86, 94–7, 126, 148, 170–2, 179, 182, 192–3. *See also* fog
Hewitt, Rachel   217
Holzapfel, Amy   206
Hong Kong Academy for Performing Arts
   The Taming of the Shrew   138–40
Hopper, Dennis   56–7
Hulls, Michael   104, 105
Hunt, Nick   9, 103–4, 106

Ibsen, Henrik   6
imagination   40, 90, 133, 157, 183, 205
immersion   15, 27, 34–5, 37–42, 44, 47, 50, 58, 74–5, 94–5
Ingold, Tim   11, 30, 36, 50–1, 56, 58
installation art   3–4, 14–15, 27–30, 35, 48, 53*f*2, 73, 77–81, 82, 85–8, 190–9, 192*f*5, 194*f*6, 197*f*7, *p*1–*p*3, *p*4, *p*8–*p*10, *p*17, *p*18–*p*19, *p*32. *See also* Carter, Lucy; Shearing, David; Shyldkrot, Yaron
intimacy   2, 39, 44, 51, 146–8
Invisible Flock
   Aurora   169–71, 177–80
Irwin, Kathleen   180

Janssens, Ann Veronica   86, 92–3
Johnson, Dominic   86–7

Kean, Charles   31–2, 31*f*1
Kendrick, Lynne   87, 99
kinaesthetics   7, 14, 165, 173, 177

labour   104–5, 107, 118
language   189, 194
Lehmann, Hans-Thies   36, 41, 173, 175
leitmotif   122, 128, 206
Lepage, Robert   4
light
   as dramaturgy   6–7, 146, 186–7, 215
   education   8, 65, 75, 159–60, 198, 214

INDEX

and environment (outside a theatre space) 2–4, 37–8, 46–52, 61–71, 77–9, 151–3, 212, 216
and feeling 7, 15, 27–81, 120, 126, 132–3, 137, 149, 165–7, 173–4, 177–9, 183, 216
as material 11, 12, 103, 132, 165, 169, 170, 175, 177, 182, 186, 194, 201, 209
as medium 47–8, 174, 178, 180
and memory 34, 39, 46–7, 58, 71, 159, 180
as metaphor 3–4, 6, 29, 35, 41, 42, 44, 84, 99, 165, 168–9, 178, 202, 211 (*see also* leitmotif)
as performer 4, 8, 14, 37, 56, 172, 187–9
as spectacle 3–4, 19, 22, 31–2, 34, 38, 64, 168, 179, 204, 212
and transformation 2, 3, 4, 5, 16, 21, 31, 45, 61, 61–71, 69*f*4, 82, 85–8, 92, 97, 140, 142, 165, 174–5, 179–80, 182–3, 185, 189, 214
as transition 34, 182–3, 211 (*see also* threshold moment)
light art. *See* installation art
light emitting diode (LED) 28, 39, 66, 68, 70, 80, 105, 141, 185, 196
light festivals 2–3, 80. *See also* son et lumière
   Diwali 35
   Festival of Britain 212
   Fêtes des Lumières, Lyon 3
   Kolding Light Festival 71–2
   The Litten Trees 3–4
   A Symphony of Lights, Hong Kong 3
lighting designers 7–8, 103, 104, 106, 107, 112–15, 117–18, 141, 153, 157–8, 195
lighting programmers 18, 23, 103, 104, 106, 107, 112–15, 117–18
limelight 33, 206, 207
linguistic ethnography 105, 112
Luckiesh, Matthew 210–11

MacAuley, David 58
McCandless, Stanley 9, 166, 211, 214, 215, 218

McGregor, Wayne 73, 75. *See also* Royal Opera House, London, *Woolf Works*
McKinney, Joslin 10–12, 19, 33, 40, 45 *n*.6, 166–8, 174
Massumi, Brian 91, 92, 169
materiality 167. *See also* light, as material; sound, as material
meaning 18–21, 166, 173–4, 176, 178–9, 201, 214, 218
Merleau-Ponty, Maurice 30, 58, 177, 206
mindfulness. *See* audience, mindfulness
Moholy-Nagy, László 211
moon/moonlight 6, 33, 39, 74, 120, 127, 137, 200
Moran, Nick 7–11, 17, 22, 23 *n*.1, 24 *n*.2, 103, 108–11, 127–8, 178, 218
motif 39, 76, 122, 128, 130, 136
music 77, 80, 81, 121, 132, 143, 146, 149, 155–6, 198, 208

narrative 42, 44, 52–5, 77–80, 109, 122, 184, 185, 187, 207, 215, 218
National Theatre, London
   Angels in America 186
   Curious Incident of the Dog in the Night Time 185
   War Horse 183
The New Opera, Esbjerg, Denmark
   Ring cycle (Richard Wagner) 119–24, 128–9
Nietzsche, Friedrich 208
NONE collective
   J3RR1 86–90, 93, *p*18
Northern Lights. *See* aurora borealis
nostalgia 34, 39, 46–7, 58, 71, 159, 180

ocular-centrism 47, 48, 82, 84, 85, 87–8, 98–9
OISTAT 24 *n*.6, 24 *n*.7
O'Neill, Eugene 6
Oshodi, Maria 84
Öztürk, Maya Nanitchkova 82

Pallasmaa, Juhani 40, 46–8, 62
Palmer, Richard 6, 10, 45 *n*.2, 144 *n*.1

INDEX

Palmer, Scott 8, 9, 11, 12, 19, 22, 23 *n*.1, 45 *n*.4, 45 *n*.5, 45 *n*.8, 166, 167, 171, 174, 181 *n*.1, 218
Pan Pan Theatre
 All That Fall 13–15, 18–20, 88
Parry, Chris 214
pedagogy. *See* light, education; teaching
perception 29, 172, 177, 191, 196–8, 201–3, 205–6
performance design. *See* scenography
performers 138, 143, 146–7, 155, 156, 159, 161, 167, 183, 195, 203, 208, 210–13, 215
phenomenology 13–14
photography 22, 24 *n*.10, 29, 74–5, 147, 197, 205–7, 213, 216
Pilbrow, Richard 8, 17, 24 *n*.2, 24 *n*.8, 166
Piscator, Erwin 212
Plato 204, 217
Process. *See* creative process; design process
projection 8, 37, 52, 55, 56, 104, 126, 128, 137, 140–1, 142, 170, 174, 201, 212–13, 216, *p*32
proprioception 29
Punchdrunk
 The Drowned Man: A Hollywood Fable 41–2, 43–4, *p*7
 It Felt Like A Kiss 41–3

RashDash
 The Darkest Corners 151–3, *p*25, *p*26
 Two Man Show 146–50, 151, *p*24
Reid, Francis 11, 24 *n*.8
Reitz, Dana
 Necessary Weather 156–7
relational performance 27–63, 77–81. *See also* immersion
rhythm 135–6, 155, 183
Rosenfeld, Sybil 204–5
Rosenthal, Jean 6, 9, 81, 178
Royal Opera House, London
 Woolf Works 73–4, *p*14, *p*15

Saraceno, Tomas
 Cosmos of the Breath 49
Scandlight 8, 24 *n*.6
scenography 10–11, 166–7
Schechner, Richard 50
Schivelbusch, Wolfgang 2–3
Schlemmer, Oskar 211
Schopenhauer, Arthur 207, 209
shadow. *See also* darkness
 affect 40, 42, 75
 directional 131, 143
 figure 29, 47, 152
 image 128, 135
 perception 67, 91, 94–8, 204, 208
 quality of light 7, 18, 86
 sidelight 158
 substance 160, 177
Shearing, David 51, 54, 60, 67
 and it all comes down to this… 52–62, 53*f*2, *p*8–*p*10
Shyldkrot, Yaron 48, 51
 Overcast 85, 94–9, *p*19
Solnit, Rebecca 57
son et lumière 3, 201, 212. *See also* light festivals
Sørensen, Tim Flohr 2, 93, 96
sound
 and atmosphere 40, 47, 171
 and dramaturgy 44, 55, 132, 189, 215
 and experience 14, 48–50, 75
 and light 20, 27, 39, 56, 77–81, 95, 110, 132, 172, 215
 as material 13, 22, 51, 62, 104–5
spectacle 3–4, 19, 22, 31–2, 34, 38, 64, 166, 168, 179, 204, 212
spectator. *See* audience
stars/starlight 16, 32, 39, 55, 124, 126–8, 200
Strindberg, August 206–7
sun/sunlight 6, 14–15, 32–3, 39, 49, 51, 55–7, 64–70, 74, 90, 120, 125, 127, 128, 137, 168–9, 200
Superflex
 It Is Not the End of the World 27–30, *p*4
sustainability 68
Svoboda, Josef 8, 21, 61, 62, 129 *n*.1, 176, 200, 213, 214, 218

teaching   8, 65, 159–60, 198, 214
technical rehearsal. *See* theatre production process
temporality   34, 183. *See also* light, as transition
Theatergraph   212
theatre building   208. *See also* architecture; auditorium
theatre criticism   10, 16, 24 *n*.10, 31, 77, 194, 195
Théâtre de Complicité. *See* Complicité
theatre production process. *See also* collaboration; design process
   cues   184–5
   equipment   126–7, 140, 148, 151–3, 156, 182, 185, 186
   plotting/programming   78, 79, 113, 143, 156, 158 (*see also* lighting programmers)
   technical rehearsal   103–4, 106, 117, 153
   technology   205, 207, 212
Thoreau, David Henry   59, 62
threshold moment   29, 34, 36, 38, 42–3, 61, 93, 95, 175
Tipton, Jennifer   10, *p*27
Tivoli Gardens   64–71, *p*12, *p*13
total theatre   131–2, 144
tuned space   13–14, 38, 39, 48

tungsten–halogen   59, 104, 139, 148, 196, 212–13
Turner, J.M.W.   95, 205
Turrell, James   35, 86, 91–2
   Bindu Shards   35
   Ganzfeld   35, 91–2, 99
twilight   40, 64–5, *p*12

University of Leeds   8, 52, 190, 193
urban environment   2–3, 5, 34, 64–71, 67*f*3, 124, 151, 216, 217, *p*2–*p*3, *p*4, *p*12–*p*13, *p*25–6, *p*32

Vasseleu, Cathryn   168, 177

Waddell, Dickens   90, 91
Wagner, Richard   6, 119–29, 207, 208
weather   14–15, 47–52, 58, 65, 68, 120
   'scenographic weather'   58–63
Welton, Martin   13, 40, 48, 45 *n*.8, 51, 83–4, 86, 93, 96
Williams, John A.   137–40, *p*22, *p*23
Williams, Katharine   *p*24, *p*25, *p*26
Wilson, Robert   4, 8, 21, 36–7, 215
World Stage Design   135, 142

Yale University   159, 211. *See also* McCandless, Stanley

Zezulka, Kelli   9, 11, 106
Zhengping, Zhou   142